The Tourism and Leisure Experience

Barcode in Back

1

ASPECTS OF TOURISM
Series Editors: **Chris Cooper** *(Oxford Brookes University, UK)*, **C. Michael Hall** *(University of Canterbury, New Zealand)* and **Dallen J. Timothy** *(Arizona State University, USA)*

Aspects of Tourism is an innovative, multifaceted series, which comprises authoritative reference handbooks on global tourism regions, research volumes, texts and monographs. It is designed to provide readers with the latest thinking on tourism worldwide and push back the frontiers of tourism knowledge. The volumes are authoritative, readable and user-friendly, providing accessible sources for further research. Books in the series are commissioned to probe the relationship between tourism and cognate subject areas such as strategy, development, retailing, sport and environmental studies.

Full details of all the books in this series and of all our other publications can be found on http://www.channelviewpublications.com, or by writing to Channel View Publications, St Nicholas House, 31-34 High Street, Bristol BS1 2AW, UK.

ASPECTS OF TOURISM
Series Editors: Chris Cooper *(Oxford Brookes University, UK)*, C. Michael Hall *(University of Canterbury, New Zealand) and* Dallen J. Timothy *(Arizona State University, USA)*

The Tourism and Leisure Experience: Consumer and Managerial Perspectives

Edited by
Michael Morgan, Peter Lugosi and
J.R. Brent Ritchie

CHANNEL VIEW PUBLICATIONS
Bristol • Buffalo • Toronto

Library of Congress Cataloging in Publication Data
A catalog record for this book is available from the Library of Congress.
The Tourism and Leisure Experience: Consumer and Managerial Perspectives/Edited by
Michael Morgan, Peter Lugosi and J.R. Brent Ritchie.
Aspects of Tourism 44
Includes bibliographical references and index.
1. Tourism. 2. Tourism--Management. 3. Leisure recreation. I. Morgan, Michael, 1948-
II. Lugosi, Peter. III. Ritchie, J. R. Brent. IV. Title. V. Series.
G155.A1T58934869 2010
910.68–dc22 2010026358

British Library Cataloguing in Publication Data
A catalogue entry for this book is available from the British Library.

ISBN-13: 978-1-84541-149-7 (hbk)
ISBN-13: 978-1-84541-148-0 (pbk)

Channel View Publications
UK: St Nicholas House, 31-34 High Street, Bristol BS1 2AW, UK.
USA: UTP, 2250 Military Road, Tonawanda, NY 14150, USA.
Canada: UTP, 5201 Dufferin Street, North York, Ontario M3H 5T8, Canada.

The policy of Multilingual Matters/Channel View Publications is to use papers that are natural,
renewable and recyclable products, made from wood grown in sustainable forests. In the
manufacturing process of our books, and to further support our policy, preference is given to
printers that have FSC and PEFC Chain of Custody certification. The FSC and/or PEFC logos
will appear on those books where full certification has been granted to the printer concerned.

Typeset by Datapage International Ltd.
Printed and bound in Great Britain by the MPG Books Group Ltd.

Contents

Contributors

Dr Barbara A. Carmichael is a Professor in the Department of Geography and Environmental Studies and the Director of NEXT Research Centre (Centre for the Study of Nascent Entrepreneurship and the Exploitation of Technology) in the School of Business and Economics at Wilfrid Laurier University, Waterloo, Ontario, Canada. She has an MBA from Durham University Business School, UK and a PhD from the University of Victoria, British Columbia. Her research interests are in tourism entrepreneurship, quality tourism experiences, special events, casino impacts, market segmentation and resident attitudes towards tourism.

Dr Scott Cohen is Lecturer in Consumer Experience and Behaviour at Bournemouth University, UK. During his doctoral research at the University of Otago, New Zealand, he carried out fieldwork with lifestyle travellers in northern India and southern Thailand. His research interests and publications centre on lifestyle, identity and experience across the contexts of tourism, leisure and sport as well as the intersections between environmental change and travel behaviour.

Nicole Ferdinand has worked in the Event Management industry for the last 10 years. She has managed a range of projects including product launches, sod turnings, meetings and conferences both as an in-house event manager and independent consultant. She joined the London Metropolitan University in 2006 and is currently a Senior Lecturer in Events Management. Her research interests include festival and events tourism, the management and marketing of the cultural industries and events management education. Nicole also serves as Editor for the *London Journal of Tourism, Sport and the Creative Industries*.

Daniel R. Fesenmaier is a Professor in the School of Tourism & Hospitality Management at Temple University and Director of the National Laboratory for Tourism and eCommerce. He is also a Visiting Principal Research Fellow at the University of Wollongong. Daniel received his PhD in Geography from the University of Western Ontario, Canada. His research interests include destination marketing, advertising evaluation and information technology and he is currently Managing Editor of the *Journal of Information Technology and Tourism*.

Darryl Gibbs is a lecturer in hospitality and other related subjects in the Cardiff School of Management at the University of Wales Institute, Cardiff. Darryl's research interests are concerned with the construction and delivery of hospitable experiences. Darryl's PhD research is a specific investigation of the motivations and perceptions of staff working in the food and beverage sector of the hospitality industry. This involves the gendered, sexual and physical nature of service work together with an exploration of the implications of emotional and aesthetic labour, natural hospitableness and the guest/host interface for hospitable experiences.

Ian Gilhespy has been a university teacher and researcher for over 20 years contributing to the areas of arts management, sports development and outdoor adventure as well as leading programmes in leisure and tourism studies. Recent publications relate to the application of visual research methods in leisure and tourism and to a pedagogic interest in the design and evaluation of blended learning materials, in particular, reusable learning objects.

Ulrike Gretzel is an Associate Professor in the Department of Recreation, Park & Tourism Sciences at Texas A&M University and Director of the Laboratory for Intelligent Systems in Tourism. She is also a Visiting Principal Research Fellow at the University of Wollongong. She received her PhD in Communications from the University of Illinois at Urbana-Champaign, USA. Her research focuses on the representation of tourism experiences through digital media and on persuasion in human-computer interactions.

Dave Harris is Professor of Leisure and Education at University College Plymouth Marjon. His research interests involve social theory and its 'application' to a number of applied fields including Higher Education and electronic teaching, Leisure and popular culture, Media and modernity, and Sociology and research methods. Details of his publications in these fields, and examples of other materials, can be found at his website: http: //www.arasite.org/. He is currently engaged in writing a book, with Prof L. Isherwood on 'radical otherness' and the implications for understanding other people.

Dr Claire Haven-Tang is Reader in Tourism and Management in the Department of Tourism, Hospitality and Events Management in Cardiff School of Management at the University of Wales Institute, Cardiff (UWIC). Recent projects undertaken for the Tourism Training Forum for Wales, Capital Region Tourism, People 1st, Visit Wales and Adventa include: exploring best practice in business and event tourism, labour market assessments, tourism industry training provision, school student perceptions of tourism careers and customising Sense of Place. Her research interests include: destination development and tourism SMEs, Sense of Place, labour market and human resource development issues.

Gayle Jennings, PhD, is Associate Professor of Tourism Management, Department of Tourism, Leisure, Hotel and Sport Management, Griffith University, Gold Coast campus. Her research agenda focuses on quality tourism experiences as well as the use of qualitative methodologies. She has sole authored and edited a number of books, written book chapters and journal articles across a range of topics relating to theoretical paradigms that inform research processes and quality tourism experiences.

Professor Eleri Jones is Director of Research in Cardiff School of Management at the University of Wales Institute, Cardiff (UWIC). Her research interests are focused on innovation, information technology and human resource management in relation to sustainable tourism development. She supervises an extensive international portfolio of research degree candidates, some in collaboration with colleagues from universities in Africa and the Middle East. She is a member of the Welsh Assembly Government's Tourism Advisory Panel which advises the Minister for Heritage. She has managed a number of European projects including BESTBET which was a European Union-funded project looking at best practice in business and event tourism.

Dr Peter Lugosi is Senior Lecturer at Bournemouth University. He has researched and published on a wide range of subjects including research ethics, hospitable spaces, consumer participation, hospitality and urban regeneration, entrepreneurship and organisational culture. His work appears in a number of journals including *Qualitative Inquiry, Space and Culture, The Service Industries Journal* and *Urban Studies.*

Kelley A. McClinchey is a doctoral student in the Department of Geography and Environmental Studies at Wilfrid Laurier University, Waterloo, Ontario, Canada. She has a Masters in Environmental Studies from Wilfrid Laurier University and her research interests include sense of place and tourist experiences, festivals and events, culinary tourism, cultural geography and mobility, and tourism entrepreneurship.

Michael Morgan is Senior Lecturer at Bournemouth University and leader of the MA European Tourism Management programme delivered by a consortium of European universities. He has written and contributed to several books on leisure and tourism marketing, including the latest edition (2009) of *Marketing in Travel and Tourism* with Victor Middleton and Alan Fyall. His current research activities into the experience of tourism have included the editing of special editions of the *International Journal of Tourism Research* and the *Journal of Foodservice.*

Dr Gianna Moscardo is a Professor in the Faculty of Law, Business and Creative Arts at James Cook University. Before joining JCU as an academic seven years ago, she worked as Project Coordinator with the CRC Reef Research, managing a series of research and extension activities aimed at enhancing the sustainability of tourism activities in Northern Australia. Her qualifications in applied psychology and sociology support her research interests in understanding how tourists make decisions, evaluate their travel experiences and respond to interpretation. In 2006 she was elected a Fellow of the UNWTO's International Academy for the Study of Tourism.

Sarah Quinlan Cutler is currently a doctoral student in the Geography and Environmental Studies Department at Wilfrid Laurier University, Canada. She has a Master's degree in Tourism Policy and Planning from the University of Waterloo, Canada and was a senior lecturer in Tourism Management at the University of Hertfordshire, UK. Her research interests include tourist experiences, visitor management, educational tourism, travel guidebooks and responsible tourism practices.

Dr Caroline Ritchie is a senior lecturer in Cardiff School of Management at the University of Wales, Cardiff. She graduated from Portsmouth Polytechnic and worked in the hospitality industry for several years before joining the Hotel, Catering and International Management Association (now the Institute of Hospitality) as their events organiser. Caroline then moved into education and began lecturing in hospitality and related subjects. Caroline's research interests are in the area of consumer behaviour as it relates to the hospitality environment and social moderate alcohol-related behaviours particularly as they relate to wine consumption and public usage.

J.R. Brent Ritchie holds the Professorship of Tourism Management in the Haskayne School of Business at the University of Calgary. He also serves as Chair of the University's World Tourism Education and Research Centre. Dr Ritchie, who was the Founding Chair of the United Nations World Tourism Organization's Tourism Education and Science Council, is the recipient of numerous awards recognizing his extensive contributions to research and publication in the field. They include the TTRA Lifetime Achievement Award and the UNWTO Ulysses Prize. In addition, he is co-author of two widely acclaimed textbooks: *TOURISM: Principles, Practices, Philosophies*, and *The Competitive Destination: A Sustainable Tourism Perspective*.

Dr Nigel L. Williams is a Senior Lecturer in Project Management in the Business Systems Department at the University of Bedfordshire. He has 15 years of experience as a Project Manager and Business Consultant for organisations in the Caribbean Region and is the Managing Director of Green PB, a clean technology start-up. His research interests include Internationalization from Small States, Process Research Methods, Experience Based Manufacturing and Project Management.

Richard Keith Wright is a lecturer within the UK Centre for Events Management at Leeds Metropolitan University. Prior to taking up his current role, he spent five years in the Department of Tourism at the University of Otago, New Zealand, completing a Masters on the regional promotion of the 2005 Lions Tour and an Auto-ethnographical PhD on the multiple identities of the sport event tourist. His primary research interests focus on the production and consumption of sport-related event tourism, and he is an active member of the ESRC-funded Sport Tourism Opportunities for Research, Mobility and International Networking Group (STORMING) Initiative.

Preface

We dedicate this volume to those academic pioneers who, many years ago, had the insight and the strength of conviction to convince the world that people do not buy 'products', or even 'services'. Rather they purchase the functionality and total experience that the product or service provides. We hope that our efforts in producing this book, will, in some meaningful way, serve to consolidate and further strengthen the contributions of these pioneers. We trust that the structure and contents of the book will provide an example of the focus we believe is necessary for ongoing work on the tourism and leisure experience. More specifically, we believe that our tripartite focus on understanding the experience, researching the experience and managing the experience, provides a useful framework for focusing the goals and associated methodologies of future research efforts and for classifying and operationalising the results of these efforts.

The need for a book offering a systematic coverage of current research and managerial practice first came to our attention as a result of the timely international conference on the 'extraordinary experience', which was hosted by my Bournemouth University colleagues in September 2007. The keynote address which I delivered to this conference sought to document the evolution of tourism experience research from its earliest beginnings, and to provide insights into the challenges we currently face as we seek to improve our understanding of the phenomenon (which we believe represents the essence of tourism and leisure). It was my hope that this documentation, and the accompanying analysis, would not only prove helpful to academic attendees – but might also enhance and facilitate the ability of practitioners in the field to more effectively deliver truly memorable tourism and leisure experiences to both residents of the communities we serve and to visitors from around the world who seek experiences that can only be realised by exploring distant horizons.

The resulting 'buzz' from this milestone event made it clear to us that the conference had indeed touched an intellectual nerve, and that its goal of stimulating more thorough study of the theoretical foundations of the tourism and leisure experience had been realised. At the same time, the buzz also made us aware that the success of the conference had highlighted the need for a means by which to encourage ongoing study of the topic and to provide some focus for such research in a more structured manner than that provided by a volume of conference proceedings. It was with this need clearly in mind that the idea for this book emerged, and we subsequently invited authors from around the world to submit chapter proposals, on a competitive basis, for this edited collection.

In conclusion, on behalf of myself and my Bournemouth colleagues [who most graciously invited me to join them in this undertaking, despite the inconveniences and inefficiencies of long-distance collaboration] we hope that the book will provide an encouragement that goes beyond the thoughts enticed from our contributors – and that this volume will be a helpful point of reference for students and researchers into the future.

J.R. Brent Ritchie, for Michael Morgan and Peter Lugosi

Introduction

MICHAEL MORGAN, PETER LUGOSI and J.R. BRENT RITCHIE

This book addresses a theme of growing importance in the tourism and leisure industries, by which we include recreation, hospitality, entertainment, events and sport. All these sectors exist to provide consumers with experiences. Some organisations, for example, tour operators who specialise in adventure tourism, seek to provide extraordinary transformational experiences; while others such as a neighbourhood café may involve more mundane experiences, which are just as important to their customers. Experience management is seen as the way to remain competitive in markets where global competition and internet technology have turned products and services into commodities, bought and sold on price alone (Schmitt, 1999, 2003). Pine and Gilmore (1999) say that developed countries are now 'experience economies', where sustainable competitive advantage can only be gained by giving the customer a unique and memorable experience. This is done through treating 'work as theatre and every business a stage'. However, more recently, Prahalad and Ramaswamy (2004) have called for a strategic approach based on shared values, allowing customers to co-create their own experiences in a search for personal growth. The emphasis has thus shifted in recent debates from narrow conceptions of staging or production to broader notions of experience creation, involving a wider range of agencies and processes (Sundbo & Darmer, 2008).

The concept of the experience economy has given rise to a growing number of books aimed at practitioners, often written by 'Customer Experience Management' consultants. Though their approach has been seen as superficial and production-orientated by academic critics, their influence can be detected in the increasingly ubiquitous promises of unique or memorable experiences made by the marketing output of the tourism and many other industries.

Academic interest in the concepts of experience also continues to grow as evidenced by the number of recent journal special editions (*Scandinavian Journal of Hospitality and Tourism*, 2007, 7:1; *Journal of Foodservice* 2008, 19:2/3; *International Journal of Tourism Research*, 2009, 11:2; *Journal of Hospitality Marketing and Management*, 2009, 18:2/3), books (Hjorth & Kostera, 2007; O'Dell & Billing, 2005; Sundbo & Darmer, 2008) and conferences in which it has been a main theme or a major track. In the last few years the organisers of these have included the Regional Studies Association, Association for Tourism and Leisure Education (ATLAS), Travel and Tourism Research Association, European Council on Hotel, Restaurant and Institutional Education (EuroCHRIE), as well as a number of universities in the UK, USA and Australia. Nevertheless, there is little evidence that practitioners of experience management have much awareness of, or make use of, the range of academic research insights into the individual consumer's experience from behavioural, sociological and anthropological approaches and methodologies that have been developing in the academic literature since the 1980s (for a comprehensive overview of this literature as it relates to tourism, see Ritchie & Hudson, 2009).

This book was inspired by a desire to draw together academic and practitioner interest in the tourist experience by combining the perspectives of the tourist consumer with that of experience managers at regional, destination and individual business levels in leisure and tourism. We invited authors working in this field to write chapters that contribute to a systematic and thematic exploration of tourism and leisure experiences either from the consumer/participant or from the managerial/operational perspective. The selected chapters are written by a mixture of well-established authors in the field and a new generation of researchers. The book, therefore, provides readers with an insight into current research and future agendas that we hope will develop the study of the topic, building on well-established texts such as Chris Ryan's *The Tourist Experience* (1997, 2002) and Jennings and Nickerson's *Quality Tourism Experiences* (2006).

While grounded in recent scholarship and research, the book is not intended to simply be a collection of research papers or case studies. Each chapter seeks to contribute to the conceptual understanding of one or more aspects of the topic, supported by a range of examples drawn from tourism, leisure, hospitality, sport and event contexts. It aims to develop a multidisciplinary perspective on experiential consumption and uses the experience paradigm to provide a critical discussion of the production and consumption of contemporary leisure and tourism. The book is organised into three broad sections: understanding experiences, researching experiences and managing experiences. The chapters in the first section attempt to understand the different dimensions of the experiences while interrogating the different factors that drive consumers and shape the nature of experiences. The chapters in the second section examine emerging approaches to researching the experience; while those in the final section focus on the organisational dimensions of creating and managing experiences.

The book begins with Sarah Quinlan-Cutler and Barbara Carmichael's chapter, which undertakes the ambitious task of charting the dimensions of the tourist experience. The model they produce shows that the tourist experience is, like all consumer experiences, preceded by motivations and expectations and results in satisfaction or dissatisfaction. However, this simplistic reduction would leave out the features that make the study of tourism and leisure experiences so complex and fascinating. The chapter highlights some of these features, the multiphasic nature of the tour or activity, the multiplicity of external influences, the role of 'place', and, the feature which most interests many of our contributors, the rich and often lasting personal significance derived from the experience in terms of emotions, knowledge, memories, self-identity and development.

It is this last theme that Scott Cohen explores. Drawing on his research into those most extreme examples of tourists, the long-term lifestyle travellers, he discusses the search for escapism, authenticity and self-identity that the literature sees as present in most types of tourism. The simple assumption that individuals seek to escape from the monotony of their daily lives to authentic experiences of other places, artefacts and cultures has been challenged by post-structualist approaches in terms both of the possibility of escape and the grounds of authenticity. In its place, there has been a shift in focus away from the authenticity of objects and towards the authenticity of subjective experiences. The individuals he interviewed talked frequently of their travels as a search for identity, for their real self, even though much current academic writing would say that they are searching for an illusion. He ends the chapter by reminding us of the claim by Pine and Gilmore that competitive advantage can come from satisfying, if only momentarily, a consumer's search for transformation. Experiences that allow participants to work and play with identity, he concludes, should not be undervalued.

If experiences of leisure and tourism are, to some extent at least, identity-work, then this work will involve participants in narratives about themselves and the people and places they encounter. Gianna Moscardo's chapter discusses the importance of stories and themes in the shaping of tourist experience. The chapter sets out the assumptions of Woodside *et al.*'s (2008) Story Telling Theory. People think narratively. They make sense of experience by telling stories. Information is absorbed and stored in the form of stories. Repeating, reliving and listening to stories is a pleasurable experience. From this position, the chapter argues that stories about a destination can play an important role in attracting visitors and in shaping their experiences during their stay. They can even play a part in encouraging sustainable behaviour by the visitors. In turn, the stories told by tourists to others also contribute to the images and representation of the destination, particularly in the era of the social web where user-generated content is more persuasive than that created by destination marketers.

The stories about the destination interact with the personal narratives of the visitors to create an experience embodied in that place. The concept of 'a sense of place' is explored in the next chapter, by Kelley McClinchey and Barbara Carmichael. This sense of place combines the physical, spatial aspects of the setting with the meanings people attach to it, through their relationships with the community, the sense of belonging or otherness and the emotional and symbolic benefits they derive from being there. The authors' conceptual model distinguishes between the collective domain – the meanings created by the physical setting and social relationships, for example, by their associations with the history and culture of particular ethnic groups – and the personal domain based on the memories and expectations such associations create for an individual based on their previous experience or life-story. Thus, the sense of place can be both reflective, and nostalgic for the past and anticipatory for future experiences. The case studies are of ethnic community festivals in urban Canada. In discussing the role of physical and social space and of the scale of the setting in how the visitor experiences these neighbourhoods, further development is given to the issues of objective, staged and existential authenticity introduced in earlier chapters. The theme of a sense of place is further developed in later chapters by Gretzel and Fesenmaier on sensory experiences, and Haven-Tang and Jones on the use of sense of place in destination marketing.

The second section of the book concerns itself with the problems of researching the complexities of the tourist experience that have been outlined in the first section. It introduces the reader to some of the directions experience research is taking in an attempt to go beyond quantitative measurement of motivational factors or the evaluation of attributes of satisfaction. Gayle Jennings' chapter reflects on the current state of experience research. She sets this in the context of the unpredictable global business environment where organisations seek to remain competitive by providing quality experiences, which are at the same time sustainable and socially-responsible. To achieve this, research will need to go beyond the quantitative, positivistic approaches that have hitherto dominated tourism research and bring in holistic evaluations based on interpretivist and constructionist insights. Such research will need to take into account the cultural differences between the established Western markets and the emerging markets of Brazil, Russia, India, China and other Asian countries in terms of what is considered a quality tourism experience. It should also look beyond the immediate company/customer transaction and instead should consider the provision of quality experiences within a holistic framework that includes and engages tourists, providers, governments, communities and the environment bearing in mind local and global contexts. The chapter gives an example of qualitative research that draws on a number of techniques to give an insider perspective on adventure tourism.

The remaining chapters in this section provide further examples of qualitative experience research based on interpretivist and constructivist paradigms. Ian Gilhespy and David Harris review the use of visual imagery in experience research. This includes the use of photographs taken by the researcher in ethnographic studies, the analysis of photographs taken by tourists and of the imagery used in tourist brochures and other marketing material. The authors point out that all these methods involve the researcher imposing an interpretation on the data; therefore, the subjectivity of the viewpoint assumed by the researcher as well as the photographer needs to be taken into account. They link this to the debate over realism in visual culture. Reality, they remind us, is never simply recorded but chosen, interpreted and framed, not always in conscious or intended ways. The selection of images and viewpoint is influenced by conventions that try to make the construction invisible and to meet the expectation of the intended audience. They refer to Urry's (2002) work on the tourist gaze and the hermeneutic circle where commercial images influence what the tourist sees and, therefore, chooses to photograph. However, the individual may resist the controlling gaze or dominant discourse and instead enact or perform their own personal experience of the tourist setting or activity drawing on a wider range of images, narratives and meanings.

Richard Wright's chapter proposes some answers to the problem of the inevitable subjectivity of any analysis of qualitative data by researchers occupying a superior position as an academic, an outsider often of a different ethnicity, class or gender from the subjects. He examines two forms of research that dissolve these barriers. The first is memory work, where the subjects of the research become 'co-researchers'. Each produces a personal narrative on the topic, and these are then shared, compared and discussed by the group. To encourage reflection, the narratives are written in the third person. This allows socially-constructed attitudes to be recognised and discussed by the group as a means of determining their self-identity. Developed to explore sensitive gender-based experiences such as physical and mental illness, it has also been used, for example, by Small (1999) to study mothers' memories of family holidays. In some cases, the reader is then challenged to become a co-researcher too and add their own reflections and reinterpretations of the experiences being addressed.

The second method Wright explores is autoethnography where the researcher becomes an insider participant in an activity and writes a first person narrative based on systematic introspection. In the words of Morgan and Pritchard (2005: 35) 'it uses our own lived experience as a resource and overcomes that sense of artificial opaqueness in much tourism scholarship'. Wright argues that this reflective approach allows for a deeper exploration of the themes of this book, such as identity, escapism, authenticity and social construction, than objective studies of consumer behaviour at a destination.

Nevertheless, there is also a need for experience research that can be applied by tourism and leisure managers in a wide range of contexts. Ulrike Gretzel and Daniel Fesenmaier's chapter on capturing the sensory aspects of a visitor experience says that while qualitative research can provide an understanding of the nature and structure of sensory experiences, it cannot provide information on the sensory appeals of a destination to a larger sample of tourists necessary to design experience offerings or experiential marketing communications campaigns. For this they suggest elicitation techniques which encourage respondents to reveal hidden feelings, beliefs and attitudes through making free unprompted lists. The chapter reviews interview-based techniques such as metaphor elicitation (Zaltman, 2003) and laddering (Grunert & Grunert, 1995) before proposing the authors' own method which is implemented through a survey questionnaire which can be applied to a larger sample of respondents. They demonstrate this through a study of the sensory associations elicited from visitors to Elkhart County, Indiana, an area known for its Amish community. The results reveal the sights, sounds, tastes and smells the visitors associate with the place and analyses them into sensory bundles elicited from different demographic and behavioural segments.

The final section of the book looks at the challenges of implementing the concepts of experience management and the findings of experience research in a management context. Claire Haven-Tang and Eleri Jones begin by providing a case study of experience management at regional level: the Wales Tourist Board's Sense of Place toolkit. They discuss the use of this tool kit with small tourism businesses in the rural county of Monmouthshire on the borders of Wales with England. Based on the assumptions that visitors are seeking experiences and expect authenticity, it encourages the development of tourism products that celebrate the unique resources of the county: its people, its history as displayed in its buildings and the survival of the Welsh language, its food, creative arts and the outdoor activities of the countryside. This case study provides readers an opportunity to consider the application in a specific context of the themes of a sense of place and the issues of authenticity, the power of stories and the subjectivity of viewpoint outlined in earlier chapters.

One of the lessons of the case study is that experience themes set by the regional tourism managers are only effective if they are adopted and implemented by the owners and staff of individual small businesses. In the next chapter Darryl Gibbs and Caroline Ritchie take the focus down to the individual business. They discuss the importance of developing an understanding of the skills required by restaurant staff to 'put on a good show' in order to meet customer expectations, enhance the hospitality experience and ensure continued custom. From a review of the literature on the analogy of service delivery as theatre they identify a number of key questions for experience management. First, management needs to understand what the customers expect from a particular service encounter – is it a functional refuelling before the next activity or an integral part of the enjoyment of the occasions? Do they want a stage-managed and scripted performance or an opportunity for socialising and unscripted moments of spontaneous enjoyment? Are the staff the leading actors or the supporting cast to enable the customers to star in their own social dramas? Gibbs and Ritchie go on to discuss the extent to which management should empower staff to go 'off-script' as 'natural hosts' and the stress to the individuals of the emotional labour involved. Underlying the discussion are issues of the nature of hospitality and the status of workers in what is often seen as a low-skill, low-wage industry.

In the next chapter Nicole Ferdinand and Nigel Williams explore an under-researched aspect of experience management, the influence of tangible cues on the leisure experience. The chapter highlights the range of meanings, functions, needs and desires that items of tourism memorabilia have for tourists. Items can be practical and functional so that they go on to be used in every day life. They can also be highly symbolic, fulfilling personal needs and desires for social status, a more authentic way of life or simple nostalgia. Thus, the chapter provides material for further discussion of what have emerged as key themes in our book – how tourism experiences, and in this case the tangible objects acquired during the trip, are interpreted in the individual's search for escapism, authenticity and self-identity. The chapter also discusses the managerial implications of these insights. Businesses and destination marketers that understand the range of needs and desires that tourism memorabilia have for tourists can obtain significant advantages from the production and sale of souvenirs.

In the closing chapter Michael Morgan revisits the central propositions of Pine and Gilmore's Experience Economy 10 years after the publication of this influential book, which popularised the concept of experience management as a business strategy. The chapter asks whether Pine and Gilmore's analysis and their predictions for the growth of an experience sector have been proved correct. Does experience management and marketing indeed deliver the sustainable competitive advantage they promised? Or were the critics quoted earlier right that it was just a passing fashion in an era of unprecedented economic growth? It explores the extent to which the concepts have been accepted by leisure and tourism managers, or by the sectors' academic community. It sets out an agenda for more systematic research into the effectiveness of experience management and marketing in attracting visitors and creating repeat business for the sector.

We hope that readers will find the book a useful overview of the current research and managerial issues in the field, one that will both stimulate them to delve deeper themselves into these fascinating and important topics and at the same time provide a resource to guide their further reading.

References

Grunert, K.G. and Grunert, S. (1995) Measuring subjective meaning structures by the laddering method: Theoretical considerations and methodological problems. *International Journal of Research in Marketing* 12, 209–225.

Hjorth, D. and Kostera, M. (eds) (2007) *Entrepreneurship and the Experience Economy*. Copenhagen: Copenhagen Business School Press.

Jennings, G.R. and Nickerson, N. (eds) (2006) *Quality Tourism Experiences*. Burlington, MA: Elsevier.

Morgan, N. and Pritchard, A. (2005) On souvenirs and metonymy: Narratives of memory, metaphor and materiality. *Tourist Studies* 5 (1), 29–53.

O'Dell, T. and Billing, P. (2005) *Experience-scapes: Tourism, Culture, and Economy*. Copenhagen: Copenhagen Business School Press.

Pine, B.J. and Gilmore, J.H. (1999) *The Experience Economy: Work is Theatre and Every Business is a Stage*. Boston, MA: Harvard Business School Press.

Prahalad, C.K. and Ramaswamy, V. (2004) *The Future of Competition: Co-creating Unique Value With Customers*. Boston, MA: Harvard Business School Press.

Ritchie, J.R.B. and Hudson, S. (2009) Understanding and meeting the challenges of consumer/tourist experience research. *International Journal of Tourism Research* 11, 111–126.

Ryan, C. (1997) *The Tourist Experience*. New York: Continuum.

Ryan, C. (2002) *The Tourist Experience* (2nd edn). New York: Continuum.

Schmitt, B.H. (1999) *Experiential Marketing: How to Get Companies to Sense, Feel, Think, Act, and Relate to Your Company and Brands*. New York: Free Press.

Schmitt, B.H. (2003) *Customer Experience Management: A Revolutionary Approach to Connecting With Your Customers*. Hoboken, NJ: John Wiley. ·

Small, J. (1999) Memory-work: A method for researching women's tourist experiences. *Tourism Management* 20, 25–35.

Sundbo, J. and Darmer, P. (eds) (2008) *Creating Experiences in the Experience Economy*. Cheltenham: Edward Elgar.

Urry, J. (2002) *The Tourist Gaze: Leisure and Travel in Contemporary Societies* (2nd edn). London: Sage.

Woodside, A.G., Sood, S. and Miller, K.R. (2008) When consumers and brands talk: Storytelling theory and research in psychology and marketing. *Psychology and Marketing* 25 (2), 97–145.

Zaltman, G. (2003) *How Customers Think-Essential Insights into the Mind of the Market*. Boston, MA: Harvard Business School Press.

Chapter 1
The Dimensions of the Tourist Experience

SARAH QUINLAN CUTLER and BARBARA A. CARMICHAEL

Introduction

Experiences are argued to be subjective, intangible, continuous and highly personal phenomena (O'Dell, 2007). The word 'experience' can refer to two different states: the moment-by-moment lived experience (*Erlebnis*) and the evaluated experience (*Erfahrung*), which is subject to reflection and prescribed meaning (Highmore, 2002). The evaluated experience is the focus of much of the tourism experience research, in which experiences are often defined as being within a person who is engaged with an event on an emotional, physical, spiritual or intellectual level (Pine & Gilmore, 1999), and is left with memorable impressions (Gram, 2005).

This chapter provides an overview of the tourist experience by tracing the various perspectives and dimensions of this topic in current research focusing on tourism as a discrete experience subject to anticipation, recollection and reflection. This review of the multiple definitions and developments of the tourist experience literature leads to the creation of a tourist experience model. This model presents the elements involved in the tourist experience, in order to help readers achieve a clearer understanding of the dynamic nature of this phenomenon.

Multiple Definitions of the Tourism Experience

The tourist experience is a complicated psychological process. Providing a succinct definition is a difficult task as this can encompass a complex variety of elements (Jennings, 2006; Selstad, 2007). Tourist experiences are arguably different from everyday experiences (Cohen, 1979, 2004; Graburn, 2001; Vogt, 1976). The act of tourism offers complex experiences, memories and emotions related to places (Noy, 2007), and it is arguably this experience of place or self in place that the individual seeks. Stamboulis and Skayannis (2003), focusing on on-site experiences, define the tourist experience as an interaction between tourists and destinations, with destinations being the site of the experience and tourists being the actors of the experience. Larsen (2007) argues that the tourist experience should be defined as a past travel-related event which

3

was significant enough to be stored in long-term memory. O'Dell's (2007) summary of arguments on the tourist experience points out that experiences involve more than the tourists. The tourism industries are also part of the generation, staging and consumption of experiences through the manipulation of place and presentation of culture.

Li (2000) reviews the various definitions of the tourist experience, which include a contrived and created act of consumption, a response to problems with 'ordinary' life, a search for authenticity and a multifaceted leisure activity. The only thing Li found to be common for all definitions is that the tourist experience is significant for the individual. Selstad (2007) defines the tourist experience as a novelty/familiarity combination involving the individual pursuit of identity and self-realisation. However, individuals experience similar activities and settings in different ways (Pine & Gilmore, 1999). Therefore, as the tourist experience is highly subjective, it can only be interpreted by reflecting on the specific individuals involved and the specific settings where experiences take place (Jennings, 2006). Most of these definitions refer to the experience at the destination; however, the experience of a tourism event begins before the trip in the planning and preparation phases and continues after the tourist returns through the recollection and communication of the events which took place (Clawson & Knetsch, 1966).

Development of the Tourist Experience Literature

In order to interpret the tourist experience, researchers need to review and evaluate the various qualities of this phenomenon. The tourist experience grew to be a key research issue in the 1960s (Uriely, 2005), becoming popular in the social science literature by the 1970s (Quan & Wang, 2004). At this time, the tourist experience was discussed by authors, such as MacCannell (1973) who related it to authenticity and Cohen (1979) who explored experience in terms of phenomenology. In the 1990s, researchers began using experience-based research approaches in an effort to develop a better understanding of the tourist experience (Andereck *et al.*, 2006). These approaches involve tourists reporting thoughts and feelings in diaries or by responding to questions. Though results tended to point to the dynamic nature of experiences, they produced little understanding of the meanings involved (Andereck *et al.*, 2006).

Mannell and Iso-Ahola (1987) discuss three dominant perspectives used to examine leisure and tourist experience: the definitional approach; the post-hoc satisfaction approach; and the immediate approach. Though the authors argued in 1987 that there was limited research using a definitional approach in tourist experience studies, this is no longer the case. Table 1.1 summarises the definitional approaches used over the past

Table 1.1 Overview of definitional approach research in tourism experiences

Definitional focus	Example of representative academic articles
Phases of experience	(Botterill & Crompton, 1996)
Modes of experience	(Cohen, 2004)
Role of authenticity	(Hayllar & Griffin, 2005; McIntosh & Prentice, 1999; Pearce, 2005; Ryan, 2003; Wang, 1999)
Relationships with self-identity	(Desforges, 2000; Galani-Moutafi, 2000; McCabe & Stokoe, 2004; Noy, 2004; Palmer, 2005; White & White, 2004)
Dimensions of specific tourist experiences	Wilderness (Patterson *et al.*, 1998) Long-haul travel (Noy, 2004; Uriely *et al.*, 2002; White & White, 2004)
Role of narrative	(Cary, 2004; Noy, 2004, 2007)
Sacredness and spirituality	(Cohen, 2004; Graburn, 2001)
Skill formation and learning	(Hunt, 2000; Pearce, 2005; Pearce & Foster, 2007)
Place and mobility	(Hayllar & Griffin, 2005; Larsen, 2001; Li, 2000)
Social relationships	(Trauer & Ryan, 2005)
Role of imagery	(Tuohino & Pitkänen, 2003)
Influential elements of experience	(Larsen, 2007; Nickerson, 2006)
Overview of tourist experience research areas	(Jennings & Nickerson, 2006; O'Dell, 2007; Quan & Wang, 2004; Uriely, 2005)

two decades that focus on the identification of elements and dimensions of the tourist experience.

The post-hoc satisfaction approach is popular in the tourist experience research. This approach focuses on psychological outcomes by examining motivations (Andersen *et al.*, 2000; Ryan, 2002a), elements of satisfaction (de Rojas & Camarero, 2008; Gram, 2005; Hudson, 2002; Oh *et al.*, 2007; Prentice *et al.*, 1998) and the assessment of experiences (Jackson *et al.*, 1996; Pritchard & Havitz, 2006).

The immediate approach examines the nature of on-site real-time experiences. Though this is popular in leisure studies, due in part to the use of the Experience Sampling Method (see Hektner *et al.*, 2007 for an overview of this technique), there are fewer studies focusing on tourism.

Such studies (see Arnould & Price, 1993; Borrie & Roggenbuck, 2001; McIntyre & Roggenbuck, 1998) concentrate on a specific activity or site rather than on the experience as a whole. However, much of the post-hoc satisfaction research is done with visitors on site (see Andersen *et al.*, 2000; de Rojas & Camarero, 2008; Gram, 2005; Oh *et al.*, 2007; Prentice *et al.*, 1998; Pritchard & Havitz, 2006), therefore it may be argued that these responses are also related to real-time experiences.

In reviewing the body of tourist experience literature, there seems to be another group of studies which fall outside of the previous three approaches discussed by Mannell and Iso-Ahola (1987). Tourist experience studies have also been undertaken from a business or attraction management approach, focusing on consumer theory, the product offered and the potential for managers to enhance tourist experiences (see Andersson, 2007; Beeho & Prentice, 1995; Gilmore & Pine, 2002; Mossberg, 2007; Pine & Gilmore, 1999; Sternberg, 1997). These studies involve the evaluation of tourist sites, activities and management techniques rather than a focus on the meaning of individual experiences. These four perspectives study the tourist experience in different ways, examining the various dimensions of experiences involved in tourism.

Dimensions of Experience: Phases, Influences and Outcomes

Though there is limited research combining the dimensions of the tourist experience, that which does exist uses frameworks based on the phases of the experience, the influences on the experience, or on important criteria or outcomes of the experience.

The use of phases to examine tourist experiences is discussed by several authors (see Borrie & Roggenbuck, 2001; Botterill & Crompton, 1996; Fridgen, 1984; Graburn, 2001; Li, 2000). Using multiple phases to describe experience comes from leisure studies which argue that leisure is a multi-phased event (Rossman & Chlatter, 2000). A model presenting this phasing of experience was developed by Clawson and Knetsch (1966) and applied to tourism (see Cohen, 1979; Graburn, 2001). The Clawson and Knetsch model involves five distinct yet interacting phases starting with anticipation, travel to site, on-site activity, return travel and recollection. Studies in tourism indicate that experiences do change over time, demonstrating this multi-phase framing (Borrie & Roggenbuck, 2001). However, these models tend to focus on outside forces only, separating phases based on time and location.

The tourist experience is also framed by evaluating the influential factors involved in shaping the outcome of the experience. In reviewing the literature on quality tourist experience, Nickerson (2006) argues that there are three interwoven influencing aspects related to this phenomenon: the traveller, the product (or destination) and the local population. The traveller arrives at a destination with ideas about the kinds of experiences which could take place. These ideas are influenced by an individual's social construction and include ideas or perceptions taken from media, product images, previous knowledge, expectations and past travel experiences (see also Chapter 5). Other influences include activities which the tourist participates in, the types of interactions the tourist has with various environments and the informal social interactions which take place (Nickerson, 2006). The tourism product generally refers to experiences with tourism industries, the public sector and formal cultural brokers (such as travel agents or tour guides). Poor experiences of services, such as transportation, accommodation and food service could lead to an overall poor experience of a destination. The attitude and sense of place fostered by the local population can also have a significant effect on the tourist's experience (Nickerson, 2006). Informal host–guest social contact can be based on numerous factors, such as local development, the distribution of tourism benefits and the quality of life of residents. Similarly, Mossberg (2007) focuses on the idea of themes as a basis for structuring the tourist experience, arguing that the major influences are physical environment, personnel, other tourists and the products/souvenirs available (see Chapter 11). These influential factors presented by Nickerson (2006) and Mossberg (2007) highlight the complex nature of tourist experiences.

The exploration of the criteria and outcomes involved in the tourist experience also frame the research. Larsen (2007) argues that the various conceptions regarding this area are too ambiguous and presents a threefold idea of the tourist experience based on expectations and events, which are constructed through memory, forming new expectancies. Hayllar and Griffin (2005) present a thematic analysis of the tourist experience of a historic district in Sydney, Australia. The data suggest that there are several essential characteristics of the tourist experience, namely intimacy/relationships, authenticity and the notion of place. It is also argued that visitors seek outcomes, such as leisure, education and social interaction (de Rojas & Camarero, 2008). McIntosh and Prentice (1999), in a study of cultural tourist experiences and authenticity, find that both affective and cognitive dimensions as well as personal dimensions need to be considered. Vogt's (1976) study on wandering youth finds that seeking experiences offering personal growth is a primary motive for travellers (see also Chapter 2). The author concludes that travel allows for greater satisfaction of needs through the experiencing diverse environments (physical settings), the ability to learn about themselves (self-identity) and the world (knowledge) and the ability to develop intense though transient relationships (social aspects).

Thus, it can be seen that previous research based on the study of different sites and tourist groups demonstrates that the tourist experience involves numerous elements. However, few researchers have attempted to analyse these elements as a whole (Ryan, 2003).

Tourist Experience: A Conceptual Model

Rather than viewing the different phases, influences and outcomes found in the research as separate entities, these can be combined into single model demonstrating the multi-phased, multi-influential and multi-outcome nature of the tourist experience (see Figure 1.1). This figure is meant to provide an organised overview of the various dimensions of the tourist experience which have been presented in the literature thus far.

Figure 1.1 is based on the dominant definitional elements of the tourist experience found in the literature. The phasic nature is represented using Clawson and Knetsch's (1966) five-phase model, but also incorporates influences and personal outcomes. In this figure, the tourist experience is

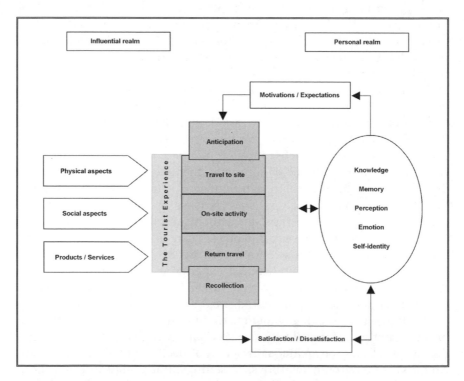

Figure 1.1 The tourist experience conceptual model of influences and outcomes

all that happens during a tourist event (travel to site, on-site activity and return travel). That being stated, the anticipatory phase and recollection phase of the tourist experience are still presented, demonstrating how the tourist experience is planned and anticipated before a trip takes places and remembered long after a trip has finished. The anticipation and recollection phases also leak into the experience itself. This is based on the idea that during travel to a site, the tourist could still be in the process of developing and refining expectations of the destination just as return travel could involve reflection on the trip which has just taken place.

During the experience, three categories of influences are presented, involving those elements which are outside the individual. The physical aspects involve spatial and place-based elements of the destination, while social aspects encompass the various social influences on experience. The influence of products and services represent factors, such as service quality, leisure activities available and the type of tourist-related products available.

The various other elements of the model are taken from findings and conclusions found in the tourist experience literature. These are incorporated into the personal realm, which involves elements within an individual. The immediate outcomes of experience are argued to be related to the overall evaluation of the trip, which can be judged through satisfaction/dissatisfaction (Ryan, 2002b). This overall evaluation can affect and is affected by elements within the personal realm, such as knowledge, memory, perception, emotion and self-identity. Though these elements could be seen as outcomes, which can change and develop after an experience through reflection and recollection, they can be impacted by the experience itself. These elements shape the experience, as tourists arrive at a destination with individual memories, perceptions of the place and people, knowledge about the world and understandings of self (Ryan, 2003; Selstad, 2007). The personal realm then feeds into motivations and expectations for future experiences, providing a cycle of motivation/expectation, experience and outcome. The remainder of this chapter will address each of the elements of the tourist experience presented in Figure 1.1 in more depth.

The influential realm

The influential realm involves elements outside of an individual which can impact upon the experience of a destination. In Figure 1.1, these influential elements are categorised as physical aspects, social aspects and products/services.

Physical aspects of destinations can be related to physical settings (natural and human made), spatial characteristics and geographical features. These physical attributes are seen as an essential influential element in understanding tourist experiences (Hayllar & Griffin, 2005; McCabe & Stokoe, 2004; Ryan, 2002a). Mossberg (2007) stresses the importance of the physical environment in the tourist consumer experience, summarising the literature in this area. The physical environment can facilitate activities, provide for social interactions and influence perceptions of tourist organisations. The tourist is seen as being uprooted from everyday environments, motivated by the spatial and cultural characteristics of destinations (McCabe & Stokoe, 2004). Mossberg (2007) argues that tourism organisations do not yet fully understand the ways in which the physical environment can affect visitor behaviour and experience. Pleasing physical aspects of destinations can lead to more positive evaluations of experiences. As there is agreement that settings are important, this is seen as an area which has the potential to be manipulated by tourism industries in order to enhance and direct experiential dimensions of tourism (Mossberg, 2007; Prentice *et al.*, 1998).

The social environment seems to be equally important in tourism experiences (Andereck *et al.*, 2006; Hayllar & Griffin, 2005; Prentice *et al.*, 1998; Selstad, 2007; Trauer & Ryan, 2005). Social aspects refer to the various social influences which can be present during tourist experiences including social settings, personal relationships, interactions with personnel, interactions with other tourists and host/guest relationships. Mossberg (2007) summarises some of the research regarding the involvement of other tourists and service personnel. Many experiences are in the presence of other people, who can influence levels of satisfaction and perceptions of quality. For example, a group of exciting and stimulating tourists will most likely enhance individual experiences. In fact, consumers can be argued to be co-producers of experiences as they are often necessary elements in the production of activities or events. This is reiterated by Andereck *et al.* (2006) who argue that social interactions influence perceived experience quality.

The role of social aspects can extend beyond the evaluation of experiences. Some researchers have argued that social aspects influence each element of the experience as they colour individual understanding. Tourist experiences bring people into contact with other people (Selstad, 2007). Therefore, the experiences of the tourist are constantly mediated through social interactions and social relationships (Selstad, 2007). Li (2000) presents an understanding of the tourist experience as an aspect of cognition where social relationships contribute to development and personal growth. Therefore, the physical and social aspects of a destination seem to permeate the experience, influencing the overall evaluation of a trip.

Stamboulis and Skayannis (2003) argue that tourist experiences can be seen as commodities related to the various products and services which enable the occurrence of experience. It can be argued that the core tourism product is experience (Prentice *et al.*, 1998); however, tangible products and tourism services (souvenirs, transportation, accommodation, facilities available, etc.) influence the overall evaluation of a trip (Ryan, 2002a). The quality of products and services during the tourist experience is deemed to be an important component (Ryan, 2003). If the quality of a specific tourist product or service meets expectations, then the consumer is satisfied (Pearce, 2005), while poor quality products and services can lead to negative attitudes towards the destination (Oh *et al.*, 2007). In tourism, products provide tangible symbols of consumption (Mossberg, 2007). de Rojas and Camarero (2008) present findings which indicate that the purchase of products intensifies the experience and is related to satisfaction. Products such as souvenirs can act as physical reminders of experiences which would otherwise remain intangible memories (Mossberg, 2007). Ryan (2002b) argues that part of the tourism product is the availability of services and activities which can satisfy the needs or desires of the individual for particular experiences. If individuals are motivated by adventure, then they will look to destinations which can offer active leisure pursuits. Similarly, if an individual is motivated by relaxation, then passive services and activities (i.e. spa services) available at the destination can meet this need. Therefore, the type and quality of products and services available at a destination can heavily influence the tourist experience.

Personal realm

The personal realm encompasses all the elements of a tourist experience which are within the individual including motivation and expectation, satisfaction/dissatisfaction, knowledge, memory, perception, emotion and self-identity.

Motivation and expectation

Much of the literature on the tourist experience highlights the importance of motivations and expectations as being related to the overall evaluation of the experience of a destination. Motivation is understood as the personal factors which influence the overall assessment of travel (Ryan, 2002b). Generally, motivations are discussed in terms of their relationship to tourist behaviour (Crompton, 1979), rather than tourist experiences. However, as motivation can be argued to contribute to the choices made and the experiences sought, it is an important element in the tourist experience. Researchers defining tourist motivations have generally done so by developing a list of reasons why people travel (see a summary of motivations in Table 1.2).

Tourist motivations are mainly characterised by the desire to escape (Burton, 1995; Crompton, 1979; Fodness, 1994; Graburn, 2001; Oh *et al.*, 2007). The idea of escape equates to a push factor. Andersen *et al.* (2000)

Table 1.2 A summary of motivations for tourist experiences

Motivation	Source
Escape	(Burton, 1995; Crompton, 1979; Fodness, 1994; Graburn, 2001; Oh *et al.*, 2007)
Education	(Burton, 1995; Crompton, 1979; Fodness, 1994; Ryan, 2002b)
Relaxation	(Burton, 1995; Crompton, 1979; Fodness, 1994; Ryan, 2002b)
Adventure	(Burton, 1995; Crompton, 1979; Fodness, 1994)
Enhancement of relationships	(Burton, 1995; Crompton, 1979; Fodness, 1994)
Exploration of self	(Crompton, 1979; Fodness, 1994; Vogt, 1976)
Prestige	(Burton, 1995; Crompton, 1979; Fodness, 1994)
Interpersonal interactions	(Crompton, 1979; Fodness, 1994)
Novelty	(Crompton, 1979; Fodness, 1994)
Recreation	(Fodness, 1994)
Health	(Fodness, 1994)
Regression	(Crompton, 1979)
Mastery	(Ryan, 2002b)

summarise the research on tourist motivation by discussing Crompton's push and pull factors. Push factors are motivations which provide the reason for leaving home, such as escape from everyday routine or relief from job stress. Pull factors are those which come from the destination, such as imagery of the landscape, activities offered and possible personal benefits available that can satisfy the push motives. Cohen (1979) argues that though motivations may be the reasons behind why people travel, they do not fully explain the tourist experience.

The focus of motivational research has been on satisfaction (Patterson *et al.*, 1998). Therefore, research has focused on whether or not the experience met the needs or desires which motivated the individual to travel, which is highly related to the role of expectations in tourist experiences.

Expectations are defined as anticipated traits, formed beliefs and predictions related to future events or states (Larsen, 2007). In much of the research, the role of expectation is generally related to the overall evaluation of experiences (see discussion in Pearce, 2005; Ryan, 2003; Vittersø *et al.*, 2000). If expectations of experiences are met or exceeded, then satisfaction will occur. Dissatisfaction occurs when experiences do not meet expectations.

Expectations are also linked to more theoretical discussions concerning the tourist gaze (Urry, 2002). Urry uses the notion of the tourist gaze to conceptualise how a tourist – influenced by media, preconceived images and ideas, and past experiences – arrives at a destination with particular assumptions about what one will see and experience. These expectations are often sought out specifically, thereby confirming preconceptions about people or places. Therefore, expectations can colour experiential choices and understanding of place, influencing whether or not the experience is satisfying. The role of expectations in satisfaction is discussed in more detail in the following section.

Satisfaction/Dissatisfaction

Satisfaction is generally discussed as an overall outcome of tourist experiences. However, as shown in Table 1.2, tourists are not motivated to travel to achieve 'satisfaction', but rather to escape, learn, relax, etc. Pearce (2005) describes satisfaction not as an end goal but as a post-experience attitude. In Fournier and Mick's (1999) phenomenological study of consumer satisfaction, the authors present the complexities of this concept, arguing that satisfaction is:

> a context-dependent process consisting of a multi-model, multi-modal blend of motivations, cognitions, emotions, and meanings, embedded in sociocultural settings, that transforms during progressive and regressive consumer–product interactions. (Fournier & Mick, 1999: 16)

The debate over how consumers of experience find satisfaction has been long standing. In tourism, satisfaction has historically been seen as the congruence between expectation and experience (when experiences meet or exceed expectations), whereas dissatisfaction is perceived to be the gap between expectation and experience (Pearce, 2005; Ryan, 1995). Many authors have questioned this approach to measuring satisfaction as it assumes satisfaction to be mainly based on expectations.

Otto and Ritchie (1996) examined satisfaction in tourism service experiences, finding several specific dimensions including hedonistic pursuits, safety and comfort, involvement in service delivery and feelings of importance which can be measured to better understand satisfaction. Arnould and Price (1993) observed that satisfaction in adventure rafting experiences was linked to communion with nature, connection with other people and renewal of the self, noting that the relationship between pre-trip expectation and satisfaction was weak. These findings indicate that satisfaction is not a simple measure of the confirmation or disconfirmation of expectations, but is based on a more rich and personal evaluation of experiences reflected in emotions, relationships and self-identity. Research also indicates that tourists have the ability to adapt to failed expectation as satisfaction can arise from other influential factors. Ryan (2002b) presents an argument that even disappointing experiences (broken down transportation, terrible meals, poor accommodation) could still lead to satisfaction as they can become trophies or stories of how the tourist overcame difficulties. Other authors voice concerns over that lack of research on the emotional value of tourism within the measure of satisfaction (Vittersø *et al.*, 2000). This is addressed by de Rojas and Camarero (2008) who define satisfaction as the evaluation of components and the feelings generated by cognitive and affective aspects of the product or service. The cognitive path involves the evaluation of quality and comparison with expectations, whereas the affective path begins when experiences reach or exceed expectations leading to feelings of pleasure. Though this approach does include affective elements, it fails to take into consideration emotion-based expectations and the evaluation of emotional elements of the experience compared to these expectations. It also fails to acknowledge the potential emotional involvement in dissatisfaction (disappointment, sadness, or even anger).

Holbrook and Hirschman (1982) explored consumer behaviour and argue that satisfaction is merely one component of experiences. Sensations, emotions, imagery and other hedonic components are related to how consumers evaluate experiential aspects of consumption. This is in agreement with Csikszentmihalyi's (1975) research which emphasises *flow* as the ideal outcome of leisure experiences, when the complete involvement in an activity results in enjoyment and pleasure. Though these arguments stress the need to go beyond satisfaction as a main outcome of the tourist experience, generally tourist events are linked to some sort of positive/satisfactory result or negative/unsatisfactory result. However, the definition of and factors involved in a satisfying outcome of a tourist experience require further discussion.

Ryan (2003) argues that the meaning of experience is also based on authenticity regarding what is being sought from the holiday. The concept of authenticity is rooted in the understanding of on-site tourist experience (Pearce, 2005), therefore it may seem strange that this element is not included in Figure 1.1. There are two reasons for this exclusion. Firstly, authenticity is understood as only being involved in the tourist experience *if* this is what is being sought from the experience. Pearce (2005) summarises research on authenticity and discusses how many researchers view the search for authenticity as being relevant only to some tourists some of the time. In Cohen's (1979, 2004) discussion on modes of tourism, it can be argued that certain types of travel (recreational and diversionary modes) do not involve authenticity as the primary goal is pleasure rather than the search for realness and deeper meaning (see Chapters 2 and 4 for further discussion on authenticity). Though some authors argue that authenticity is the goal of tourist experiences (Mannell & Iso-Ahola, 1987), in looking at the motivations for travel (outlined previously in Table 1.2) this goal does not seem to be present. Motivations such as escape and relaxation can be of primary importance in tourist trips, therefore the evaluation of the authenticity of foods, performances, events, or objects is not necessarily considered by the tourist. Secondly, if authenticity is involved in the tourist experience, it can be seen as being related to the process of evaluating experiences (satisfaction/dissatisfaction). Hayllar and Griffin (2005) prize authenticity as an essential characteristic of the tourist experience in historic districts as tourists noted the authentic character of the site as important. Therefore, authenticity becomes a way to measure overall satisfaction rather than an element in its own right. However, this argument seems to only be valid when discussing objective or constructed authenticity.

In Wang's (1999) paper on authenticity, the author argues for various applications, categorising authenticity as being related either to objects or to experiences. Wang outlines three different approaches to authenticity in tourism (see Table 1.3).

Based on Wang's (1999) definitions, existential authenticity could be argued to be involved in all elements of the tourist experience if that leads to a real emotional or cognitive reaction. Even in the seeking of pleasure, the individual may be seeking authentic feelings of pleasure, rather than those which are contrived. This would make authenticity almost synonymous with experience and it would therefore be encompassed within the personal realm (see Chapter 2 for further discussion on authenticity as it relates to identity, escape and experience).

Table 1.3 Three approaches to authenticity in tourism (see Wang, 1999)

Objective authenticity	*Constructive authenticity*	*Existential authenticity*
Authentic tourist experiences are related to the experience of authentic objects.	Authentic tourist experiences are centred on symbolic authenticity, related to how individuals perceive and interpret tourist objects.	Authentic tourist experiences are not based on objects, but rather on the personal feelings involved in tourist activities. Authenticity is related to the achievement of finding an authentic self or state of being.

Knowledge

Knowledge is a cognitive aspect of the tourist experience which involves learning and education. There is an argument that all tourism involves experiential learning as it broadens our understanding of places and people (Li, 2000; Smith & Jenner, 1997). However, there is little research available on knowledge and learning in tourism, though this is deemed to be an important part of the experience (Li, 2000; McIntosh & Prentice, 1999; Ryan, 2003). Pearce (2005) argues that this is due to the limited commercial interest in how and what tourists learn as learning and reorganising individual world views are not applicable to consumer purchases.

Much of the research associated with learning in tourism can be found in literature on the educational value of field trips (Ritchie *et al.*, 2003). Several studies have identified specific skills and learning outcomes related to field work and travel experiences. In synthesising the findings from the literature, four main categories of learning and skill development in tourist experiences emerge:

- Cognitive development: discovery of knowledge and mental skills.
- Affective development: discovery of feelings or emotional responses.
- Psychomotor development: discovery of manual or physical skills.
- Personal development: discovery of self.

The specific attributes outlined in the literature which fall within the four main categories of learning and skill development are listed in Table 1.4.

The attributes outlined in Table 1.4 demonstrate the potential educational and knowledge-based aspects of tourism. It is unclear whether or not these aspects are specifically sought out by the tourist or are simply a result of experiences or a combination of both. It is also unclear how knowledge and educational development relate to the evaluation of a tourist event. This lack of insight suggests that more specific research into the relationship between knowledge and the tourist experience is warranted.

Memory

Memory is an important element in the tourist experience (Larsen, 2007; Pine & Gilmore, 1999). Noy argues that tourism practices are the resources for experience, which are accessible only in the form of representations through memory. Memories can be defined as filtering mechanisms which link the experience to the emotional and perceptual outcomes of a tourist event (Oh *et al.*, 2007).

The discussion on memory and its relationship with experiences is not new. Fridgen (1984), in a review of the literature on environmental

Table 1.4 Skills and learning outcomes associated with tourist experiences

Cognitive development	
Communication skills	(Gmelch, 1997; Pearce & Foster, 2007)
Critical thinking skills	(Pearce & Foster, 2007)
Cultural learning and awareness	(Berwick & Whalley, 2000; Byrnes, 2001; Davidson-Hunt & Berkes, 2003; Li, 2000; Litvin, 2003; Pearce & Foster, 2007)
Decision-making skills	(Gmelch, 1997; Pearce & Foster, 2007)
Environmental learning/ Cognitive mapping	(Byrnes, 2001; Guy *et al.*, 1990; Walmsley & Jenkins, 1992)
Geographic knowledge	(Roper, 2002)
General knowledge of history	(Pearce & Foster, 2007)
Global understanding	(Byrnes, 2001; Li, 2000; Vogt, 1976; Wilson, 1988)
Heightened awareness of home country	(Wilson, 1988)
Knowledge of world issues	(Li, 2000; Pearce & Foster, 2007, Wilson, 1988)
Linguistic skills	(Gmelch, 1997; Pearce & Foster, 2007)
Management of financial and material resources	(Gmelch, 1997; Pearce & Foster, 2007)
Problem-solving skills	(Byrnes, 2001; Gmelch, 1997; Pearce & Foster, 2007)
Research skills	(Pearce & Foster, 2007)
Time management	(Pearce & Foster, 2007)
Affective development	
Dealing with pressure and stress	(Gmelch, 1997; Pearce & Foster, 2007)
Making and maintaining relationships	(Arnould & Price, 1993; Pearce & Foster, 2007; Vogt, 1976)
Strengthening relationships	(Arnould & Price, 1993; Trauer & Ryan, 2005)
Patience	(Byrnes, 2001; Noy, 2004; Pearce & Foster, 2007)
Responsibility	(Gmelch, 1997; Pearce & Foster, 2007)
Tolerance of others	(Noy, 2004; Pearce & Foster, 2007)

Table 1.4 (*Continued*)

Psychomotor development	
Information literacy (media and information technology)	(Pearce & Foster, 2007)
Mastery over tools	(Arnould & Price, 1993)
Physical skill enhancement	(Arnould & Price, 1993)
Personal development	
Adaptability/Flexibility	(Byrnes, 2001; Gmelch, 1997; Hunt, 2000; Pearce & Foster, 2007)
Independence	(Gmelch, 1997; Pearce & Foster, 2007)
Interpersonal competence/ Self-awareness	(Arnould & Price, 1993; Kuh, 1995; Noy, 2004; Pearce & Foster, 2007; Vogt, 1976; White & White, 2004)
Leadership	(Hunt, 2000; Kuh, 1995)
Maturity	(Gmelch, 1997; Noy, 2004)
Open-mindedness in considering other viewpoints	(Litvin, 2003; Pearce & Foster, 2007)
Self-confidence	(Gmelch, 1997; Hunt, 2000; Pearce & Foster, 2007)
Self-initiated activity/ Self-motivation	(Pearce & Foster, 2007)
Self-transition	(Noy, 2004; White & White, 2004)
Teamwork	(Arnould & Price, 1993; Byrnes, 2001; Pearce & Foster, 2007)

psychology and tourism, notes that memory interacts with the evaluation of tourist experiences. Negative events tend to fade while positive events are recalled with more accuracy. This importance of memory as an influential aspect of experience is reiterated by Selstad (2007) and Cary (2004). Though memory is seen as the outcome of experience, it can also be actively involved in the interpretation and transformation of experience through narration (Selstad, 2007). The narration of memory allows experiences to change, indicating that experiences are not closed items; they can continually evolve within tourist discourse. This is necessary to keep in mind, as tourists are not passive recipients of destination experiences, but are involved in the production of meaning (Selstad, 2007). Cary (2004) reiterates this argument, stating that there are differences between actual experiences and the later representation of experiences in narratives, as these representations are based on memory. Further discussion on the role of narratives in experiences can be found in Chapter 3.

In taking a cognitive approach to the study of tourist experience, one must consider the mental memory processes, as this memory will be all that remains after the experience has ended (Larsen, 2007). Therefore, it can be argued that memory is the most influential aspect of tourist experiences, as it can have a strong influence on other factors, such as perception.

Perception

Perception is how sensory inputs are processed, organised and interpreted (Larsen, 2007), and is defined as a process where meaning is attributed to an environment, event or object (Reisinger & Turner, 2004). Perception is influenced by an individual's inner psychology including motivations, emotions, values, opinions and worldviews as well as the characteristics of the environment.

Larsen (2007) argues that perception as a mental process allows us to evaluate our tourist experiences. The evaluation of experiences can result from the similarities and differences between perception and expectation (Reisinger & Turner, 2004) making perception a powerful determinant of tourist satisfaction (Ryan, 2003). The importance of perception is reiterated by Selstad (2007) who argues that perception is at the core of experience, interacting with our evaluation and memory of an event. The meaning we take from an experience is based on a perception which is socially constructed. The tourist carries with him/her pre-set ideas, values and knowledge which colour the interpretation of experiences (Selstad, 2007). Reisinger and Turner (2004) present three types of perception: those of other people; those of ones self; and those of perceptions. In tourism this involves how tourists perceive others, how tourists perceive themselves and how tourists perceive how they are perceived by others. These perceptions are constantly interacting with experiences to develop and challenge interpretations of events, activities and objects making perception a vital element of the tourist experience.

Emotion

The affective dimension of the tourist experience was discussed briefly in relation to satisfaction and knowledge, but warrants additional discussion regarding emotion in the tourist experience.

Tourism is argued to offer complex emotions related to destinations (Noy, 2007). These emotions are understood as outcomes of tourist events (Oh *et al.*, 2007) which influence the evaluation of experiences (Chang, 2008; de Rojas & Camarero, 2008; Holbrook & Hirschman, 1982; Nettleton & Dickinson, 1993; Vitterso *et al.*, 2000). Emotional responses are also argued to influence perceptions and memories of experiences (Chang, 2008; Trauer & Ryan, 2005). Arnould and Price (1993) studied rafting as an extraordinary experience and found that these experiences involve intense emotions. The authors argue that these emotional outcomes are highly related to the relationships that develop during the experience. Trauer and Ryan (2005) argue that emotional elements involving personal relationships create memory and these memories can reinforce intimacies where places are seen as a centre for emotional exchange. White (2005) summarises the literature on emotion in tourism where emotional states can influence the relationship between people and places. This idea of emotional attachments to physical place is encompassed in the concept of sense of place.

Though sense of place is argued to involve spatial and cognitive elements (Farnum *et al.*, 2005; Stokowski, 2002), it is most often linked with emotion (Stokowski, 2002). Kyle and Chick (2007) and Jorgensen and Stedman (2006) argue that this concept involves the emotions (place attachment), beliefs (place identity) and behavioural commitments (place dependence) of individuals to a geographic setting. In summarising the research, both Farnum *et al.* (2005) and Stedman (2003) argue that place attachment – the emotional or affective bond which develops between humans and the environment – is a core concept in sense of place.

There are arguments in sense of place literature which relate to its applicability to the tourist experience. Hawkins and Backman (1998) studied the sense of place in visitor conflict and found that tourists experience a bond with the landscape. The authors even observed a degree of ownership amongst some visitors who resented other visitors they perceived to be less involved with the area. Kianicka *et al.* (2006) examined tourist and resident relationships to local landscape and found that the tourist's sense of place was shaped mainly by the characteristics of the area (i.e. beauty) and the leisure activities available. The depth of emotional attachment to places was consistent in both tourists and residents, as was the importance of environmental features (Kianicka *et al.*, 2006). This then demonstrates that emotional bonds can form between the tourist and the destination. Given the potential emotional and spatial variables that can influence experience, it is interesting to note that this has not been given much attention in the tourist experience literature.

Self-identity

Travel and tourism is seen as a transitional experience which can shape the way in which we understand our own identity (Desforges, 2000; Palmer, 2005; Selstad, 2007; Vogt, 1976; White & White, 2004). Therefore, the tourist experience is something which can affect our everyday life through changes in self-identity and self-perception.

The general theme of self-identity involves questions related to the kind of person an individual perceives themselves to be. Desforges (2000) relates the ideas of identity in tourism to Urry's (2002) and MacCannell's (1973) ideas of tourist experiences, arguing that the anticipation of trips, the experience of places and the narratives presented upon return are involved in processes of redeveloping self-identity. Noy (2004) agrees, discussing how the understanding of experiences allow for stories of identity to be told and this can manifest into the validation of a transformed self. Vogt's (1976) study on wandering youth discusses how travel experiences are specifically sought out as opportunities for personal growth and transformation.

Identity involves the connections between individuals and society as well as individualistic senses of person (Desforges, 2000). This is reiterated by Galani-Moutafi (2000) who argues that self-identity through the tourist experience is linked to the comparison between the individual and the 'other'. Therefore, the evaluation of the identity of other cultures is a way to then formulate the tourist's own identity.

The relationship between identity and travel has been empirically researched in long-haul tourist groups. White and White (2004) studied older adults, finding that travel can facilitate transition during periods of life change, suggesting that tourism serves as a right of passage as individuals move from an old way of life to new ways of living. Desforges (2000) interviewed long-haul tourists from the UK and concluded that the experiences of tourism are used to narrate and represent identity. More research is needed on the relationship between self-identity and the tourist experience within other tourist groups.

Conclusion

This chapter has provided an overview of the tourist experience, presenting definitions of this area and four dominant perspectives (definitional approach, post-hoc satisfaction approach, immediate approach and business or attraction management approach) which have developed through the examination of leisure and tourist experience research. This overview has demonstrated that though interest in the tourist experience is increasing in the academic literature in recent decades, there are still numerous areas which require further investigation to have a better understanding of this phenomenon. One under-researched area in tourism is the immediate or in the moment evaluation of experiences. Recent advances in mobile technology offer opportunities to tap into these tourism experiences while they are occurring. Currently, the authors are involved in a research project that uses such technologies within the educational tourism context.

The previous discussion of the various influences and outcomes presented in Figure 1.1 is based on a summary of those aspects most often associated with the tourist experience in the literature. However, this model is not meant to be all encompassing, as the tourist experience needs further investigation to discover and document the complexities and relationships of these various elements. More in-depth research is needed on how physical settings, social settings and product/service attributes can affect an experience. There is also considerable disagreement in the literature as to how experiences are evaluated by the tourist. More research is needed to:

- determine the extent to which satisfaction is an appropriate measure of experiences in tourism;
- examine how authenticity is involved in the tourist experience;
- evaluate how knowledge or learning relates to experiences;
- examine the importance of internal and external factors in influencing quality tourism experiences;
- understand the affective dimension of the tourist experience including how emotion interacts with expectations, perceptions and the evaluation of events; and
- examine how positive and negative experiences vary for different types of tourists.

This chapter intended to present the various dimensions involved in the tourist experience, providing a summary of those dimensions and relationships in the tourist experience conceptual model. Many of the ideas and arguments presented in this chapter will be addressed in more detail throughout this text.

References

Andereck, K., Bricker, K.S., Kerstetter, D. and Nickerson, N.P. (2006) Connecting experiences to quality: Understanding the meanings behind visitors' experiences. In G. Jennings and N.P. Nickerson (eds) *Quality Tourism Experiences* (pp. 81–98). Burlington, MA: Elsevier Butterworth-Heinemann.

Andersen, V., Prentice, R. and Wantanabe, K. (2000) Journeys for experiences: Japanese independent travellers in Scotland. *Journal of Travel and Tourism Marketing* 9, 129–151.

Andersson, T.D. (2007) The tourist in the experience economy. *Scandinavian Journal of Hospitality and Tourism* 7 (1), 46–58.

Arnould, R.J. and Price, L.L. (1993) River magic: Extraordinary experience and the extended service encounter. *Journal of Consumer Research* 20 (1), 24–45.

Beeho, A.J. and Prentice, R. (1995) Evaluating the experiences and benefits gained by tourists visiting a socio-industrial heritage museum: An application of ASEB Grid Analysis to Blists Hill Open-Air Museum, The Ironbridge Gorge Museum, United Kingdom. *Museum Management and Curatorship* 14 (3), 229–251.

Berwick, R.F. and Whalley, T.R. (2000) The experiential bases of culture learning: A case study of Canadian high schoolers in Japan. *International Journal of Intercultural Relations* 24 (3), 325–340.

Borrie, W. and Roggenbuck, J.W. (2001) The dynamic, emergent, and multi-phasic nature of on-site wilderness experiences. *Journal of Leisure Research* 33 (2), 202–228.

Botterill, D.T. and Crompton, J.L. (1996) Two case studies exploring the nature of the tourist's experience. *Journal of Leisure Research* 28 (1), 57–82.

Burton, R. (1995) *Travel Geography* (2nd edn). Harlow: Pearson Education.

Byrnes, D. (2001) Travel schooling: Helping children learn through travel. *Childhood Education* 77 (6), 345–350.

Cary, S.H. (2004) The tourist moment. *Annals of Tourism Research* 31 (1), 61–77.

Chang, J.C. (2008) Tourists' satisfaction judgments: An investigation of emotion, equity, and attribution. *Journal of Hospitality & Tourism Research* 32 (1), 108–134.

Clawson, M. and Knetsch, J.L. (1966) *Economics of Outdoor Recreation*. Baltimore, MD: Johns Hopkins.

Cohen, E. (1979) A phenomenology of tourist experience. *Sociology* 13 (2), 179–201.

Cohen, E. (2004) *Contemporary Tourism: Diversity and Change*. Oxford: Elsevier.

Crompton, J. (1979) Motivations for pleasure travel. *Annals of Tourism Research* 6 (4), 408–424.

Csikszentmihalyi, M. (1975) *Beyond Boredom and Anxiety*. San Francisco, CA: Jossey-Bass.

Davidson-Hunt, I. and Berkes, F. (2003) Learning as you journey: Anishinaabe perception of social-ecological environments and adaptive learning. *Conservation Ecology* 8 (1), 5. Accessed 03.06.10.

de Rojas, C. and Camarero, C. (2008) Visitors' experience, mood and satisfaction in a heritage context: Evidence from an interpretation center. *Tourism Management* 29 (3), 525–537.

Desforges, L. (2000) Traveling the world: Identity and travel biography. *Annals of Tourism Research* 27 (4), 926–945.

Farnum, J., Hall, T. and Kruger, L.E. (2005) *Sense of Place in Natural Resource Recreation and Tourism: An Evaluation and Assessment of Research Findings*. Portland, OR: US Department of Agriculture, Forest Service, Pacific Northwest Research Station.

Fodness, D. (1994) Measuring tourist motivation. *Annals of Tourism Research* 21 (3), 555–581.

Fournier, S. and Mick, D.G. (1999) Rediscovering satisfaction. *Journal of Marketing* 63 (4), 5–23.

Fridgen, J.D. (1984) Environmental psychology and tourism. *Annals of Tourism Research* 11 (1), 19–39.

Galani-Moutafi, V. (2000) The self and the other: Traveler, ethnographer, tourist. *Annals of Tourism Research* 27 (1), 203–224.

Gilmore, J.H. and Pine, B.J. (2002) Differentiating hospitality operations via experiences: Why selling services is not enough. *Cornell Hotel and Restaurant Administration Quarterly* 43 (3), 87–96.

Gmelch, G. (1997) Crossing cultures: Student travel and personal development. *International Journal of Intercultural Relations* 21 (4), 475–490.

Graburn, N.H.H. (2001) Secular ritual: A general theory of tourism. In V.L. Smith and M. Brent (eds) *Hosts and Guests Revisited: Tourism Issues of the 21st Century* (pp. 42–50). New York: Cognizant Communication.

Gram, M. (2005) Family holidays. A qualitative analysis of family holiday experiences. *Scandinavian Journal of Hospitality and Tourism* 5 (1), 2–22.

Guy, B.S., Curtis, W.W. and Crotts, J.C. (1990) Environmental learning of first-time travelers. *Annals of Tourism Research* 17 (3), 419–431.

Hawkins, G. and Backman, K.F. (1998) An exploration of sense of place as a possible explanatory concept in nature-based traveler conflict. *Tourism Analysis* 3, 89–102.

Hayllar, B. and Griffin, T. (2005) The precinct experience: A phenomenological approach. *Tourism Management* 26 (4), 517–528.

Hektner, J.M., Schmidt, J.A. and Csikszentmihalyi, M. (2007) *Experience Sampling Method: Measuring the Quality of Everyday Life*. London: Sage.

Highmore, B. (2002) *Everyday Life and Cultural Theory*. London: Routledge.

Holbrook, M.B. and Hirschman, E.C. (1982) The experiential aspects of consumption: Consumer fantasies, feelings and fun. *Journal of Consumer Research* 9 (2), 132–140.

Hudson, B.J. (2002) Best after rain: Waterfall discharge and the tourist experience. *Tourism Geographies* 4 (4), 440–456.

Hunt, J.B. (2000) Travel experience in the formation of leadership: John Quincy Adams, Frederick Douglass and Jane Addams. *Journal of Leadership and Organizational Studies* 7 (1), 92–106.

Jackson, M., White, G.N. and Schmierer, C.L. (1996) Tourism experiences within an attributional framework. *Annals of Tourism Research* 23 (4), 798–810.

Jennings, G. (2006) Perspectives on quality tourism experiences: An introduction. In G. Jennings and N.P. Nickerson (eds) *Quality Tourism Experiences* (pp. 1–22). Burlington, MA: Elsevier Butterworth-Heinemann.

Jennings, G. and Nickerson, N.P. (eds) (2006) *Quality Tourism Experiences*. Burlington, MA: Elsevier Butterworth-Heinemann.

Jorgensen, B.S. and Stedman, R.C. (2006) A comparative analysis of predictors of sense of place dimensions: Attachment to, dependence on, and identification with lakeshore properties. *Journal of Environmental Management* 79 (3), 316–327.

Kianicka, S., Buchecker, M., Hunziker, M. and Muller-Boker, U. (2006) Locals' and tourists' sense of place: A case study of a swiss alpine village. *Mountain Research and Development* 26 (1), 55–63.

Kuh, G.D. (1995) The other curriculum: Out-of-class experiences associated with student learning and personal development. *The Journal of Higher Education* 66 (2), 123–155.

Kyle, G. and Chick, G. (2007) The social construction of a sense of place. *Leisure Sciences* 29 (3), 209–225.

Larsen, J. (2001) Tourism mobilities and the travel glance: Experiences of being on the move. *Scandinavian Journal of Hospitality and Tourism* 1 (2), 80–98.

Larsen, S. (2007) Aspects of a psychology of the tourist experience. *Scandinavian Journal of Hospitality and Tourism* 7 (1), 7–18.

Li, Y. (2000) Geographical consciousness and tourism experience. *Annals of Tourism Research* 27 (4), 863–883.

Litvin, S.W. (2003) Tourism and understanding: The MBA study mission. *Annals of Tourism Research* 30 (1), 77–93.

MacCannell, D. (1973) Staged authenticity: Arrangements of social space in tourist settings. *The American Journal of Sociology* 79 (3), 589–603.

Mannell, R.C. and Iso-Ahola, S.E. (1987) Psychological nature of leisure and tourism experience. *Annals of Tourism Research* 14 (3), 314–331.

McCabe, S. and Stokoe, E.H. (2004) Place and identity in tourists' accounts. *Annals of Tourism Research* 31 (3), 601–622.

McIntosh, A.J. and Prentice, R. (1999) Affirming authenticity: Consuming cultural heritage. *Annals of Tourism Research* 26 (3), 589–612.

McIntyre, N. and Roggenbuck, J.W. (1998) Nature/person transactions during an outdoor adventure experience: A multi-phasic analysis. *Journal of Leisure Research* 30 (4), 401–422.

Mossberg, L. (2007) A marketing approach to the tourist experience. *Scandinavian Journal of Hospitality and Tourism* 7 (1), 59–74.

Nettleton, B. and Dickinson, S. (1993) Measuring emotional responses of park users. *Australian Parks & Recreation* Autumn, 14–18.

Nickerson, N.P. (2006) Some reflections on quality tourism experiences. In G. Jennings and N.P. Nickerson (eds) *Quality Tourism Experiences* (pp. 227–236). Burlington, MA: Elsevier Butterworth-Heinemann.

Noy, C. (2004) This trip really changed me: Backpackers' narratives of self-change. *Annals of Tourism Research* 31 (1), 78–102.

Noy, C. (2007) The poetics of tourist experience: An autoethnography of a family trip to Eilat. *Journal of Tourism and Cultural Change* 5 (3), 141–157.

O'Dell, T. (2007) Tourist experiences and academic junctures. *Scandinavian Journal of Hospitality and Tourism* 7 (1), 34–45.

Oh, H., Fiore, A.M. and Jeoung, M. (2007) Measuring experience economy concepts: Tourism applications. *Journal of Travel Research* 46 (November), 119–132.

Otto, J.E. and Ritchie, J.R.B. (1996) The service experience in tourism. *Tourism Management* 17 (3), 165–174.

Palmer, C. (2005) An ethnography of Englishness: Experiencing identity through tourism. *Annals of Tourism Research* 32 (1), 7–27.

Patterson, M., Watson, A., Williams, D. and Roggenbuck, J.W. (1998) An hermeneutic approach to studying the nature of wilderness experiences. *Journal of Leisure Research* 30 (4), 423–452.

Pearce, P. (2005) *Tourist Behaviour: Themes and Conceptual Schemes*. Clevedon: Channel View Publications.

Pearce, P.L. and Foster, F. (2007) A "University of Travel": Backpacker learning. *Tourism Management* 28, 1285–1298.

Pine, B.J. and Gilmore, J.H. (1999) *The Experience Economy: Work is Theatre & Every Business a Stage*. Boston, MA: Harvard Business School Press.

Prentice, R.C., Witt, S.F. and Hamer, C. (1998) Tourism as experience: The case of heritage parks. *Annals of Tourism Research* 25 (1), 1–24.

Pritchard, M.P. and Havitz, M.E. (2006) Ratios of tourist experience: It was the best of times and it was the worst of times. *Tourism Analysis* 10, 291–297.

Quan, S. and Wang, N. (2004) Towards a structural model of the tourist experience: An illustration from food experiences in tourism. *Tourism Management* 25, 297–305.

Reisinger, Y. and Turner, L.W. (2004) *Cross-Cultural Behaviour in Tourism: Concepts and Analysis*. Oxford: Elsevier Butterworth-Heinemann.

Ritchie, B.W., Carr, N. and Cooper, C. (2003) Schools' educational tourism. In B.W. Ritchie (ed.) *Managing Educational Tourism* (pp. 130–180). Clevedon: Channel View Publications.

Roper, A.S.W. (2002) *2002 Global Geographic Literacy Survey*. National Geographic Education Foundation. On WWW at http://www.nationalgeographic.com/geosurvey2002/download/RoperSurvey.pdf. Accessed 5.11.07.

Rossman, J.R. and Chlatter, B.E. (2000) *Recreation Programming: Designing Leisure Experiences*. Champaign, IL: Sagamore.

Ryan, C. (1995) *Researching Tourist Satisfaction: Issues, Concepts, Problems*. London: Routledge.

Ryan, C. (ed.) (2002a) *The Tourist Experience* (2nd edn). London: Continuum.

Ryan, C. (2002b) From motivation to assessment. In C. Ryan (ed.) *The Tourist Experience* (2nd edn, pp. 58–77). London: Continuum.

Ryan, C. (2003) *Recreational Tourism: Demand and Impacts*. Clevedon: Channel View Publications.

Selstad, L. (2007) The social anthropology of the tourist experience. Exploring the "Middle Role". *Scandinavian Journal of Hospitality and Tourism* 7 (1), 19–33.

Smith, C. and Jenner, P. (1997) Market segments: Educational tourism. *Travel & Tourism Analyst* 3, 60–75.

Stamboulis, Y. and Skayannis, P. (2003) Innovation strategies and technology for experience-based tourism. *Tourism Management* 24 (1), 35–43.

Stedman, R.C. (2003) Is it really just a social construction? The contribution of the physical environment to sense of place. *Society & Natural Resources* 16 (8), 671–685.

Sternberg, E. (1997) The iconography of the tourism experience. *Annals of Tourism Research* 24 (4), 951–969.

Stokowski, P.A. (2002) Languages of place and discourses of power: Constructing new senses of place. *Journal of Leisure Research* 34 (4), 368–382.

Trauer, B. and Ryan, C. (2005) Destination image, romance and place experience—an application of intimacy theory in tourism. *Tourism Management* 26 (4), 481–491.

Tuohino, A. and Pitkänen, K. (2003) The transformation of a neutral lake landscape into a meaningful experience – interpreting tourist photos. *Tourism and Cultural Change* 2 (2), 77–93.

Uriely, N. (2005) The tourist experience: Conceptual developments. *Annals of Tourism Research* 32 (1), 199–216.

Uriely, N., Yonay, Y. and Simchai, D. (2002) Backpacking experiences: A type and form analysis. *Annals of Tourism Research* 29 (2), 520–538.

Urry, J. (2002) *The Tourist Gaze* (2nd edn). London: Sage.

Vittersø, J., Vorkinn, M., Vistad, O.I. and Vaagland, J. (2000) Tourist experiences and attractions. *Annals of Tourism Research* 27 (2), 432–450.

Vogt, J.W. (1976) Wandering: Youth and travel behavior. *Annals of Tourism Research* 4 (1), 25–41.

Walmsley, D.J. and Jenkins, J.M. (1992) Tourism cognitive mapping of unfamiliar environments. *Annals of Tourism Research* 19 (2), 268–286.

Wang, N. (1999) Rethinking authentocitiy in tourism experience. *Annals of Tourism Research* 26 (2), 349–370.

White, C.J. (2005) Culture, emotions and behavioural intentions: Implications for tourism research and practice. *Current Issues in Tourism* 8 (6), 510–531.

White, N.R. and White, P.B. (2004) Travel as transition: Identity and place. *Annals of Tourism Research* 31 (1), 200–218.

Wilson, A.H. (1988) Reentry: Toward becoming an international person. *Education and Urban Society* 20 (2), 197–210.

Chapter 2

Searching for Escape, Authenticity and Identity: Experiences of 'Lifestyle Travellers'

SCOTT COHEN

Introduction

Since the 1970s, it has been argued that escaping from the pressures of one's 'home' society in order to search for more 'authentic' experiences is a primary driver in tourist motivation. On a broader level, escaping *from* in order *to* is reflective of Iso-Ahola's (1982) characterisation of leisure and tourism experiences as two-fold: dependent not only on an idea of escape or avoidance, but also on a process of seeking. Indeed, consumer experiences in the leisure and tourism industries can be linked to a notion of searching. Morgan (2006: 305) noted that the word 'experience' itself has been generally used in leisure and other industries 'to describe the essence of what customers are seeking and paying for'.

If individuals are seeking 'experiences' through the vehicles of leisure and tourism, how can researchers begin to understand experiences from a participant perspective? Certainly, this is a complex question that is not satisfied with the simple assumption that individuals seek to escape to authentic experiences. Nonetheless, the theories surrounding escapism and authenticity have been historically relied upon in various attempts to understand participant experiences in leisure and tourism. However, recent poststructural approaches have questioned both the possibility of escape and the grounds for authenticity, hoping to bury both of these concepts on the basis of their relativity.

Deconstruction has threatened the validity of the meanings and rewards that individuals may perceive in experiences by favouring discourse over subjectivities. The resultant backlash has re-emphasised 'self', as individual worldviews have been relied upon to re-justify escape as a state of mind and shift the focus of authenticity away from 'objectivity' and instead towards the authenticity of subjective experiences. With this movement has come a wealth of research on identity as the notion of searching for a stronger sense of self has gained momentum as a useful tool in understanding leisure and tourism experiences.

In line with these theoretical shifts in trying to understand individual realities, this chapter (re)examines the dialectics surrounding escapism,

27

authenticity and identity in the context of leisure and tourism experiences. Attempt is made to not only discuss escapism, authenticity and identity from a modern perspective, but to also give voice to poststructural discourses without losing sight of the meanings and values that individuals still place on subjective experiences. As such, the chapter is first focused on the broad theoretical debates surrounding escapism, authenticity and identity, while the latter part of the chapter uses an illustrative case study. The case study, based on interpretive findings from the author's fieldwork with 'lifestyle travellers' in India and Thailand in 2007, provides a research-based example of the roles that escapism, authenticity and identity may play in participant experiences.

Escapism

Within modern literature on tourist motivation, the need to escape has long been posited as a key motivator for why some individuals go on holiday (Crompton, 1979; Dann, 1977; see also Chapter 1). Escapism has been described as a push factor, which refers to factors that predispose an individual to travel (Dann, 1977). Crompton (1979: 416) noted that the desire to 'escape from a perceived mundane environment', or in other words, the tedium of routine, formed one of the major motives driving vacation behaviour. In Riley's (1988: 317) description of long-term budget travellers, she held that her respondents were 'escaping from the dullness and monotony of their everyday routine, from their jobs, from making decisions about careers, and desire to delay or postpone work, marriage, and other responsibilities'. Iso-Ahola (1982) broadly suggested that individuals may try to escape dimensions of both their personal and interpersonal worlds.

From a psychology perspective, Baumeister (1991) commented that individuals may be trying to escape their current ideas of 'self'. He also suggested that escape may be temporarily achieved by 'shrinking' down the self to its bare minimum. Pine and Gilmore (1999) noted that 'escapist experiences' correspond with a complete immersion of a participant in an activity, a dimension that has also been called upon in Csikszentmihalyi's (1975) description of the concept of flow experience. The feeling of flow experience has been described as an enjoyable and focused concentration in which one experiences a loss of self-consciousness (Csikszentmihalyi, 1990). Hence, being in flow means temporarily escaping one's ideas of self.

A number of researchers have indicated wider aspects of modern Western society from which tourists may try to escape. Dann (1977: 187) suggested that a tourist may wish to 'get away from it all', so as to escape a feeling of isolation that may be felt in everyday life as the result of perceiving one's home society as anomic. Anomie is a sociological term used to describe situations where social 'norms' are conflicting or non-integrated (Roberts, 1978). When applied at the individual level, a derivative of anomie, anomia, can be used to describe someone who feels alienated and unable to direct her/his life meaningfully in a social context (Dann, 1977; Roberts, 1978).

Having supported a view that Western society may be perceived as anomic, Ateljevic and Doorne found in focus groups with long-term travellers that they had 'pessimistic perceptions of global capitalism and its associated lifestyle' (2000: 135) and an 'increasing dissatisfaction with the Western way of life' (2000: 133) that caused the travellers to view travel as a form of escape, which in turn allowed for 'personal growth'. This perspective was reinforced in Maoz's (2007: 126) study of Israeli backpacker motivations, in which the participants 'attempt to escape what they describe as a very materialistic, stressed and harsh society' and as such perceived a reversal of their previous 'conformist' lives. Davidson (2005: 36) found that 'many travellers imagine and experience travel as a route to "finding one's own space" outside the social, political and economic contradictions of life at home'. Thus, as suggested by Richards and Wilson (2004: 5) in their discussion of the nomad as an idealised form of travel, travel may be experienced as 'liberation from the constraints of modern society'. In this sense, travel is Romanticised as an exercise of 'self-directed idealism', for which striving to fulfil imaginative ideals is an integral part of the experience (Campbell, 1987: 213).

While the need to escape has been frequently suggested as a motivator for tourism experiences, it must be reminded that motivations are multidimensional, need to be contextualised and are changing over time (Crompton, 1979; Goeldner & Ritchie, 2006; Ryan, 1997a, 1997b). As such, holidays may be periods of escape for some individuals at certain times (Ryan, 1997a), but for those for which escape is relevant, it may also be working in tandem with other needs and desires. Nonetheless, as a supposed means of resisting pressures and dissatisfaction with one's home society, tourism has been regularly used in modern attempts to allow alienated individuals escape from the constraints of a perceived mundane existence and/or the anomie of Western society.

More recently, however, the possibility of actual escape, not just through tourism and leisure, but through all aspects of life, has come under scrutiny as the increasing commodification of experiences has highlighted the underlying social construction of many, if not all, forms of escape. Most people would view a quest to escape as a 'projection' out from the values of their society (Rojek, 1993). Within modern literature on escape attempts, there has existed an underlying assumption that a dominant reality exists that individuals may attempt to resist (Cohen & Taylor, 1992). This 'paramount reality' would have 'objectively specifiable circumstances' such as, for instance, a daily timetable, an occupational career and/or domestic routines (Cohen & Taylor, 1992: 3). However,

Cohen and Taylor (1992: 15) pointed out that in recent years poststructural discourse has done much to deconstruct the notion of a paramount reality as:

> ...what 'the collapse of meta-narratives' implies is that there is no single meaning system or metaphor that we can use to obtain a sense of the world from which we want to distance ourselves or against which we want to construct an alternative.

In other words, rather than there being an underlying paramount reality, what seems real is that which is most successfully presented as real, however, such a reality is actually just one experiential mode among many (Cohen & Taylor, 1992). Hence, poststructural thought argues that it is not possible to talk about escape when there is no all-encompassing reality from which to escape. As Rojek (1993: 212) fatalistically held: 'There is no escape'.

Even though the impossibility of actual escape has been suggested, there are still reasons to consider escape as a useful metaphor. In addition to this book, other researchers have considered the poststructural rejection of escape but have still found it important and relevant to explore the experiences of individuals who may seek to escape (see Cohen & Taylor, 1992; Macbeth, 2000). As Cohen and Taylor (1992: 234) concluded: 'None of our scepticism or pessimism should hide our continual amazement and delight at how people keep up this struggle, how they keep trying to dislodge the self from society'. As the rewards that individuals may hope to derive from tourism and leisure experiences are dependent both on a perception of escape and a process of seeking, the focus of this chapter is next turned to the notion of authenticity and then to identity, two concepts that have oft been used in trying to answer what individuals might be seeking through tourism and leisure experiences.

Authenticity

The search for authenticity has been a reoccurring theme in attempts to understand tourists over the last four decades (Reisinger & Steiner, 2006). However, authenticity has a much longer history within existential philosophy where it has referred to experiencing one's authentic 'self' (Golomb, 1995). Yet, authenticity's source in existential philosophy has only been recently recognised within tourism studies (Steiner & Reisinger, 2006), where it has been introduced as 'existential authenticity' (Wang, 1999). Prior to an existential conceptualisation of authenticity based on self, tourism scholarship had focused on the authenticity of toured objects.

The entry point for discussions on the authenticity of toured objects in tourism scholarship is most commonly traced to Boorstin's (1964) lamentation of the loss of the possibility of 'real' travel. Boorstin (1964) criticised the growth of mass tourism and characterised tourists as a growing body of 'cultural dopes' satisfied by contrived 'pseudo-events'. In response, MacCannell (1976) posited that tourists were not satisfied with pseudo-events, but were instead alienated moderns in search of an authenticity to be found outside of the anomie of modernity. Thus, in a MacCannellian sense, tourism is seen again in a two-fold light as both a Romantic escape from the anomie of 'inauthentic' modernity and, in turn, a quest for authenticity.

Cohen (1988) suggested that MacCannell's views on authenticity assumed that the commoditisation of an experience was destructive to the authenticity of the experience for both locals and tourists. However, as cultures and societies are not frozen in time, but are dynamic, cultural products that were originally considered inauthentic can eventually become authentic over time (Sharpley, 2003). Cohen (1988) referred to this process as 'emergent authenticity', which recognised that authenticity is not a 'primitive given', but is instead negotiable.

Wang (1999) attempted to clarify the authenticity debate by first dividing the authenticity of toured objects into two usages: objective authenticity and constructive authenticity. Objective authenticity is an extraction of authenticity from museum terminology (Wang, 1999), where it is used to describe whether objects are genuine, real or unique (Sharpley, 2003). On the other hand, constructive authenticity, which allows for an emergent aspect to authenticity, considers authenticity as variable, socially constructed interpretations of the genuiness of a toured object, including toured 'Others' (Reisinger & Steiner, 2006; Wang, 1999).

Reisinger and Steiner (2006: 69) have aimed criticism at the utility of objective and constructive authenticity in understanding tourism experiences as they have claimed that the 'perspectives on the authenticity of objects are numerous, contradictory and irreconcilable'. They also reminded that through a poststructural lens, the boundaries between originals and copies have been dissolved. Thus, while the modern tourist has been associated with a serious quest for authenticity, for individuals who might fit Urry's (2002) description of a 'post-tourist', the authenticity of toured objects is irrelevant as tourism may instead be aligned with a 'playful search for enjoyment' (Cohen, 1995: 21).

Wang (1999) also identified existential authenticity as a third way of using authenticity, which does not rely on the authenticity of toured objects. Existential inquiry into the idea of an 'authentic self' has a rich philosophical history with existential philosophers such as Kierkegaard, Nietzsche, Heidegger, Camus and Sartre each having been concerned with the search for an authentic self (Golomb, 1995). As opposed to objective and constructive authenticity, which are judgements of the authenticity of external objects or activities, existential authenticity has been described as a subjective state of being in which one believes one has experienced one's 'true self' (Berger, 1973; Wang, 1999). Existential authenticity is suggested to have wider power in explaining tourist experiences as it can account for phenomena that are difficult to objectify such as nature experiences and interactions between tourists (Reisinger & Steiner, 2006; Wang, 1999).

Existential authenticity is described as a process of 'being in touch with one's inner self, knowing one's self, having a sense of one's own identity and then living in accord with one's sense of oneself' (Steiner & Reisinger, 2006: 300). Thus, existential authenticity clearly rests on the notion that an individual is able to maintain an integrated sense of self. However, poststructural discourse that has attempted to devalue the notion of the authentic in terms of the original has also cast significant doubt on the possibilities of experiencing a stable sense of self. While Wang (1999) argued that a deconstruction of the authenticity of toured objects had opened the way for alternative experiences of existential authenticity, other theorists such as Gergen (1991: 7) have instead suggested that the multiplicity of incoherent and disconnected relationships that exist in postmodernity 'pull us in myriad directions, inviting us to play·such a variety of roles that the very concept of an "authentic self" with knowable characteristics recedes from view'. Hence, for postmoderns, experiencing one's authentic self loses all meaning as a 'bombardment' of external images erodes the sense of an authentic core (Cote & Levine, 2002: 41).

Thus, while the focus of authenticity in tourism studies may have shifted from toured objects to perceived experiences of one's authentic self (Kim & Jamal, 2007; Steiner & Reisinger, 2006; Wang, 1999), poststructural perspectives continue to call for authenticity in all its forms to be buried entirely. Disagreement over the utility of authenticity in understanding tourist experiences has been paralleled by a prolific increase in tourism research pertaining to identity. This is not surprising considering that existential authenticity and concepts of identity both rely on concerns over notions of 'self'.

Identity

The accumulation of tourism experiences has been proposed as one vehicle through which individuals engage in the (re)formation of identity (Desforges, 2000; Neumann, 1992; Noy, 2004), often as part of a search for personal growth or a 'subjective sustained sense of self' (Finnegan, 1997: 68). From the point of view of individual experience, identity can be understood as the sum of reflections on the subjective experience of embodied self (Cote & Levine, 2002), or as McAdams (1997: 63) stated: 'Identity is the story that the modern I constructs and tells about the me'.

Searching for identity has been argued as pervasive in modern society as the meta-narrative of self as an inner moral source with a potential that should be cultivated still pervades and drives much of Western society (Baumeister, 1986; McAdams, 1997).

Constituting a coherent sense of self, however, has become a difficult process in modernity as social organisation has changed so that choice has increasingly replaced obligation or tradition as a basis in self-definition (Cote & Levine, 2002). While personal identity is still largely constituted by broader societal forces such as nationality, class, gender, race, ethnicity and peer reference, among others, the need to link together disparate experiences into an individual life narrative has now become an increasingly important underpinning of identity (Richards & Wilson, 2006). Thus, for many modern individuals, constructing and maintaining a stable identity has become an ongoing issue (Bauman, 1996; Lanfant, 1995). As identities in contemporary times have become increasingly fragmented and fractured (Hall, 1996), most modern Western individuals still seek an idea of self that reflects unity and purpose, a cultural expectation that one's identity reflects 'a patterned and purposeful integration of the me' (McAdams, 1997: 60). In this sense, identity can act as an 'anchoring' or sense-making device (Kuentzel, 2000: 87).

In the context of tourism, Neumann (1992: 177) held that tourist sites 'are places where people find themselves working towards forms of self-realization and meaning, attempting to fill experiential vacancies that run through contemporary life'. As Rojek (1993: 178) noted, 'the traveller views travel experience as a resource in the quest for self-realization'. But while individuals may use tourism as a means of, and/or a place for, attempting to reinforce a coherent sense of identity, discursive theory has meanwhile deconstructed the popular modern view of the self as a developmental project (Baumeister, 1986).

Foucault (1988) aimed to deconstruct the reflective dimension of self by situating it historically in linguistics. The reflective self signifies the human capacity to put 'ourselves at a distance from our own being' and to 'turn a kind of mirror' on our body, social interactions and consciousness, and try to 'examine, judge, and sometimes regulate or revise it' (Seigel, 2005: 5). Through linguistic practice, or what Foucault (1988) referred to as 'technologies of the self', individuals are encouraged to learn socially condoned procedures for systematically reflecting upon their own thoughts, feelings and behaviours (Danziger, 1997). Thus, rather than the modern notion that one's 'true self' can be slowly and arduously actualised (Cohen & Taylor, 1992), discursive theory has located the reflective self as culturally contingent, and as such, socially constructed.

Selves are not just reflective, however, but are also socially relational and embodied (Seigel, 2005). Correspondingly, while discursive theory has discredited the humanistic perspective of self-realisation or self-actualisation (Maslow, 1971) that has rested on the notion of a reflective self, research on self and identity in the social sciences that has conceptualised selves as situational and performative has gained speed. Beginning with symbolic interactionism and the dramaturgical metaphors of Goffman (1959), sociology brought to the fore of the discussion on self the idea that 'selves are constructed, modified and played out in interaction with other people', meaning that rather than one fixed self, each individual has multiple selves that are permeable and contextually dependent (Vaughan & Hogg, 2002: 101).

While a Foucauldian view of self certainly draws 'attention to the socially positioning power of discourses', it has also been criticised as 'an extreme ephemeralist position that has no interest in the embodied self' (Holland, 1997: 171). Butler's (1990) work on the performativity of gender offers a useful perspective on identity constitution that may help to bridge the gap between the power of discourse and embodied selves, which re-opens theoretical possibilities for cultural and individual change (Bell, 2008). Bell (2008: 174) observed that as a theory of identity, 'performativity has come to mean that we perform multiple and shifting identities in history, language, and material embodiments'. Butler noted that identity constitution is an embodied performance that is processual, wherein individuals are always 'on the stage' and 'within the terms of the performance' (1990: 277), yet 'just as a script may be enacted in various ways, and just as the play requires both text and interpretation' so can individuals 'expand the cultural field bodily through subversive performances of various kinds' (1990: 282).

Thus, while all performances are citations, or enacted ways of doing, for instance, class, sexuality, gender, ethnicity, age and abilities, identities are also performative in that they are negotiated in and through a process of becoming (Bell, 2008). The theatrical metaphor of 'kinesis' offers insight into the performative nature of identity constitution as a process of 'breaking and remaking' in which performances not only mirror and sustain normative boundaries but can also subvert and transgress them (Bell, 2008: 13). An understanding that identity is not a fixed given, but is always in process, indicates that experiences can be opportunities for individuals to (re)produce a sense of personal identity. This may hold especially relevant during tourism and leisure experiences when individuals may perceive a higher degree of choice than in other aspects of their daily lives (Graburn, 1983; Neulinger, 1981).

Understanding Experiences of Lifestyle Travellers

While the earlier sections have discussed general theoretical issues surrounding escapism, authenticity and identity in tourism and leisure experiences, the chapter now turns to a case study in the context of tourism to illustrate how the concepts discussed may manifest in 'real' life. The author, with several years of long-term travel experience himself, conducted in-depth, semi-structured interviews with 25 'lifestyle travellers', while having undertaken participant observation over three months in northern India and southern Thailand in 2007. The inquiry was focused on interpreting why these individuals travelled as a lifestyle and the subjective meanings they may have placed upon their travel experiences. The criteria for selecting lifestyle travellers were a fluid combination of self-definition of travel as one's lifestyle and multiple trips of approximately six months or more. A number of interesting insights from the participant perspective relating to escapism, authenticity and identity emerged from the study.

The subjective experiences of many of the lifestyle travellers gave empirical support to the importance of perceived escape as a travel motivation and push factor (Crompton, 1979; Dann, 1977), as individuals frequently cited the desire to escape as a reason for why they had decided to go travelling. Several of the interviewees felt that escapism played a significant role in why they had first chosen to go travelling, and for some, why they had continued to travel. As Thomas (English, 29) observed, 'For me it was escapism at the beginning, purely and utterly escapism'. However, it seemed that escapism may have played a lessening role over time for some of the lifestyle travellers, which reflected Ryan's (1997a) suggestion that holidays may be periods of escape for some individuals at certain times. As Julie (German, 27) attested when asked if her motivation for travel had changed over time: 'Now I don't have to escape anymore. The first travelling was just an escape. But now I have such a nice life'.

The lifestyle travellers at times described escape in terms of their immediate personal worlds, but more often characterised their escapes as a broader movement away from the perceived values of their home societies. Charlotte (Canadian, 26) summed up travel as a perceived escape from one's immediate reality: 'In a lot of ways, I think it's an escape; that you want to escape the present reality that you've created for your self'. Respondents described feeling 'boxed in' by the expectations of their family and peers. This included not only expectations to work and pursue adult responsibilities such as raising a family, but also to act, behave and/or even dress in a certain manner. When asked what she generally liked about travel, Jackie (English, 26) focused on the anonymity that the travel experience seemed to allow:

> When you're at home, there's always pressure from the people around you and the people that know you who expect you to do a

certain thing. But when nobody knows you, they don't expect you to act in a certain way. I suppose it's the freedom of being anonymous.

Here, as with Davidson's (2005: 36) depiction of travel as an imagined route to 'finding one's own space', travel had afforded Jackie the opportunity to feel she had 'broken out' from previous patterns of behaviour, a process which may have been more difficult when spatially under the thumb of familiar social expectations.

A general dissatisfaction with the idea of fulltime work or 'responsibility' also pervaded many of the interviews. As Brendon (Irish, 26) commented on why he travelled as a lifestyle: 'Escapism is definitely a huge part of it. Adult responsibilities seem a million miles away and you're not thinking about rent, it's definitely to escape.' Many respondents felt trapped by their home society and attempted to escape it by physically moving outside the boundaries of it. Julie (German, 27) said of her life back in Germany prior to travel – 'I felt like a bird in a cage'. Moreover, Fiona (New Zealander, 23) recalled her disappointment in returning to what she perceived as a mundane life in New Zealand after her first long trip away: 'There was just so much routine, it was just all the same and people didn't seem to be going anywhere, everyone just in a rut'. Respondents commonly felt negatively towards falling into a 'routine life', which credited the notion that individuals may desire to escape from a perceived mundane environment (Crompton, 1979; Riley, 1988).

In terms of escaping a perceived anomie in their home societies, many of the lifestyle travellers noted value differences with 'Western society' over the importance of naturalness, materiality, money and the drive to succeed. Julie (German, 27) described how she no longer identified with what she perceived as the dominant German lifestyle: 'When I was three weeks at home it was horrible, absolutely horrible, because everything's inside. Everyone is trying to be the best in everything, it's terrible, and it's all about money.' A strong ethic of anti-materialism, which runs deeply through the traveller lifestyle and largely rests on the belief that one needs nothing more than the contents of a backpack, may have helped some of the lifestyle travellers to have felt they were freer from Western consumerism. Hence, the perception among many of the lifestyle travellers of Western society as anomic supported previous tourism research that has aligned travellers with feelings of alienation (Ateljevic & Doorne, 2000; Dann, 1977; Maoz, 2007).

Alternatively, it can be suggested that while these lifestyle travellers may somewhat escape the cycle of working in order to buy tangible goods, that they are instead held captive by the need to purchase experiences.

When asked if travel allowed for freedom from consumerism, Thomas (English, 29) responded:

> This is modern materialism, we're sold this dream and we buy in to it. Experience things and see new things. But linking it with freedom, if you've got a free mind, you're not bound by anything.

Rather than being deterred by the commodification of experience in the travel context, Thomas focused instead on the importance of escape and freedom as states of mind. Thus, while actual escape may not be possible, the subjective experience of feeling or believing one has escaped may satisfy some individuals.

Commercialised tourist escape routes beg questions of the authenticity of toured objects. However, the concept of authenticity, both in its toured object and existential capacities, did not emerge directly as a relevant theme in discussions with the participants. Rather than voicing concern over the authenticity of experiences with the 'Other', the lifestyle travellers did, however, express a desire to experience their 'true selves' through travel. Hence, many of the respondents indirectly touched upon the discourse of existential authenticity (Kim & Jamal, 2007; Steiner & Reisinger, 2006; Wang, 1999), yet did so through using a vocabulary of self and identity. This indicated that the boundaries between perceptions of existential authenticity and identity constitution may be blurred as both concepts can be linked to the subjective experience of one's perceived 'true self'.

The concept of searching for self, a form of identity work, was frequently cited among the lifestyle travellers as a motivating factor for their engagement in lifestyle travel. However, while some of the lifestyle travellers consciously undertook a search for a more secure sense of self through travel, others instead recognised their identity work retrospectively. Yet, as Simon (Swiss, 50), the oldest of the respondents, suggested: 'I think everyone looks, searching for their self'. It was common for the lifestyle travellers to view travel as a developmental process of learning about their 'inner self', which was characteristic of Maslow's (1971) humanistic perspective of self-actualisation. Tamara (Canadian/Indian, 34), who had been travelling for the majority of the last 17 years, summed up the assumption of many of the lifestyle travellers that an inner self existed and could be discovered and developed in having said: 'Travelling is really about your self, about learning what's inside of your self'. In several instances, learning about the self was communicated as processual and based in daily experience:

> Everyday you learn about you. Everyday you know you more and more. You know who you are more and more. Maybe it's really important to know who you are. For me, it's really important. (Eric, French, 35)

For Eric, who had sold his business in France in order to travel and work in Asia indefinitely, learning about the self was an ongoing exercise in which striving towards an idealised or felt 'true' self was an important part of the experience (Campbell, 1987).

Some of the respondents viewed 'self-discovery' as more fruitfully undertaken when physically away from their home environments as travel often allowed for the experience of new and different situations. This was supported by Ehud (Israeli, 34), who when asked about travel's role in regards to identity, related that it was helpful to be away from one's comfort zone in order to get to know the self better:

> It gives you angles, gives you experiences, as you experience yourself in different situations you know yourself better. As much as you break your routine, your chain, you will know yourself better.

The new experiences that the travel context had presented Ehud were placed in contrast to the 'chains' of mundane life, thus again pointing to leisure and tourism experiences as a two-fold process of avoidance and seeking (Iso-Ahola, 1982). Through negotiating situations in which one was unsure of how to act, respondents expressed that they could test themselves and learn from the experience.

> All these things that you endure and then you experience and that you learn so much about yourself that you don't even know is within your self and that might not even have a chance to come out if you didn't travel. (Tamara, Canadian/Indian, 34)

As such, challenging experiences were perceived by some of the respondents as potentially transformational moments in the search for self. As Fiona (New Zealander, 23) communicated about her travel experiences: 'I guess it felt empowering, and just having those experiences as your own made me feel stronger'.

In contrast to the intense work week he considered as typical of his home society, Alec (Scottish, 34) suggested that travel may provide a freer sense of space and time that can lead individuals to the feeling that something has 'shifted inside':

> Maybe having moments of reflection and inner inquiry leads you to some sort of feeling. Maybe that's one aspect of why travellers have that, just purely from that we have time and freedom to allow that experience to happen. Not necessarily saying it happens for every-body of course, but there's a lot more opportunity and potential for those people to even inquire into those things and possibly have some kind of understanding or experience or something, some shift inside just because they have the chance to.

The maxim of 'finding one's self' through travel was even somewhat lampooned by Laura (Canadian, 28), who seemed to realise for the first time during the interview that she had used travel as a means of addressing identity questions:

> I think it was when I first went to England, when I was thinking, ok, well, maybe I just need another year off to find myself. I used that term, ha, ha. Maybe I need to leave the country and actually live somewhere else and find myself in a different country where I don't know anyone and I can sort of start fresh and go from there. I don't know anyone so I can be whoever I want, change my personality, which I always sort of figured I'd do but hasn't really happened.

With her latter words, rather than seeking an internal self, Laura seemed to have embraced the idea of changing her environment so that she could be whoever she wanted. Laura may have inadvertently hinted at a concept of identity that has the potential for multiple selves or performances. In a similar vein, when asked what 'grabbed him' when he first started travelling, Barry (English, 32) related: 'I suppose it is that, kind of, you can just shed a life each time you change places. You can just change your life each time you want to go somewhere new'. For Laura and Barry, self was not necessarily an innate object to be developed, but instead multiple and open to various performances (Bell, 2008; Butler, 1990). In contrast to the majority of the other lifestyle travellers, these latter views on identity were more representative of the trend in the social sciences to conceive of selves as relational, multiple and contextually dependent (Danziger, 1997; Finnegan, 1997; Vaughan & Hogg, 2002) rather than as an individual developmental project (Maslow, 1971; Neumann, 1992). Thus, the divergence in views on self among the lifestyle travellers reflected oppositional theoretical perspectives on self and identity that have run through the broader academic literature.

Conclusion

Modern theories on seeking escapism, authenticity and identity point to each of these concepts as critical in understanding dimensions of tourism and leisure experiences. Although the actual possibility of escape, an objective basis for authenticity and the concept of self have all been subject to deconstruction, the lifestyle travellers in this study seemed to have taken little heed of the supposed 'illusion' at the basis of their searching efforts. Indeed, the case study has demonstrated that some individuals still seek experiences that allow for feelings of escape and a stronger sense of identity, and that meaning and value may be attached to experiences that provide for these perceptions.

Though the lifestyle travellers regularly cited tourism as a means of escape from the constraints of a perceived mundane existence and/or the anomie of Western society (Crompton, 1979; Dann, 1977), concern over the authenticity of experiences with the Other was not voiced. Instead, many of the respondents indirectly touched upon issues of existential authenticity using a vocabulary of self and identity. This indicates that identity discourse may be a more useful theoretical lens for discussing 'self' than the existential conceptualisation of authenticity introduced to tourism studies by Wang (1999). While many of the lifestyle travellers sought to experience their 'true self', reflecting a widely held humanistic assumption that an inner self exists that can be transformed and developed (Baumeister, 1986; McAdams, 1997), there were also participant perspectives that alluded to selves as relational and performative, which instead pointed to opposing theories on identity constitution (for instance, Butler, 1990; Finnegan, 1997). Hence, there was a theoretical tension in perspectives on self and identity among the lifestyle travellers.

In their discussion of the 'experience economy', Pine and Gilmore (1999) suggested that a competitive edge will be gained by providers who are able to momentarily satisfy a consumer's search for personal transformation. Such transformational experiences reflect encounters in which a participant feels that she/he has changed as the result of an experience. To perceive self-transformation or self-change is a narration of identity (Noy, 2004). In this light, experiences that can provide a temporary perception of escape as well as allow participants to work and play with identity should not be under-valued.

References

Ateljevic, I. and Doorne, S. (2000) Tourism as an escape: Long-term travelers in New Zealand. *Tourism Analysis* 5, 131–136.

Bauman, Z. (1996) From pilgrim to tourist – or a short history of identity. In S. Hall and P. du Gay (eds) *Questions of Cultural Identity* (pp. 18–36). London: Sage.

Baumeister, R.F. (1986) *Identity: Cultural Change and the Struggle for Self*. New York: Oxford University Press.

Baumeister, R.F. (1991) *Escaping the Self: Alcoholism, Spirituality, Masochism, and Other Flights from the Burden of Selfhood*. New York: Basic Books.

Bell, E. (2008) *Theories of Performance*. Los Angeles, CA: Sage.

Berger, P.L. (1973) 'Sincerity' and 'authenticity' in modern society. *The Public Interest* 31, 81–90.

Boorstin, D.J. (1964) *The Image: A Guide to Pseudo-Events in America*. New York: Harper & Row.

Butler, J. (1990) Performative acts and gender constitution: An essay in phenomenology and feminist theory. In S. Case (ed.) *Performing Feminisms: Feminist Critical Theory and Theatre* (pp. 270–282). Baltimore, MD: Johns Hopkins University Press.

Campbell, C. (1987) *The Romantic Ethic and the Spirit of Modern Consumerism.* Oxford: Basil Blackwell.

Cohen, E. (1988) Authenticity and commoditization in tourism. *Annals of Tourism Research* 15, 371–386.

Cohen, E. (1995) Contemporary tourism – trends and challenges: Sustainable authenticity or contrived post-modernity? In R. Butler and D. Pearce (eds) *Change in Tourism: People, Places, Processes* (pp. 12–29). London: Routledge.

Cohen, S. and Taylor, L. (1992) *Escape Attempts: The Theory and Practice of Resistance to Everyday Life.* London: Routledge.

Cote, J.E. and Levine, C.G. (2002) *Identity Formation, Agency, and Culture: A Social Psychological Synthesis.* Mahwah, NJ: Lawrence Erlbaum.

Crompton, J. (1979) Motivations for pleasure vacation. *Annals of Tourism Research* 6 (4), 408–424.

Csikszentmihalyi, M. (1975) *Beyond Boredom and Anxiety.* San Francisco, CA: Jossey-Bass.

Csikszentmihalyi, M. (1990) *Flow: The Psychology of Optimal Experience.* New York: HarperCollins.

Dann, G. (1977) Anomie, ego-enhancement and tourism. *Annals of Tourism Research* 4 (4), 184–194.

Danziger, K. (1997) The historical formation of selves. In R.D. Ashmore and L. Jussim (eds) *Self and Identity: Fundamental Issues* (pp. 137–159). New York: Oxford University Press.

Davidson, K. (2005) Alternative India: Transgressive spaces. In A. Jaworski and A. Pritchard (eds) *Discourse, Communication and Tourism* (pp. 28–52). Clevedon: Channel View Publications.

Desforges, L. (2000) Traveling the world: Identity and travel biography. *Annals of Tourism Research* 27 (4), 926–945.

Finnegan, R. (1997) Storying the Self': Personal narratives and identity. In H. Mackay (ed.) *Consumption and Everyday Life* (pp. 66–111). London: Sage.

Foucault, M. (1988) Technologies of the self. In L. Martin, H. Gutman and P. Hutton (eds) *Technologies of the Self: A Seminar with Michael Foucault* (pp. 16–49). London: Tavistock.

Gergen, K.J. (1991) *The Saturated Self: Dilemmas of Identity in Contemporary Life.* New York: Basic Books.

Goeldner, C.R. and Ritchie, J.R.B. (2006) *Tourism: Principles, Practices, Philosophies* (10th edn). Hoboken, NJ: John Wiley.

Goffman, E. (1959) *The Presentation of Self in Everyday Life.* Middlesex: Penguin.

Golomb, J. (1995) *In Search of Authenticity: From Kierkegaard to Camus.* London: Routledge.

Graburn, N. (1983) The anthropology of tourism. *Annals of Tourism Research* 10 (1), 9–33.

Hall, S. (1996) Introduction: Who needs 'Identity'. In S. Hall and P. du Gay (eds) *Questions of Cultural Identity* (pp. 1–17). London: Sage.

Holland, D. (1997) Selves as cultured: As told by an anthropologist who lacks a soul. In R.D. Ashmore and L. Jussim (eds) *Self and Identity: Fundamental Issues* (pp. 160–190). New York: Oxford University Press.

Iso-Ahola, S.E. (1982) Toward a social psychological theory of tourism motivation: A rejoinder. *Annals of Tourism Research* 9 (2), 256–262.

Kim, H. and Jamal, T. (2007) Touristic quest for existential authenticity *Annals of Tourism Research* 34 (1), 181–201.

Kuentzel, W.F. (2000) Self-identity, modernity, and the rational actor in leisure research. *Journal of Leisure Research* 32 (1), 87–92.

Lanfant, M. (1995) Introduction. In M. Lanfant, J. Allcock and E.M. Bruner (eds) *International Tourism: Identity and Change* (pp. 1–23). London: Sage.

Macbeth, J. (2000) Utopian tourists – cruising is not just about sailing. *Current Issues in Tourism* 3 (1), 20–34.

MacCannell, D. (1976) *The Tourist: A New Theory of the Leisure Class*. New York: Schocken.

Maoz, D. (2007) Backpackers' motivations: The role of culture and nationality. *Annals of Tourism Research* 34 (1), 122–140.

Maslow, A. (1971) *The Farther Reaches of Human Nature*. Middlesex: Penguin.

McAdams, D.P. (1997) The case for unity in the (post)modern self: A modest proposal. In R.D. Ashmore and L. Jussim (eds) *Self and Identity: Fundamental Issues* (pp. 46–78). New York: Oxford University Press.

Morgan, M. (2006) Making space for experiences. *Journal of Retail and Leisure Property* 5, 305–313.

Neulinger, J. (1981) *The Psychology of Leisure* (2nd edn). Springfield, IL: Charles C Thomas.

Neumann, M. (1992) The trail through experience: Finding self in the recollection of travel. In C. Ellis and M.G. Flaherty (eds) *Investigating Subjectivity: Research on Lived Experience* (pp. 176–201). Newbury Park, CA: Sage.

Noy, C. (2004) This trip really changed me: Backpackers' narratives of self-change. *Annals of Tourism Research* 31 (1), 78–102.

Pine, J.B. and Gilmore, J.H. (1999) *The Experience Economy: Work is Theatre & Every Business a Stage*. Boston, MA: Harvard Business School Press.

Reisinger, Y. and Steiner, C.J. (2006) Reconceptualizing object authenticity. *Annals of Tourism Research* 33 (1), 65–86.

Richards, G. and Wilson, J. (2004) Drifting towards the global nomad. In G. Richards and J. Wilson (eds) *The Global Nomad: Backpacker Travel in Theory and Practice* (pp. 3–13). Clevedon: Channel View Publications.

Richards, G. and Wilson, J. (2006) Developing creativity in tourist experiences: A solution to the serial reproduction of culture? *Tourism Management* 27, 1209–1223.

Riley, P.J. (1988) Road culture of international long-term budget travelers. *Annals of Tourism Research* 15, 313–328.

Roberts, K. (1978) *Contemporary Society and the Growth of Leisure*. London: Longman.

Rojek, C. (1993) *Ways of Escape: Modern Transformations in Leisure and Travel*. Houndmills: MacMillan Press.

Ryan, C. (1997a) The chase of a dream, the end of a play. In C. Ryan (ed.) *The Tourist Experience: A New Introduction* (pp. 1–24). London: Cassell.

Ryan, C. (1997b) Similar motivations – diverse behaviours. In C. Ryan (ed.) *The Tourist Experience: A New Introduction* (pp. 25–47). London: Cassell.

Seigel, J. (2005) *The Idea of the Self: Thought and Experience in Western Europe since the Seventeenth Century*. Cambridge: Cambridge University Press.

Sharpley, R. (2003) *Tourism, Tourists and Society*. Huntingdon: Elm.

Steiner, C.J. and Reisinger, Y. (2006) Understanding existential authenticity. *Annals of Tourism Research* 33 (2), 299–318.

Urry, J. (2002) *The Tourist Gaze* (2nd edn). London: Sage.

Vaughan, G.M. and Hogg, M.A. (2002) *Introduction to Social Psychology* (3rd edn). Frenches Forest: Pearson Education.

Wang, N. (1999) Rethinking authenticity in tourism experience. *Annals of Tourism Research* 26 (2), 349–370.

Chapter 3
The Shaping of Tourist Experience: The Importance of Stories and Themes

GIANNA MOSCARDO

Introduction

Stories are such a common part of our lives that it is sometimes easy to overlook their central role in the way we communicate with each other, understand and make sense of the world and its events, and store our memories. The importance of stories as a core element in human cognition and social interaction has long been recognised by psychologists (Schank & Abelson, 1977), sociologists (Durkheim *et al.*, 1995) and anthropologists (Holloway, 1997). In tourism research, however, much of the existing focus has been on narratives in general with only a few researchers explicitly analysing tourist stories (Hsu *et al.*, 2009). This chapter argues that stories and themes are critical elements in understanding tourist experiences and that we need to develop integrative conceptual frameworks in order to better understand the nature of tourist experiences. The overall aim of the chapter is to integrate concepts and issues from research into both the role of stories and themes in tourism and factors contributing to positive tourist evaluations, in order to improve our understanding of tourist experiences.

The chapter will follow an approach suggested by Fournier (1998) for understanding brand relationships in marketing and Gorke (2001) for analysing entertainment as public communication. After defining key terms, this chapter will identify major themes and concepts in existing research into stories and themes in tourism and major findings from, and theoretical approaches to, research into tourist experiences. The chapter will then highlight the convergence between these two areas before suggesting how stories and themes might fit within a systems model of the tourist experience. This systems model will then be used to highlight areas for further research as well as suggesting some practical implications.

Defining Key Terms

It is important to begin by defining and distinguishing between the various concepts that are central to this chapter – narratives, stories, myths, themes and tourist experiences. It is generally agreed that narratives are the broader more abstract concept with stories being a particular type of narrative (Brewer & Lichtenstein, 1982). According to Adaval and Weyer (1998: 208), narratives can be defined as 'knowledge structures that consist of a sequence of thematically and temporally related events. Subsumed under this heading are... stories (anecdotes that have a beginning, a plot and an end)'. Brewer and Lichtenstein (1982) also argue that there are several types of narrative and these are distinguished by their primary intent. There are narratives designed to inform such as news stories, narratives designed to persuade such as advertisements and narratives designed to entertain which are stories.

Myths can be seen as specific types of stories. Hennig (2002) argues that myths are stories that use cultural symbols and particular sequences of actions to refer to and reinforce important values and behaviours for a social or cultural group. Woodside *et al.* (2008: 98) define myths as 'a traditional story about heroes or supernatural beings, often explaining the origins of natural phenomena or aspects of human behaviour'. In the first approach it could be argued that myths can develop and change over time to suit cultural needs, while in the second it is believed that there exist certain universal archetypes for the characters in these stories and their plots that do not change over time.

An alternative to the idea of myths is that of universal themes for stories put forward by evolutionary psychologists (Davis & Mcleod, 2003; Sugiyama, 2001). Themes can be defined as the main thing to be learnt from a narrative, the moral of the story, the single big idea that is being communicated or the take home message (Moscardo *et al.*, 2007). According to evolutionary psychologists, narratives are a universal way to communicate information and storytelling is an ability that all individuals have in all cultures (Sugiyama, 2001). They argue that that the key role of a story is to pass on information about a theme that could be of value in ensuring ongoing social success and survival (Davis & Mcleod, 2003). Cross-cultural studies of the major topics or themes across a number of different types of stories including those reported in the news, folk tales and other forms of literature confirm the existence of some recurring and universal themes (Davis & Mcleod, 2003; Sugiyama, 2001). These can be categorised into:

- Themes related to survival, including information on animals, pain and death.
- Themes related to reproduction, including family, marriage and children.
- Themes related to social success, including play, friendship, reputation, group membership, loyalty, heroism and altruism (from Brochu & Merriman, 2002; Davis & Mcleod, 2003; Sugiyama, 2001).

At the most general level experience can be defined as 'a continuous process of doing and undergoing that provides meaning to the individual' (Boswijk *et al.*, 2005: 2). Shaw and Ivens (2005: 6) go onto define a customer experience, which exists within the realm of commercial consumption, as 'an interaction between an organization and a customer. It is a blend of an organization's physical performance, the senses stimulated and emotions evoked, each intuitively measured against customer expectation across all moments of contact'. Boswijk and colleagues (2005) and Moscardo (2008) highlight the complexity of the experience concept, noting that existing definitions vary on many dimensions, including the relative importance of the individual versus the setting in contributing to the experience, the extent to which expectations play a role in experience and whether experience is seen as a continuous process or a specific instance bounded in time and place (see Chapter 1 for further discussion of the temporal dimension of the tourist experience). Tourism offers a particular type of consumption experience and so for the purpose of this chapter a tourist experience will be defined as a continuous process made up of a set of events or activities occurring at a destination that often involve contact with tourism-related organisations and their personnel, and are driven by expectations of some sort of benefit.

Themes and Stories in Tourism Research

Tourism research related to themes and stories can be classified into three main types: studies of destination representations in marketing and media, research that directly analyses tourist stories and research into the role of narratives, stories and themes in interpretive settings. The following sections will briefly describe each area using some recent papers to illustrate key points. It is important to note these are not comprehensive reviews of each area but rather seek to highlight key points emerging from the research. There is also extensive use of tourist stories and narrative analysis of tourist responses as a tool to study other aspects of the tourist experience. Nimrod (2008), for example, analysed narratives and themes in the travel stories told by retirees in order to analyse the role of travel in their lives and how they negotiated various constraints to travel. Obenour *et al.* (2006) used backpacker stories to explore service quality and Desforges (2000) used travel biographies to examine the role of tourism in the development and enhancement of self-identity. In each case though, the focus is not on the nature of the stories or the role of narratives or stories in the tourist experiences.

Destination representations

There is a long tradition in tourism research of seeking to understand the representations of places and people that are associated with destinations (Mercille, 2005). These representations provide stories about destinations that are aimed at attracting tourists and/or providing meaning to their experiences. They are typically analysed by exploring narratives about destinations present in:

- promotional material such as guide books (Bhattacharyya, 1997), destination brochures (Ateljevic & Doorne, 2002) or websites (Choi *et al.*, 2007);
- presentations given by tour guides (Lugosi & Bray, 2008);
- media portrayals of destinations such as in magazines and movies (Mercille, 2005); and
- in the descriptions given by tourists (Mercille, 2005).

Jenkins (2003) describes a circle of representation that links these various sources of narratives about destinations. Destination marketers generate representations of destinations that contain narratives about the significance of the place or people who live there, stories that support the narratives and icons that mark key elements of the narratives. These representations can also be described in other media portrayals of destinations such as in literature, movies and in the news media. Tourists select destinations based on these representations, and often organise their behaviour in the destination to match the narratives and to collect the icons in some way (Chronis, 2005). Tourists then reproduce the narratives in the stories they tell about their experiences (Jenkins, 2003). It is important to recognise that this is not a closed circle. There may be multiple and conflicting representations of destinations and tourists' own experiences can create changes in the representations they pass on to others in their travel stories (Jenkins, 2003; Mercille, 2005).

Some of the work on destination representations has argued for the importance of myths and specific destination stories as part of the narratives generated by the various participants in the process. Chronis (2005), for example, provides evidence that tourists at heritage attractions often act out parts of the stories that they associate with site. Hennig (2002) goes further to argue that there are six specific myths used extensively in tourism representations. These are:

- 'Nature as a redeeming and renewing force' (Hennig, 2002: 175).
- The noble savage living in harmony with nature.
- Proximity to art and artists as a way to transcend everyday experience.
- Opportunity for individual freedom and self-realisation.
- Travel as liberation from inequality.
- Finding paradise.

Focusing on tourist stories

There is an increasing focus in consumer behaviour more generally on the importance of stories and themes in the way customers respond to advertising (Adaval & Wyer, 1998), connect to other consumers in brand communities or tribes (Veloutsou & Moutinho, 2009) and engage in consumption experiences (Arnould & Thompson, 2005). Several of the ideas expressed in this research have been developed by Woodside and colleagues in the context of tourist stories about Chinese cities (Hsu *et al.*, 2009) and Italian cities (Woodside *et al.*, 2007). In both cases the focus of the analysis was on the structure of the stories themselves with a particular emphasis on the ways in which the tourists dealt with tension arising from unbalanced cognitive states. These studies are part of a larger programme to develop a storytelling theory to explain customer relationships with brands. Table 3.1 summarises the main assumptions of, and propositions put forward for, this theory.

Woodside and colleagues (Woodside *et al.*, 2007, 2008) argue for the development of storytelling theory as a key element in consumption experiences presenting evidence that people do structure their travel stories in the ways listed in Table 3.1, and that the existence of various archetypes is important in the development of destination images. It is important to note that there is another level at which these stories, myths and roles may exist – that of the larger narrative of the tourist's own life story. According to Desforges (2000), travel and destination choices and experiences contribute to the self-identity of tourists and can make important contributions to their own biographies (see also Chapter 2).

Woodside *et al.* (2007) specifically argue that there are some archetypal roles for protagonists in these consumption stories and these are hero, antihero, creator, change master, power broker, wise old man, loyalist, mother of goodness, little trickster and enigma. These are similar to those proposed in studies of literature by Campbell (2008). It is also proposed that there are some common archetypal story plots based on universal myths and that the use of these plots is likely to make marketing efforts more effective (Woodside *et al.*, 2007). As noted previously there does exist, however, some debate over this idea of archetypes and universal myths with some arguing for more context-specific myths (Hennig, 2002) and others arguing for the importance of themes rather than myths (Davis & Mcleod, 2003).

Narratives, stories and themes in interpretive settings

Interpretive settings such as museums, art galleries, science centres, historic and archaeological sites, zoos and aquaria and guided and self-guided tours of both cultural and natural heritage areas, are common

Table 3.1 Assumptions and propositions of Woodside *et al.*'s (2008) story telling theory

Assumptions
People think narratively
Most information is stored in memory in stories
Repeating, reliving, listening to stories is a pleasurable experience and often involves archetypal myths
Brands and products can play a role in enacting a specific archetype
People seek to make sense of experience by telling stories
Propositions
Narrative storytelling requires customers to have a consumption experience
Storytelling can apply to a range of consumption experiences from high risk to mundane
Consumption stories often match the plot lines provided in brand promotion or from archetypal myths
Consumers often present themselves as being goal-directed in their stories
Stories inform the reader/listener about the thoughts of the protagonists
Consumption stories often include some sort of epiphany or personal realisation
The stories are structured around a series of events
The stories often include a crisis or turning point and/or its resolution
Situations are usually presented as clear-cut
Storytellers often provide a summary in terms of a lesson learnt

elements of many tourist experiences. In this context, interpretation can be seen as a form of informal education or persuasive communication aimed at providing tourists with information about the visited place both to improve their understanding of its significance (see e.g. Lugosi & Bray, 2008) and to encourage conservation attitudes (Moscardo & Ballantyne, 2008). A consistent finding in evaluations of the interpretation provided in these settings is that the use of stories to present information is a more effective technique than presenting lists of facts in terms of the amount of attention tourists pay to the interpretation, the amount of new information they learn and remember and the likelihood of them engaging in behaviours seen as desirable by the setting managers (Strauss, 1995).

The use of themes to provide a framework for information is also an effective way to assist visitors to develop meaning from their interpretive experiences (Moscardo *et al.*, 2007). Despite this recognition of the importance of stories and themes in effective interpretation, there has been little discussion of how or why stories and themes are valuable in these settings.

Understanding Tourist Experiences

The recent growth in interest in experiences in various types of commercial consumption is driven by two main forces. Firstly, there are the broader social and economic trends described by Pine and Gilmore (1999) in their proposed shift from a service to an experience economy. Secondly, the development of marketing into relationship marketing and branding and the recognition of the value of providing rewarding experiences for customers as part of the development of strong brand relationships between customers and businesses for enhanced competitiveness (Fournier, 1998). Tourism researchers have, however, been exploring the concept of experiences for quite some time (Uriely, 2005). In both these areas of research, customer experience in general and tourist experience in particular, the major focus of the research to date has been on identifying the elements that are related to positive outcomes and evaluations of the experiences. Table 3.2 summarises the most common and consistent findings from both these areas.

A Systems Framework of the Role of Themes and Stories in Tourist Experiences

The discussion so far can be seen as generating three key conclusions.

- Stories and themes have emerged as playing an important role in several different places in the overall tourist experience.
- There has been little discussion of why stories and themes might be important in tourist experiences.
- There is considerable convergence in the findings of several different approaches to understanding customer and tourist experiences.

It is the core argument of this chapter that a framework for understanding where stories and themes might fit into the overall system surrounding a tourist experience may be a useful first step in integrating these different approaches and suggesting areas for further research. Figure 3.1 presents such a systems framework. It is important to note that this framework sits within a larger system in which travel plays a role in the overall story of the individual tourist's life.

Table 3.2 Factors associated with effective and rewarding customer and tourist experiences

Strong, clear and consistent **theme** supported by design of servicescape (Benckendorff *et al.*, 2006; Berry & Carbone, 2007; McGoun *et al.*, 2003; Moscardo, 2008; Pine & Gilmore, 1999)
Built around a narrative/story – a story that allows customers to play a desirable role, provides opportunity for customers to create their own stories to tell others (McGoun *et al.*, 2003; Pine & Gilmore, 1999)
Perceived authenticity – on many dimensions including access to original or real objects, places or people, genuine social interactions with staff and others in the setting and the opportunity to engage in activities seen as reflecting one's true self (Benckendorff *et al.*, 2006; Mascarenhas *et al.*, 2006; Moscardo, 2008; Pine & Gilmore, 1999)
Interactive, participatory and engaging – offering clear opportunity for customers to be active **co-creators** of the experience (Benckendorff *et al.*, 2006; Boswijk *et al.*, 2005; Mascarenhas *et al.*, 2006; Moscardo, 2008; Poulsson & Kale, 2004)
Unique, rare, novel and/or **surprising features** (Benckendorff *et al.*, 2006; Mascarenhas *et al.*, 2006; Moscardo, 2008; Poulsson & Kale, 2004)
Easy to access – physical, virtual and mental access, easy to get to, easy to get around and easy to understand (Benckendorff *et al.*, 2006; Boswijk, *et al.*, 2005; Moscardo, 2008)
Multi-sensory (Benckendorff *et al.*, 2006; Moscardo, 2008; Pine & Gilmore, 1999)
Emotive – have affective elements (Kwortnik & Ross, 2007; Mascarenhas *et al.*, 2006; Trauer & Ryan, 2005)
Opportunities to be social – to interact in a social collective (Hollenbeck *et al.*, 2008; Schembri, 2009; Trauer & Ryan, 2005)
Personal relevance – connections to personal history, meets individual needs, can be personalised, can make choices (Benckendorff *et al.*, 2006; Hollenbeck *et al.*, 2008; Moscardo, 2008; Poulsson & Kale, 2004)
Total immersion in the experience setting (Benckendorff *et al.*, 2006; Berry & Carbone, 2007; Moscardo, 2008; Pine & Gilmore, 1999)
Opportunities for **learning** (Benckendorff *et al.*, 2006; Boswijk *et al.*, 2005; Hollenbeck *et al.*, 2008; Poulsson & Kale, 2004)

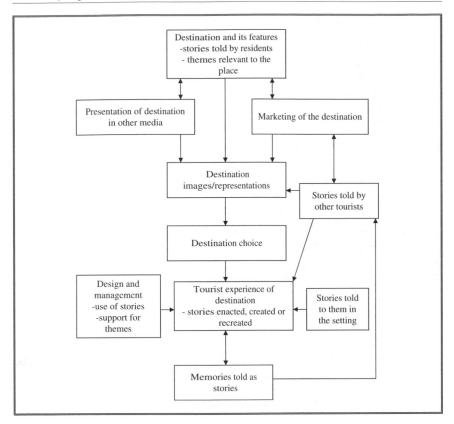

Figure 3.1 Framework for considering role of stories in tourist experiences

The framework suggests that stories exist in several parts of the tourism system starting with the stories of residents and the themes connected to destination places because of their environment, history, location or culture. These destination places are then developed and presented in various ways by tourism marketing. This marketing, the images of the destination presented in other media, stories told by other tourists and, in some case, the stories and themes presented by the residents themselves, are sources of information that contribute to the destination image that tourists may have. This destination image is one of the key variables in destination choice. Thus, any stories or themes that have been presented or are associated with the destination may have an influence on destination choice. Once in the destination, stories can be told to the tourists by other visitors, by locals, guides or tourism staff. Themes can be presented and supported by the design and management of tourist experience settings. Tourists can listen to, perform and/or create stories during their experiences and these are then presented to others as memories of the trip.

Research Implications

A consideration of the framework suggests that there are four main areas for research and examination: the role of stories in effective destination branding, the role of stories in destination choice, the significance of stories told by others and the connection between tourist stories and sustainability.

Stories, themes and effective destination marketing

In the same way that stories are an effective way to structure information in interpretation, there is evidence that the use of stories in travel promotion is also an effective form of advertising (Adaval & Wyer, 1998; Kwortnik & Ross, 2007; Woodside *et al.*, 2007). Woodside and colleagues have argued that the use of unique stories can help create effective destination brands (Hsu *et al.*, 2009; Woodside *et al.*, 2008). In particular, it has been proposed that the use of traditional myths with archetypal protagonists as the most effective option (Bodkin *et al.*, 2009; Hsu *et al.*, 2009). But there is little evidence to support these latter claims and some debate over the existence and importance of modern versus traditional myths. If, as Hennig (2002) argues, there exist a set of modern myths specific to tourism consumption, then this raises the question of linking specific types of myths, stories or themes to particular products, or in the case of tourism, particular destinations or forms of travel. It may be that some stories and themes provide a stronger justification for consumption than others (Kwortnik & Ross, 2007). In order to address these issues research is needed into:

- the range of myths or themes used in tourist stories compared to other types of consumption in order to understand if there are tourism-specific myths;
- the effectiveness of different types of story or themes in creating competitive brands; and
- possible links between types of story or theme and particular types of destination or forms of travel.

Stories, themes and destination choices

If it is possible to suggest that certain types of stories or themes may be better used for certain products then it is also possible to suggest that certain types of stories or themes may be better used to attract certain market segments. Fournier's (1998) discussion of the benefits sought from consumption suggests that consumers may have different needs at different lifecycle stages and Adaval and Weyer's (1998) work suggests that different personality types may seek different myths or roles in stories related to consumption. The research question raised in this instance is – do different tourists, based on personality, motivation, social identity and/or life cycle stage, seek different stories or find different themes more appealing than others when choosing a destination?

Given that most destinations have multiple markets, is it possible to associate different destinations with multiple themes or stories? Research by Gattrell and Collins-Kreiner (2006) at a specific attraction suggests that it is possible for multiple tourist stories to be associated with a place and for these not to create conflict. But this evidence is from one site only and further research into the possible combinations of stories and/or themes is required to better understand this issue.

Stories told by others

Tourists can be exposed to a range of different stories associated with a destination, both before and during their actual destination experiences. In addition to the sources already discussed, there are three other sources of stories that need to be considered – stories told by service personnel at the destination, stories told by friends and family and stories told by other tourists. There is an emerging discussion in the broader customer experience literature on the importance of the stories told by the service staff that customers interact with during their consumption experiences (Shaw & Ivens, 2005). This discussion suggests that it is important that staff have positive stories to tell about their own experiences of a brand or company and that staff are aware of and support the stories and themes that are being presented for the brand (Hollenbeck *et al.*, 2008). Stories told by friends and family and other tourists can be important sources of information about places. But stories told by friends and family have the additional element of nostalgia and the possibility of re-enacting stories linked to family or group traditions (Dann, 1996).

Another critical area to consider in any discussion of the stories told by other tourists is that of the social web (Gruber, 2008). Stories told by tourists in their blogs need particular attention for several reasons. Firstly, the use of travel blogs, defined as online travel diaries or ongoing narrative presented on the internet, is substantial and growing rapidly (Litvin *et al.*, 2008). Singh *et al.* (2008) provide statistics that suggest that there are more than 60 million blogs on the internet and 50–70,000 are added daily. While not all of these are travel blogs, tourist experiences are a common topic in web stories and the existence of travel blogs has significant implications for the nature of tourism (Wang *et al.*, 2002). Secondly, these travel blogs are sources of information that can influence destination images and choices both informally and formally through the incorporation of favourable blogs in destination marketing (Choi *et al.*, 2007; Litvin *et al.*, 2008). Thirdly, travel blogs can provide an additional set of stories to guide behaviour at destinations. Given the combination of visual imagery with text used in most blogs these additional stories can also guide re-enactments. Finally, blogs connect individuals to virtual communities who could offer an alternative reference point for tourist behaviour. It is possible that tourists may change their behaviour and therefore their experiences because they are aware of their virtual audience. This raises many research issues and management challenges.

Stories, themes and sustainability

There are three main ways in which stories and themes connect to sustainability issues in tourism. Firstly, there is the issue of the match between the stories and themes developed in tourism marketing and those that destination communities see as most appropriate (Walker, 2008). One of the major concerns that emerged from research into representations is that the destination images created by tourism marketers may conflict with the way residents wish to see themselves (Ashworth, 2003), in turn contributing to negative social impacts and the disempowerment of destination communities in the tourism develop-ment process (Moscardo & Pearce, 2003). This suggests that the sustainability of tourism could be improved if greater attention was paid by tourism developers and marketers to the themes and stories destination communities associate with these places.

The second way stories and themes can be linked to the sustainable development of tourism is through their influence on where tourists go and how they behave while at the destination. Tourists' pursuit of behaviours highlighted in inappropriate stories may create a range of negative environmental and social impacts. On the other hand, it may be possible to use stories and themes in a positive way encouraging a spread of benefits throughout a destination, highlighting areas or activities of local significance that could benefit from tourism income and providing examples of behaviours less likely to have negative impacts (Moscardo, 1996).

The third link between stories and themes and sustainability is through their contribution to effective interpretation and positive tourist experiences. The review of literature in the previous sections noted the importance of using stories and themes to structure information in the design of effective interpretation. Given that the aim of interpretation is to encourage minimal impact behaviours and the conservation of heritage, it can be argued that the use of stories and themes is important in encouraging sustainable behaviour and attitudes in tourists.

Management Implications

Although many research questions have been identified and the framework presented is a preliminary one requiring further analysis and revision, a number of applied directions can be presented based on the available research evidence. Firstly, it is clear that the use of stories in the development of destination images is likely to produce higher levels of tourist awareness and intention to visit. These stories can be about the destination itself, its residents or from other visitors about their own experiences of the places visited. Secondly, stories and themes can also be used to organise information for presentation to tourists when they arrive in the setting both within specific attractions and for the overall destination. Finally it can be proposed that providing tourists with opportunities to participate in the re-enactment or creation of stories as part of their activities while in the destination is likely to support many of the factors that have been shown to enhance experience development and evaluation. In terms of experience management, though, it seems that it is important to find a balance between providing sufficient detail in stories to help visitors have a clear understanding of a destination and still allowing opportunities for tourists to create their own stories.

Conclusions

This chapter has argued for greater attention to be paid to the role of stories and themes in tourist experiences. Evidence from a range of different research areas provided support for this argument. A systems framework has been proposed which sets out various places in the tourist experience system where stories might have an influence on tourist cognition and behaviour. The framework presented is a preliminary one offered as an initial point in further developing an understanding of the importance of stories and themes in experience.

References

Adaval, R. and Wyer, R.S. Jr. (1998) The role of narratives in consumer information processing. *Journal of Consumer Psychology* 7 (3), 207–245.
Arnould, E.J. and Thompson, C.J. (2005) Consumer culture theory (CCYT): Twenty years of research. *Journal of Consumer Research* 31, 868–882.
Ashworth, G.J. (2003) Heritage, identity and places for tourists and host communities. In S. Singh, D.J. Timothy and R.K. Dowling (eds) *Tourism in Destination Communities* (pp. 79–98). Wallingford: CABI.
Ateljevic, I. and Doorne, S. (2002) Representing New Zealand: Tourism imagery and ideology. *Annals of Tourism Research* 29 (3), 648–667.
Benckendorff, P., Moscardo, G. and Murphy, L. (2006) Visitor perceptions of technology use in tourist attraction experiences. In G. Papageorgiou (ed.) *Cutting Edge Research in Tourism* (available as pdf on CVD).
Berry, L.L. and Carbone, L.P. (2007) Build loyalty through experience management. *Quality Progress* 40 (9), 26–32.
Bhattacharyya, D.P. (1997) Mediating India: An analysis of guidebook. *Annals of Tourism Research* 29 (3), 371–389.

Bodkin, C.D., Amato, C. and Peters, C. (2009) The role of conflict, culture, and myth in creating attitudinal commitment. *Journal of Business Research* 62 (10), 1013–1019.

Boswijk, A., Thijssen, T. and Peelen, E. (2005) *A New Perspective on the Experience Economy.* Online document. On WWW at http://www.experience-economy.com/wp-content/UserFiles/File/Article%20Lapland5.pdf. Accessed 03.06.10.

Brewer, W.F. and Lichtenstein, E.H. (1982) Stories are to entertain: A structural-affect theory of stories. *Journal of Pragmatics* 6, 473–486.

Brochu, L. and Merriman, T. (2002) *Personal Interpretation: Connecting Your Audience to Heritage Resources.* Fort Collins, CO: The National Association for Interpretation.

Campbell, J. (2008) *The Hero with a Thousand Faces* (3rd edn). Oakland, CA: New World Library.

Choi, S., Lehto, X.Y. and Morrison, A.M. (2007) Destination image representations on the web: Content analysis of Macau travel related websites. *Tourism Management* 28, 118–129.

Chronis, A. (2005) Coconstructing heritage at the Gettysburg storyscape. *Annals of Tourism Research* 32 (2), 386–406.

Dann, G.M.S. (1996) *The Language of Tourism: A Sociolinguistic Perspective.* Wallingford: CABI.

Davis, H. and Mcleod, S.L. (2003) Why humans value sensational news – an evolutionary perspective. *Evolution and Human Behavior* 24, 208–216.

Desforges, L. (2000) Travelling the world: Identity and travel biography. *Annals of Tourism Research* 27 (4), 926–945.

Durkheim, E., Cosman, C. and Cladis, M.S. (1995) *The Elementary Forms of Religious Life.* Oxford: Oxford University Press (first published in 1912).

Fournier, S. (1998) Consumers and their brands: Developing relationship theory in consumer research. *Journal of Consumer Research* 24, 343–373.

Gattrell, J.D. and Collins-Kreiner, N. (2006) Negotiated space: Tourists, pilgrims, and the Baha'i terraced gardens in Haifa. *Geoforum* 37, 765–778.

Gorke, A. (2001) Entertainment as public communication: A systems-theoretic approach. *Poetics* 29, 209–224.

Gruber, T. (2008) Collective knowledge systems: Where the social web meets the semantic web. *Web Semantics* 6, 4–13.

Hennig, C. (2002) Tourism: Enacting modern myths. In G.M.S. Dann (ed.) *The Tourist as a Metaphor of the Social World* (pp. 169–188). Wallingford: CABI.

Hollenbeck, C.R., Peters, C. and Zinkham, G.M. (2008) Retail spectacles and brand meaning: Insights from a brand museum case study. *Journal of Retailing* 84 (3), 334–353.

Holloway, I. (1997) *Basic Concepts for Qualitative Research.* London: Blackwell.

Hsu, S-Y., Dehuang, N. and Woodside, A.G. (2009) Storytelling research of consumer's self-reports of urban tourism experiences in China. *Journal of Business Research* 62 (12), 1223–1254.

Jenkins, O.H. (2003) Photography and travel brochures: The circle of representation. *Tourism Geographies* 5 (3), 305–328.

Kwortnik, R.J. Jr. and Ross, W.T. Jr. (2007) The role of positive emotions in experiential decisions. *International Journal of Research in Marketing* 24 (4), 324–335.

Litvin, S.W., Goldsmith, R.E. and Pan, B. (2008) Electronic word-of-mouth in hospitality and tourism management. *Tourism Management* 29, 458–468.

Lugosi, P. and Bray, J. (2008) Tour guiding, organisational culture and learning: Lessons from an entrepreneurial company. *International Journal of Tourism Research* 10 (5), 467–479.

Mascarenhas, O.A., Kesavan, R. and Bernacchi, M. (2006) Lasting customer loyalty. *Journal of Consumer Marketing* 23 (7), 397–405.

McGoun, E.G., Dunkak, W.H., Bettner, M.S. and Allen, D.E. (2003) Walt's street and Wall Street: Theming, theatre and experience in finance. *Critical Perspectives on Accounting* 14, 647–661.

Mercille, L. (2005) Media effects on image: The case of Tibet. *Annals of Tourism Research* 32 (4), 1039–1055.

Moscardo, G. (1996) Mindful visitors: Creating sustainable links between heritage and tourism. *Annals of Tourism Research* 23 (2), 376–387.

Moscardo, G. (2008) Understanding tourist experience through mindfulness theory. In M. Kozak and A. DeCrop (eds) *Handbook of Tourist Behavior* (pp. 99–115). London: Routledge.

Moscardo, G. and Ballantyne, R. (2008) Interpretation and tourist attractions. In A. Fyall, A. Leask and S. Wanhill (eds) *Managing Tourist Attractions* (2nd edn) (pp. 237–252). London: Elsevier.

Moscardo, G., Ballantyne, R. and Hughes, K. (2007) *Designing Interpretive Signs: Principles in Practice*. Denver: Fulcrum.

Moscardo, G. and Pearce, P.L. (2003) Presenting destination: Marketing host communities. In S. Singh, D.J. Timothy and R.K. Dowling (eds) *Tourism in Host Communities* (pp. 253–272). Wallingford: CABI.

Nimrod, G. (2008) Retirement and tourism themes in retirees' narratives. *Annals of Tourism Research* 35 (4), 859–878.

Obenour, W., Patterson, M., Pedersen, P. and Pearson, L. (2006) Conceptualization of a meaning-based research approach for tourism service experiences. *Tourism Management* 27, 34–41.

Pine, B.J. and Gilmore, J.H. (1999) *The Experience Economy.* Boston, MA: Harvard Business School Press.

Poulsson, S.H.G. and Kale, S.H. (2004) The experience economy and commercial experiences. *The Marketing Review* 4 (3), 267–277.

Schank, R.C. and Abelson, R.P. (1977) *Scripts, Plans, Goals, and Understanding.* Hillsdale, NJ: Lawrence Erlbaum.

Schembri, S. (2009) Reframing brand experience: The experiential meaning of Harley-Davidson. *Journal of Business Research* 62, 1299–1310.

Shaw, C. and Ivens, J. (2005) *Building Great Customer Experiences* (2nd edn). New York: Palgrave MacMillan.

Singh, T., Veron-Jackson, L. and Cullinane, J. (2008) Blogging: A new play in your marketing game plan. *Business Horizons* 51, 281–292.

Strauss, S. (1995) The passionate fact: An overview of storytelling in interpretation. *InterpEdge* 2 (2), 27–28.

Sugiyama, M.S. (2001) Food, foragers, and folklore: The role of narrative in human subsistence. *Evolution and Human Behavior* 22, 221–240.

Trauer, B. and Ryan, C. (2005) Destination image, romance and place experience – an application of intimacy theory in tourism. *Tourism Management* 26, 481–491.

Uriely, N. (2005) The tourist experience: Conceptual development. *Annals of Tourism Research* 32 (1), 199–216.

Veloutsou, C. and Moutinho, L. (2009) Brand relationships through brand reputation and brand tribalism. *Journal of Business Research* 62 (3), 314–322.

Walker, K. (2008) Tools to enhance community capacity to critically evaluate tourism activities. In G. Moscardo (ed.) *Building Community Capacity for Tourism Development* (pp. 86–100). Wallingford: CABI.

Wang, Y., Yu, Q. and Fesenmaier, D.R. (2002) Defining the virtual tourist community: Implications for tourism marketing. *Tourism Management* 23, 407–417.

Woodside, A.G., Cruickshank, B.F. and Dehuang, N. (2007) Stories visitors tell about Italian cities as destination icons. *Tourism Management* 28 (1), 162–174.

Woodside, A.G., Sood, S. and Miller, K.R. (2008) When consumers and brands talk: Storytelling theory and research in psychology and marketing. *Psychology and Marketing*, 25 (2) 97–145.

Chapter 4

The Role and Meaning of Place in Cultural Festival Visitor Experiences

KELLEY A. MCCLINCHEY and BARBARA A. CARMICHAEL

Introduction

Community cultural festivals are special events that occur in public spaces, specifically community centres, parks, sidewalks or closed streets. They celebrate aspects of culture such as music, performing arts, crafts and handiwork, games, sports, and the production and consumption of food (Yeoman *et al.*, 2004). Festival visitors generate meaningful experiences from the festival based on its physical location, the type of event and its social environment. Cultural festival experiences bridge a gap between leisure and tourism experiences because they are short in duration (usually one to three days), tend to attract local residents, friends, family and past residents or visitors who have travelled a short distance to attend the event (McKercher *et al.*, 2006).

Urban areas include cultural festivals as part of their tourism strategies in order to create distinctive place images and experiences (Richards & Wilson, 2006). There is a renewed focus for urban areas to create vibrant attractive urban spaces and unique experiences for consumers rather than simply marketing products for consumption (Pine & Gilmore, 1999). Festivals are one part of these places marketing initiatives because they succeed 'by providing a space and time away from everyday life in which intense extraordinary experiences can be created and shared' (Morgan, 2008: 91).

Festival visitor experiences have garnered the attention of researchers focusing on visitor satisfaction, motivation, evaluation as well as experience (Kim *et al.*, 2002; Lade & Jackson, 2004; Morgan, 2008). However, the role of place and the meaning of place in festival experiences are also important components of the consumer experience. It is evident that festivals contribute to a community's sense of place, belonging and identity (De Bres & Davis, 2001; Derrett, 2003; Quinn, 2003). But as the number of festivals grow annually there are concerns about the over-production of events leading to negative implications such as festivalisation, the commodification of culture and loss of cultural authenticity (Getz, 2007). The commodified production of events may also lead to 'placeless' festivals, what MacLeod (2006) suggests are generic events, with no specific attachment to place or authentic cultural experience. This is an important concern for managers trying to instil unique place experiences. Therefore, how can we understand the role and meaning of place in the festival experience?

While meanings of place with regard to the images of festivals, attractions and destinations are important, understanding the meaning of place to tourists' experience and the role of place in consumer behaviour deserves attention. Place meanings may be one element in the creation of a tourist experience, but, from a cultural perspective, places serve as storehouses of meanings that capture value in use and frame expectations for experiences...Places are the venues for tourism experiences, the context for social–psychological interaction, and the phenomena by which this behaviour can be described, explained and predicted (Snepenger *et al.*, 2007: 310).

This chapter focuses on place and the meaning of place in the context of cultural festival visitor experiences. It conceptualises festival visitor experiences from a geographical understanding of place and the meaning of place through time and space. A brief discussion of place and the tourist experience will connect the themes to the festival experience before a detailed explanation is given of the conceptualisations of senses of place relating to cultural festival experiences. The description of the conceptual framework will be exemplified with cultural festival experiences in urban neighbourhoods of Toronto, Ontario, Canada. These examples are from a larger study on place meanings and festivals in urban ethnic neighbourhoods.

Space as Meaningful Place

Historically, understandings of place were as a spatial science where quantitative studies examined patterns and regularities in spatial phenomena. Place was then studied as locations with uniqueness and individuality (e.g. Sauer, 1956). However, a humanistic approach to geography evolved which sought to reconceptualise place in the context of human experiences; how people made relationships with places (Crang, 1998). Thus, it was understood that people could attach meanings to place, feel a sense of belonging to place and that place plays an important role in the formation of our identities (Holloway & Hubbard, 2001).

Geographers such as Relph (1976) and Tuan (1980) have referred to this humanistic approach to place as having a 'sense of place'. In particular, Relph devised various notions of 'insideness' and 'outsideness' based on people's level of experience with place. Insiders' feel at one with a place and have deep experiences with place, whereas outsiders feel alienated or perceive place as little more than the background or setting for activities. Relph defines a sense of place as originating from lived experience, understanding the intangible essence of a place and experiencing place as an insider. Tuan perceives that an individual develops a sense of place by knowing the place intimately and reacts to it emotionally; the place becomes significant to the individual. In other words, individuals are 'rooted' in places. Senses of place can also be influenced by ecological (physical landscape), social (relationships with others) and ideological (prevailing social and economic systems) elements (Eyles, 1985). There-fore, both individual and collective experiences are important in generating a sense of place.

The meaning of place is a complex phenomenon comprised of a variety of different interpretations. Place attachment, place dependence and place identity all refer to a variety of people's relationships and experiences with place whether it is for utilitarian or hedonic purposes (Holloway & Hubbard, 2001; Snepenger *et al.*, 2004; Wickham & Kerstetter, 2000). A *sense of place* is a holistic concept referring to affective or emotional dimensions (place attachment), cognitive dimensions (place identity) and conative or behavioural dimensions (place dependence) (Jorgensen & Stedman, 2006). In other words, a sense of place is composed of an individual's relationship with a community, a feeling of belonging to a place and a combination of both the social and physical environment (Butz & Eyles, 1997; Mazanti & Ploger, 2003; Mazumdar *et al.*, 2000; Shamai & Ilatov, 2005).

The dimensions of sense of place also coincide closely with the elements of the event visitor experience. Morgan (2008) adapts a model that integrates pull factors, push factors, social relationships, festival design, cultural meanings, symbolic meanings and personal benefits of the festival experience. It is concluded through the application of this event experience model that the key to a successful festival exists in creating a space that includes the social interactions and personal experiences of the visitors (Morgan, 2008). Others also suggest that 'place' in which tourism experience occurs may be conceptualised on a number of scales and involves different geogra-phical elements (Carmichael, 2005; Carmichael & McClinchey, 2009). More specifically, meanings ascribed to place are multi-dimensional and occur within a variety of spaces, scales and through time. A conceptual framework is presented in this chapter which displays the multi-dimensional aspect of place meanings in the context of urban cultural festival experiences.

Place Meaning and the Tourist Experience

Long-term residents of a place naturally produce a strong sense of place due to rootedness, but people who have spent only short periods of time in a place, perhaps while travelling, are said to have a sense of place due to a fleeting appreciation of it (Hay, 1998). Perhaps, visitors and tourists can even develop a deep connection and experience with a place. This is especially true since 'places have symbolic content either in their own right or because of the sentiments they represent...[which] are often shared and may be based on a place's reputation or people's activities in or memories of a place' (Eyles, 1985: 83).

Place meanings are examined and measured at different scales, in connection with tourists' experiences and within a variety of places (e.g. Gross & Brown, 2006; Lane & Waitt, 2007). However, Andrews (2005) moves beyond the idea of the static component of place by considering how tourists use their bodies and how their bodies, including the visual, olfactory and auditory senses, are directed to engage with the experience of their holidays and contribute to creating place. Subsequently, through the use of the senses tourists embody a sense of place, 'the embodiment becomes a reflexive process in which their awareness of who they are not and where they are not is heightened and feeds into understandings and constructions of their sense of self' (Andrews, 2005: 256). Visitors to a place may also experience levels of attachment similar to Relph's conceptualisations of sense of place. Chang's (2005) examination of Singapore's Little India District illustrates how 'insiders' feel at one with a place and have deep experiences with place and 'outsiders' may feel alienated where place is little more than a background or setting for activities (Chang, 2005). These examples illustrate the complexity in establishing a sense of place through personal feelings, emotions and memories as well as people's level of attachment, identity and dependence with place.

Leisure and tourism experiences are also subjective, emotional and laden with symbolic meaning (Holbrook & Hirschman, 1982) which shows a relationship with the dimensions of place perceptions. Tourist experiences are perceived as multi-component with peak experiences and supporting consumer experiences which are perceived to differ from daily routine experiences as one is believed to travel away from daily routines to experience something new, different and unique (Quan & Wang, 2004). Motivations for tourism specifically relate to the notion of extraordinary, unexpected experiences and perhaps the opportunity to glimpse something new, real and different (MacCannell, 2001; Urry, 1995). Festivals have also connected us to those ideals since they enable us to experience either a real place or a mythical place (Bell, 2003). Therefore, many relationships exist between the visitors' experience and their senses of place further complicated by the subjectivity of the type of setting and social space, personal emotions and level of authentic experience.

The Multi-dimensions of Sense of Place in Cultural Festival Visitor Experiences

It is evident that complexity exists not only in understanding the components of a sense of place but also in the components of a visitor's experience (see Chapter 1). However, by approaching this from a geographical perspective it displays the multi-dimensions of sense of place in the context of a cultural festival visitor's experience (Figure 4.1).

There are two inclusive domains as part of an individual's sense of place that being the *collective* domain and the *personal* domain. The collective domain includes the meanings of place as influenced by festival experiences with others or in the presence of others. The personal domain encompasses individual perceptions of place. The personal domain includes both the present place experiences and two *temporal* dimensions to sense of place: (1) a reflective state or nostalgia for past place experiences, and (2) an anticipatory state or the potential for future place experiences. Both of these temporal dimensions are influenced by

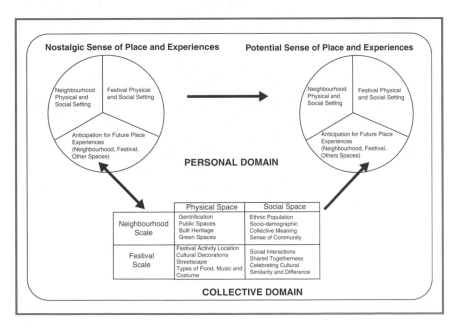

Figure 4.1 Multi-dimensional conceptual framework of sense of place

the present sense of place perceptions and experiences at the festival and in the neighbourhood.

Each temporal aspect of the sense of place experience, present, past and future, has two other geographical dimensions. The first is the *spatial* dimension, which consists of the physical space/environment and the social space/environment. The second is the *scale* dimension, which consists of the neighbourhood setting and the festival setting. These geographical dimensions of time, space and scale through the sense of place experience will be discussed further in the succeeding discussion.

Physical Space in the Neighbourhood Setting

Collective domain – present sense of place and experience

Collective experiences in the neighbourhood can impact place perceptions and festival experiences. For instance, the more positive the experience and sense of place, the more likely the visitor will attend the festival and anticipate sharing the festival experience with the community. The more negative the neighbourhood experience, the more likely the visitor will have feelings of apathy or antagonism for the event and may communicate this to others.

Physical space in the neighbourhood is important in not only maintaining positive consumer experiences on a daily basis but also impacts perceptions related to the festival as festivals exist in public spaces. The cleanliness and maintenance of parks, squares, gardens and other shared open spaces is part of the neighbourhood setting and can affect visitor experiences. For example, Kyle *et al.* (2004) discovered that respondents who identified more closely with the place identity dimension were more critical of the social and environmental conditions along the Appalachian Trail. For these respondents, disruptions to the setting were viewed negatively in their experiences of the trail.

The physical space of the neighbourhood also includes built heritage such as the age, architectural style and level of gentrification of buildings. Built heritage is recognised as part of many people's sense of belonging and cultural identity (Tweed & Sutherland, 2007). Furthermore, ethnic architectural design and heritage is important in establishing a sense of place identity for immigrant residents and visitors. For example, the construction of a China Gate in an Asian retail neighbourhood in Toronto, Canada, was a significant architectural and cultural symbol not only for the residents but also for the Asians who visit the neighbourhood regularly for consumer experiences (Zhuang, 2008). Similarly, Mazumdar *et al.* (2000) specifically showed that architectural design is an important component of place identity as it retains the memories of Vietnam for refugees in Little Saigon, California, and creates a connection to Vietnam for those born in America.

Built heritage in the neighbourhood and the types of consumer experiences available may be embedded in a particular ethnic heritage but these are not immune to change. This is the case with the neighbourhood of Little Portugal in Toronto (Teixeira, 2007). Traditionally, consumer experiences within the neighbourhood related to Portuguese culture such as bakeries and delis and specifically a sausage smoke house. However, recent gentrification and the increase in housing prices have created an influx of younger, more affluent consumers who create the demand for other experiences. Similarly, the Roncesvalles neighbourhood in Toronto which was once a distinctly Polish neighbourhood is now a multi-ethnic community. However, most of the original Polish businesses and institutions remain today even though the neighbourhood is rapidly evolving. Thus, the built heritage of Roncesvalles Avenue upon quick observation remains similar to that of previous generations. But with closer examination, it is peppered with newer businesses that attract a diverse resident and visitor consumer population. Therefore, the traditional Polish businesses attract visitors and residents whose sense of place includes the memory of a predominantly Polish neighbourhood, yet the gentrification of the neighbourhood satisfies the place and consumer experiences of newer visitors.

The previous example illustrates how types of retail shops, restaurants and concession stands in public spaces and streetscapes contribute to the physical space of the neighbourhood. Chessell (2002) also explores the role of Italian traditions such as sitting at outdoor cafes, visiting market stalls as well as attending festivals in Australia's outdoor Mediterranean-style public spaces in authenticating a cosmopolitan sense of place. These collective experiences in a specific physical space such as the Italian piazza connect with the personal space through our senses. Thus, senses enable a collective experience in the neighbourhood to become a personal experience.

Social Space in the Neighbourhood Setting

Collective domain – present sense of place and experiences

Social spaces contribute to meanings of places by allowing people to identify with their neighbourhood through relationships with family and friends. Hidalgo and Hernandez (2001) reveal that social attachment in a neighbourhood is greater than physical attachment. Shamai and Ilatov (2005) also state that sense of place is a combination of the physical (environmental) and social (as well as personal) interactions in a place.

Stronger social attachments contribute to a greater sense of belonging and community within the neighbourhood setting. This is especially true in urban ethnic communities with a specific immigrant population as they are impacted by the social space dimension in different ways than other neighbourhoods. Ethnic enclaves, in particular, produce significant spaces for two types of social interaction, that of their adopted places as well as that of the life and culture of the place from which they emigrated (Mazumdar *et al.*, 2000). This creates a complexity and subjectivity in attempting to understand the role and meaning of place in neighbourhood and festival experiences.

Ethnic representation in the neighbourhood and at the festival also impacts place meanings in the neighbourhood's social space. For example, if the neighbourhood has an affluent and dominant ethnic group able to make decisions for the neighbourhood then the less advantaged ethnic groups may feel resentment and discontent and thus have negative meanings attached to the neighbourhood. The neighbourhood of York-Eglinton in Toronto offsets conflict among the dominant Italian and Caribbean ethnic groups by hosting the International Street Festival which is representative of all groups in the community.

On the other hand, ethnic representation might be an issue for the Roncesvalles neighbourhood. The neighbourhood has evolved from a predominantly Polish neighbourhood to one that is more multi-cultural and now includes a 'young artist vibe'. Some festival visitors commented on the Polish theme of the festival. One visitor said there were 'too many signs in Polish'. A visitor mentioned 'community segregation' as being a negative aspect of the festival and another visitor commented that 'non-European music doesn't suit the area (like rock music)'. In contrast, other festival visitors to the Polish Festival specifically mentioned the community and cultural experiences as the best part of the festival for the neighbourhood. Visitors mentioned how the festival is 'an example of the true heritage', shows 'the diversity yet the history of the area', displays 'the different cultures and has opened [it] up culturally'. Other visitors pointed out a connection to community as the festival 'brings people together and because [it] brings people close'. Furthermore, one visitor said that 'people born after the community can learn something [about culture]'. Some visitors specifically mentioned that the festival connects visitors to the Polish culture. This exemplifies how festival experiences can influence neighbourhood experiences and vice versa.

Other aspects that contribute to the neighbourhood setting and social space dimension are issues that relate to feeling at home in the neighbourhood in terms of public safety, crime levels and feeling comfortable in public spaces. For example, some festival visitors to the Taste of Lawrence festival in the Wexford Heights neighbourhood of Toronto commented on the fact that a lack of crime made them feel better about their neighbourhood and able to feel happier about the festival. A few visitors even commented that the festival experience made them feel a stronger connection with the community, and that the festivals also acted as a deterrent against gang-like activity.

Physical Space in the Festival Setting

Collective domain – present sense of place and experience

The design of the festival setting in the neighbourhood space is an important contribution to festival visitor experiences. The cleanliness of the festival grounds, the availability of parking, needs of visitors such as washrooms, the amount of physical space available for visitors to walk, sit and see the sites at the festival can have an impact on the perception and image the visitors have of the festival. Wickham and Kerstetter (2000) discovered that place attachment is positively related to an individual's perception of crowding. As an individual's attachment to their community increases so do their positive feelings about crowds; however, visitors who may not be residents of the neighbourhood may have a negative experience if they perceive the festival space to be too crowded. Another example shows how the needs of visitors in the festival space affects place perceptions. At the Roncesvalles Polish Festival visitors commented on the lack of public washroom facilities. In order to encourage positive festival experiences, festival organisers ensured they provided more lavatory facilities for the following year's festival.

The actual theme, brand and design of the festival can give visitors a connection to the neighbourhood or affect their senses of place as well. As Morgan (2008) suggests, the design of the event needs to play into the five senses creatively to give the customer that compelling reason to attend. The Taste of Lawrence festival in Wexford Heights and the Taste of Little Italy festival in Little Italy have a theme in the neighbourhood based on a collective experience of tasting, seeing and smelling the foods available in these neighbourhoods. It is not only to celebrate the ethnic foods from businesses in the neighbourhood but also to celebrate in a wider scale the ethnic diversity. Thus, the physical space of the neighbourhood setting is connected to the physical space and setting of the festival.

Similarly, for the Polish Festival in Roncesvalles, the physical space is important for the festival setting in terms of visitors' festival experiences. Situating the festival along Roncesvalles Avenue and closing the street enable festival visitors not only to experience the festival but also to experience the neighbourhood. Visitors are able to visually identify with the variety of businesses lining Roncesvalles whether it is a delicatessen, an independent book retailer, an Indian restaurant, Asian food market or a unique clothing store. Simultaneously, visitors witness the festival symbols that mark and identify the neighbourhood with the Polish culture such as Polish flags, banners of the festival sponsors (a Polish brand of vodka and pierogies supplier), the vivid smells of Polish sausage, sauerkraut and pierogies, the Polish music echoing from the main stage mixing with the scents of Thai and Indian food and an eclectic blend of other festival attractions.

Social Space in the Festival Setting

Collective domain – present sense of place and experiences

Community festivals provide an opportunity for many social interactions and experiences. One of the motivations of festival attendees is doing things with the family (Bowen & Daniels, 2005; Kim *et al.*, 2002). Community cultural festivals can be shown to provide a sense of place for residents and increase their sense of community by offering connections, belonging, support, empowerment and participation (De Bres & Davis, 2001; Derrett, 2003).

Ethnic festivals are also found to contribute to a sense of place identity since they provide spaces for community members and visitors (immigrant and non-immigrant) to celebrate ethnic culture. The Cultural Festival of India, an event that took place in New Jersey during 1991 presented a general and extravagant vision of India for Indian as well as non-Indian Americans (Shukla, 1997). Thus, the social space at the festival provides visitors with the opportunity to have a variety of experiences regardless of background or previous cultural experiences.

Visitors to the Roncesvalles Polish Festival made reference to the social space of the festival when they were asked what they perceived to be the most positive aspect of the festival. One respondent stated 'the whole community comes together' and another commented that, 'seeing everyone out enjoying the neighbourhood and seeing what it is all about'. One visitor described the festival experience as 'one of peace and comfort – the whole community is here – the multi-culturalism; we show our culture; we're all one'.

Cultural experiences at festivals can exist in many different forms which may result in subjectivity and complexity in understanding the consumer experience. Ethnic cultural experiences may be commodified for the purposes of selling the experience to visitors or an authentic representation of culture enabling visitors to experience a more 'real' rather than imaginary experience. With regard to Italian festivals in Italian ethnic heritage neighbourhoods, collective or group memory shared by visitors at the festivals who may have never experienced authentic Italian culture share a 'myth' of culture instead (Bell, 2003). This may be the case in Corso Italia with its Fiesta and in Little Italy with the Taste of Little Italy. While these neighbourhoods have evolved from being predominantly Italian to becoming more multi-cultural, their Italian 'focused' festivals celebrate the heritage of the neighbourhood while also including other ethnic cultural experiences through food, music and entertainment. Thus, the displays of Italian culture may be authentic enough for neighbourhood and festival visitor experiences but may not be in terms of a deeply authentic Italian experience. Furthermore, the authenticity of tourism experiences (existential authenticity and relative authenticity) suggests that visitors create their own interpretations of what is authentic (Timothy & Boyd, 2006; Wang, 1999).

Personal Space, Sense of Place and Nostalgic and Anticipatory Experiences

Personal domain – nostalgic sense of place and experiences

Senses of place involve an affective dimension where experiences in the social and physical space are individual, subjective and emotional. Nostalgia is perceived by some researchers to be an aspect of the tourist experience at cultural heritage events and attractions (Caton & Almeida Santos, 2007), whereas, other scholars suggest that tourists are 'insightful' or 'mindful', integrating new information with their own memories of personal experiences (McIntosh & Prentice, 1999). Built heritage, even if it is a symbolic representation of a place somewhere else, connects the physical setting with the emotional significance of places. Memories of heritage from one generation to the next unite communities across historical eras (Yeoh & Kong, 1996). Furthermore, 'personal memories of events, people and places often differ markedly not only across individuals and groups but over time' (Chang & Huang, 2005: 268). Therefore, present experiences occurring in the neighbourhood and at the festival have the potential to invoke memorable past place experiences.

In some urban neighbourhoods, the familiarity of the physical space is apt to encourage a positive consumer experience. Visitors to the neighbourhood prefer to visit businesses with which they have a habit of purchasing goods whether it is to the local butcher, fresh fruit and vegetable market or to the neighbourhood coffee shop. This is especially the case in the Kensington Market neighbourhood of Toronto where regular patrons purchase goods from familiar producers. New York's Little Italy and Chinatown shops selling locally produced and prepared foods give visitors and residents a sense of familiarity as they purchase handmade sausages, fresh pastas or noodle dishes from roadside stalls (Fernando, 2005).

Festival visitors perceive the festival space in a variety of ways because their experiences are shaped by their own memories as well as their experiences with the festival (Voase, 2002). Feelings of nostalgia or memories of past place experiences can bring about either positive place meanings (as in a memorable travel experience) or negative place meanings (as in having to leave a home country due to political conflict). For example, in the neighbourhood of York-Eglinton, the Italian residents maintain a strong nostalgic sense of place that coincides with the image of people socialising over espresso at Italian cafes, of the hardships of coming to the country during challenging times and struggling to fit into a new community with little help from social services and local government (Heath-Rawlings, 2007). These perceptions conflict with other place perceptions of the more recent Caribbean immigrants who relate to the Italian experience but perceive the neighbourhood as benefiting from a more vibrant, inclusive place image.

The physical space of the neighbourhood also connects with the festival space and with our senses which is a personal understanding of place. Sense of place brings into play not only the commonly understood five senses of touch, taste, hearing, smell and sight but also animation and feeling (Derrett, 2003). These are important components of the physical space and are also referred to as sensual geographies (Rodaway, 1994). 'Sensoryscapes' that create rich urban experiences through 'visualscapes', 'olfactoryscapes' and 'soundscapes' sharpen our senses (Mazumdar, 2003). Fernando (2005) describes how the familiar smells of ethnic foods and the sights and sounds at outdoor markets, food stalls and restaurants in Little Italy and Chinatown, New York, contribute to a holistic place experience.

Senses also enable a collective experience in the neighbourhood to become a very personal nostalgic experience. For example, upon visiting one of the neighbourhoods before one of the festivals I (first author) walked into a Portuguese café and saw the delicate custard tarts that I remembered from my vacation to Portugal several years earlier:

> I was immediately reminded of my wonderful experience there, not to any village or attraction in particular but to the memory of having travelled there before. I was instantly taken back with memories of the very hot summer in Lisbon and Porto, the Portuguese baked goods, the Algarve, the windy, misty hills of Sintra, the cool breezes off the Atlantic coast, the peaceful cultural sites, the strong yet sweet taste of Port and the pleasantness of people as I tried my best to speak their language. In the bakery I immediately said 'Obrigado' to the young server behind the counter. To his very pleasant surprise, he grinned widely and said your welcome in his native tongue. I said I had visited Portugal and we had an instant connection, 'It is a beautiful country, no?' He asked and I replied, 'Oh yes, I had a wonderful time there!' My nostalgic sense of place for Portugal influenced my present sense of place for this café in downtown Toronto. It enabled me to have a deeper connection to the neighbourhood and also with my Portuguese server. Now, I will have fond memories of this café and their delicious custard tarts.

On the other hand, the custard tarts brought forth a different personal experience for the person I was travelling with [second author]. She had recently travelled to Asia and having been to Macau she noticed many people purchasing Portuguese custard tarts. Upon seeing, smelling and tasting the delicate pastry in the café she had a different nostalgic sense of place experience; her memories were of Macau.

Nostalgic senses of place may be of past place experiences of the neighbourhood and other locations but they may also be memories of the festival setting as well. Sights, sounds, smells and tastes may remind someone of the festival, specifically, which will either instil a positive sense of place because it was a memorable experience or it may result in a negative sense of place as those memories are different from their present place experience.

While festival and neighbourhood experiences can be very personal and subjective, they can also be collective and connect to everyone because of wider dimensions through time, space and scale. Perceptions of unity and camaraderie within a neighbourhood enable individuals to feel a personal affection for the physical and social spaces of the neighbourhood and may even remind them of familiar places some-where else. Nostalgic senses of place can not only remind us of a physical setting but of the social interactions that existed in that space. Manzo (2005: 83) reveals how 'viewing relationships to places as a reflection of our journey in the world also enables us to see how feelings of comfort, belonging and self-affirmation can transcend physical boundaries of the residence and be found in a variety of settings. In an increasingly globalised world, this particular understanding of place meaning may be more illustrative than more traditional notions of home'.

As previously discussed, along with multi-cultural sights at cultural festivals are the characteristic smells that accompany ethnic foods, the ability to touch certain handicrafts, taste the delicious flavours traditional to other nations as well as hear the familiar or unfamiliar sounds of cultural music and singing. Festival spaces, as do neighbourhood spaces, connect people with their sensuous geographies and thus contribute to their emotional senses of place and a personal memory, imagination or nostalgia for other experiences (Shukla, 1997). Visitor experiences at the Roncesvalles Polish Festival showed that several visitors indicated the Polish food, music, costumes and dances as the most positive aspects of the festival. For example, visitors at the festival who are meeting up with family and friends who have once lived in the neighbourhood are able to reminisce, while the festival conjures up feelings of nostalgia for past festival and neighbourhood experiences. One visitor alluded to a past visitor experience at the festival as a place to 'meet my old friends'.

A stronger sense of community and belonging can encourage visitors to the festival to have more celebratory experiences. Therefore, even in places where the collective meanings are challenged the festival's role is important as it reminds visitors who they are and who they are not, all while gaining an appreciation for all. Mazanti and Ploger (2003) focus on the often incompatibility between the political symbolic construction of place (outside understanding/construction) and the residents' social construction of place (inside understanding/construction). They reveal how urban residents living in deprived urban neighbourhoods create meaningful place identities, conceive their place of residence and use their place in everyday life (Mazanti & Ploger, 2003). Waitt (2008) suggests that urban festival spaces offer creative possibilities through temporarily suspending social relations and blurring boundaries allowing sites for negotiation and hope.

Personal domain – anticipatory place experiences

The conceptual diagram displays a connection between the physical space in the neighbourhood and the personal memories of past place experiences. However, experiences in the neighbourhood and the personal perceptions of those experiences can also give a glimpse into future place perceptions or anticipatory senses of place. For example, a visit to an Italian restaurant or outdoor café in the once predominantly Italian neighbourhood of Corso Italia may instil a sense of anticipation for a future trip to Italy. Experiences at the Fiesta in Corso Italia may give a glimpse into what collective experiences are like in Italian piazzas. Similarly, the ethnic architectural symbols and signs along with the scents of Asian dishes and outdoor food stalls in Chinatown may enable a visitor to glimpse aspects of a cultural experience that they would like to experience again whether it is through an actual trip to Asia or to simply return to the neighbourhood. Present place experiences in the neighbourhood can enable visitors to gain a sense of place which will allow them to anticipate with excitement for the festival. Furthermore, present place experiences in the neighbourhood may encourage the anticipatory sense of place for future travel experiences to somewhere far away. Festival visitors who may be new to the festival and neighbourhood may participate in or observe various social interactions and feel they are having a new place experience.

Conclusion

This conceptual framework deconstructs senses of place in the context of cultural festival visitor experiences. It widens the understanding of the dimensions of place experiences showing how community cultural festivals limited in space have a broader application for nostalgic and memorable experiences of the neighbourhood, festival and other places. It also illustrates how present place experiences can connect to anticipatory senses of place for future experiences whether it is at the festival, in the neighbourhood or some other place. Studies have explored the role of nostalgia in the experience of tourists and visitors (Caton & Almeida Santos, 2007), but the role of place perceptions and how they may connect to past and future place experiences are aspects of this framework that deserve more attention.

The geographical understanding of place and the festival experience demonstrates how meanings of place consist of multi-components through space, scale and time. While the conceptual model implemented in this chapter illustrates the components as separate, they prove to be inter-connected and complex. Similarly, Gustafson (2001: 9) found three themes to classify meanings of place (self, others and environment), but found that the meanings of place expressed by his respondents were 'often situated in the relationship between self/others and/or environment rather than just unambiguously belonging to just one of these categories'. Furthermore, visitor experiences involving cultural heritage are multi-faceted and do not always fit within a theoretical interpretation (Caton & Almeida Santos, 2007). Thus, it is important to acknowledge how each of the components are impacted by the personal, emotional dimension as this influences experiences on the physical and social dimensions.

Collective memory binds people together under a shared identity (Chang & Huang, 2005), but ethnic festivals attract visitors of many different backgrounds which may result in different perceptions and experiences. Furthermore, urban neighbourhoods once dominated by a specific ethnic heritage evolve over time which creates planning and management challenges that exceed the scale of the festival. Therefore, festival organisers and urban managers/planners need to ensure that the festival is representative of the true cultural heritage of the neighbour-hood space so that an ethnic cultural experience is one that can be shared in the festival space and connect the personal domain with the collective domain in a positive place experience.

Another concern for urban managers, marketers and festival organi-sers is to ensure that the cultural representation of the festival and the neighbourhood space are not commodified for the purposes of festival visitor consumption. Even though existential authenticity is based on visitors' own perceptions and experiences of the festival product, they may grow tired of the staged performances and cultural representations. Senses of place will become increasingly negative as visitors perceive the experience as boring and fleeting rather than exciting and lasting. After all, it is the deeply unique experiences that Pine and Gilmore (1999) suggest are the key to creating more than just consumable products. This means that festival organisers should encourage resident/visitor input regarding the festival on an on-going basis in order to ensure that cultural festival experiences are true neighbourhood experiences.

This conceptual model demonstrates how the cultural festival experience is interlaced with meanings of place. While this chapter describes the model using examples of cultural festivals in urban ethnic neighbourhoods, stronger empirical and case study analysis is needed to illustrate the full potential of its application. A more narrative approach, which enables the deeper connections among place experiences to emerge, would be a more conducive approach to applying this conceptual framework in other cultural festival situations (Morgan, 2008; Schnell, 2003). Furthermore, the model shows how subjective place meanings are in relation to the cultural festival experience and that traditional marketing research, branding and product image formation may not be the most appropriate way to view cultural festival marketing and management. This is especially important as there is mounting competition for urban areas, even in the already unique ethnic neighbourhoods of Toronto, to produce and maintain vibrant urban spaces and creative, extraordinary experiences.

References

Andrews, H. (2005) Feeling at home: Embodying Britishness in a Spanish charter tourist resort. *Tourist Studies* 5 (3), 247–266.

Bell, D. (2003) Mythscapes: Memory, mythology, and national identity. *British Journal of Sociology* 54 (1), 63–81.

Bowen, H.E. and Daniels, M.J. (2005) Does the music matter? Motivations for attending a music festival. *Event Management* 9 (3), 155–164.

Butz, D. and Eyles, J. (1997) Reconceptualizing senses of place: Social relations, ideology and ecology. *Geografiska Annaler* 79B, 1–25.

Carmichael, B.A. (2005) Understanding the wine tourism experience for winery visitors in the Niagara Region, Ontario, Canada. *Tourism Geographies* 7 (2), 185–204.

Carmichael, B.A. and McClinchey, K.A. (2009) Exploring the importance of setting to the rural tourism experience for rural commercial home entrepreneurs and their guests. In P. Lynch, A. McIntosh and H. Tucker (eds) *Commercial Homes in Tourism: An International Perspective* (pp. 73–86). London: Routledge.

Caton, K. and Almeida Santos, C. (2007) Heritage tourism on route 66: Deconstructing nostalgia. *Journal of Travel Research* 45 (4), 371–386.

Chang, T.C. (2005) Place, memory and identity: Imagining 'New Asia'. *Asia Pacific Viewpoint* 46 (3), 247–253.

Chang, T.C. and Huang, S. (2005) Recreating place, replacing memory: Creative descruction at the Singapore River. *Asia Pacific Viewpoint* 46 (3), 267–280.

Chessell, D. (2002) Italian festivals in Australia's Little Italys: The use of public spaces in Italian-Australian commercial precincts to create a cosmopolitan 'sense of place'. *Events and Place Making: Proceedings of International Event Research Conference*. On http://www.acem.uts.edu.au/pdfs/Proceedings.pdf. Accessed 03.06.10. Sydney: University of Technology.

Crang, M. (1998) *Cultural Geography*. London: Routledge.

De Bres, K. and Davis, J. (2001) Celebrating group and place identity: A case study of a new regional festival. *Tourism Geographies* 3 (3), 326–337.

Derrett, R. (2003) Making sense of how festivals demonstrate a community's sense of place. *Event Management* 8, 49–58.

Eyles, J. (1985) *Senses of Place*. Warrington: Silverbrook Press.

Fernando, N. (2005) Taste, smell and sound: On the street in Chinatown and Little Italy. *Architectural Design* 75 (3), 20–25.

Getz, D. (2007) *Event Studies: Theory, Research and Policy for Planned Events*. Oxford: Elsevier.

Gross, M. and Brown, G. (2006) Tourist experience in a lifestyle destination setting: The roles of involvement and place attachment. *Journal of Business Research* 59, 696–700.

Gustafson, P. (2001) Meanings of place: Everyday experience and theoretical conceptualizations. *Journal of Environmental Psychology* 21, 5–16.

Hay, R. (1998) A rooted sense of place in cross-cultural perspective. *Canadian Geographer* 42 (3), 245–266.

Heath-Rawlings, J. (2007) In search of its soul: Once Italian, now largely West Indian, an Eglinton West neighbourhood struggles to find an identity. *Toronto Star*. On WWW at http://www.yorkbia.com/newsletter/star.pdf. Accessed 03.06.10.

Hidalgo, M.C. and Hernandez, B. (2001) Place attachment: Conceptual and empirical questions. *Journal of Environmental Psychology* 21, 273–281.

Holbrook, M. and Hirschman, E. (1982) The experiential aspects of consumption: Consumer fantasies, feelings and fun. *Journal of Consumer Research* 9 (12), 132–139.

Holloway, L. and Hubbard, P. (2001) *People and Place: The Extraordinary Geographies of Everyday Life*. Harlow: Pearson Education.

Jorgensen, B.S. and Stedman, R.C. (2006). A comparative analysis of predictors of sense of place dimensions: Attachment to, dependence on, and identification with lakeshore properties. *Journal of Environmental Management* 79, 316–327.

Kim, K., Uysal, M. and Chen, J.S. (2002) Festival motivation from the organizer's point of view. *Event Management* 7 (2), 127–134.

Kyle, G., Graefe, A., Manning, R. and Bacon, J. (2004) Effects of place attachment on users' perceptions of social and environmental conditions in a natural setting. *Journal of Environmental Psychology* 24, 213–225.

Lade, C. and Jackson, J. (2004) Key success factors in regional festivals: Some Australian experiences. *Event Management* 9, 1–11.

Lane, R. and Waitt, G. (2007) Inalienable places: Self-drive tourists in Northwest Australia. *Annals of Tourism Research* 34 (1), 105–121.

Manzo, L.C. (2005) For better or worse: Exploring multiple dimensions of place meaning. *Journal of Environmental Psychology* 25, 67–86.

MacCannell, D. (2001) Tourist Agency. *Tourist Studies* 1 (1), 23–37.

MacLeod, N.E. (2006) The placeless festival: Identity and place in the post-modern festival. In D. Picard and M. Robinson (eds) *Festivals, Tourism and Social Change* (pp. 222–237). Clevedon: Channel View Publications.

Mazanti, B. and Ploger, J. (2003) Community planning – from politicized places to lived spaces. *Journal of Housing and the Built Environment* 18, 309–327.

Mazumdar, S. (2003) Sense of place considerations for quality of urban life. In N. Guteroy and A. Ozsoy (eds) *Quality of Urban Life: Policy vs. Practice* (pp. 83–97). Istanbul: Istanbul Technical University.

Mazumdar, S., Mazumdar, S., Docuyanan, F. and McLaughlin, C.M. (2000) Creating a sense of place: The Vietnamese-Americans and Little Saigon. *Journal of Environmental Psychology* 20, 319–333.

McIntosh, A.J. and Prentice, R.C. (1999) Affirming authenticity: Cosuming cultural heritage. *Annals of Tourism Research* 26 (3), 589–612.

McKercher, B., Mei, W.S. and Tse, T.S.M. (2006) Are short duration cultural festivals tourist attractions? *Journal of Sustainable Tourism* 14 (1), 55–66.

Morgan, M. (2008) What makes a good festival? Understanding the event experience. *Event Management* 12, 81–93.

Pine, J. and Gilmore, J. (1999) *The Experience Economy.* Boston, MA: Harvard Business School Press.

Quan, S. and Wang, N. (2004) Towards a structural model of the tourist experience: An illustration from food experiences in tourism. *Tourism Management* 25, 297–305.

Quinn, B. (2003) Symbols, practices and myth-making: Cultural perspectives on the Wexford Festival Opera. *Tourism Geographies* 5 (3), 329–349.

Relph, E. (1976) *Place and Placelessness.* London: Pion.

Richards, G. and Wilson, J. (2006) Developing creativity in tourist experiences: A solution to the serial reproduction of culture. *Tourism Management* 27, 1209–1223.

Rodaway, P. (1994) *Sensuous Geographies: Body, Sense, and Place.* London: Routledge.

Sauer, C. (1956) The education of a geographer. *Annals of the American Association of Geographers* 46, 287–299.

Schnell, S.M. (2003) Creating narratives of place and identity in "Little Sweden, USA". *Geographical Review* 93 (1), 1–29.

Shamai, S. and Ilatov, Z. (2005) Measuring sense of place: Methodological aspects. *Tijdschrift Voor Economische En Sociale Geografie* 96 (5), 467–476.

Shukla, S. (1997) Building diaspora and nation: The 1991 'cultural festival of India'. *Cultural Studies* 11 (2), 296–315.

Snepenger, D., Murphy, L., Snepenger, M. and Anderson, W. (2004) Normative meanings of experiences for a spectrum of tourism places. *Journal of Travel Research* 43, 108–117.

Snepenger, D., Snepenger, M., Dalby, M. and Wessol, A. (2007) Meanings and consumption characteristics of places at a tourism destination. *Journal of Travel Research* 45, 310–321.

Teixeira, C. (2007) Toronto's Little Portugal: A neighbourhood in transition. *Centre for Urban and Community Studies-Research Bulletin #35.* University of Toronto. On WWW at http://www.urbancentre.utoronto.ca/pdfs/researchbulletins/CUCSRB35Teixeira.pdf. Accessed 03.06.10.

Timothy, D. and Boyd, S. (2006) Heritage tourism in the 21st century: Valued traditions and new perspectives. *Journal of Heritage Tourism* 1 (1), 1–16.

Tuan, Y. (1980) Rootedness verses sense of place. *Landscape* 24, 3–8.

Tweed, C. and Sutherland, M. (2007) Built cultural heritage and sustainable urban development. *Landscape and Urban Planning* 83, 62–69.

Urry, J. (1995) *Consuming Places.* London: Routledge.

Voase, R. (2002) Rediscovering the imagination: Investigating active and passive visitor experience in the 21st century. *International Journal of Tourism Research* 4 (5), 391–399.

Waitt, G. (2008) Urban festivals: Geographies of hype, helplessness and hope. *Geography Compass* 2 (2), 513–537.

Wang, N. (1999) Re-thinking authenticity in tourism experience. *Annals of Tourism Research* 26 (2), 349–370.

Wickham, T.D. and Kerstetter, D.L. (2000) The relationship between place attachment and crowding in an event setting. *Event Management* 6, 167–174.

Yeoh, B. and Kong, L. (1996) The notion of place in the construction of history, nostalgia and heritage in Singapore. *Singapore Journal of Tropical Geography* 17 (1), 52–65.

Yeoman, I., Robertson, M., Ali-Mcknight, J., Drummond, S. and McMahon-Beattie, U. (eds) (2004) *Festival and Events Management: An International Arts and Culture Perspective*. Oxford: Elsevier Butterworth-Heinemann.

Zhuang, Z.C. (2008) Ethnic retailing and the role of municipal planning. Unpublished PhD dissertation,University of Waterloo, Waterloo, Ontario.

Part 2
Researching the Experience

Chapter 5

Research Processes for Evaluating Quality Experiences: Reflections from the 'Experiences' Field(s)

GAYLE JENNINGS

Researching Experiences: Why Research the Quality of Experiences?

The beginning of the 21st century has been a time of ever-increasing consumption and (re)production of experiences across global landscapes, which cross temporal, spatial, cultural, geopolitical, economic and virtual boundaries. The world is filled with consumers, and with providers, only too eager to assuage their needs. Within recreation, hospitality, entertainment, events, sports and travel sectors (collectively called tourism and leisure industries in this book), consumptive and (re)productive processes are manifest and manifold. Relatedly, in this environment, consumption and (re)production are constantly niche-ing, tailorising, re-inventing and innovating in order to establish difference, uniqueness and distinction. Value-adding strategies are continuously being developed, with both value for money criteria and high-end market positionings being emphasised. Experience efficiencies and cost-cutting measures are given strategic importance. The latter are even more so being adopted, at the time of writing this chapter, in the wake of the economic crisis of October 2008 and its flow-on consequences. All of the aforementioned measures represent efforts by tourism and leisure providers to attract consumers to their experience-oriented products/ services and to maintain and increase market share.

To do this may be more complicated than this initial overview may suggest. In the current situation, the tourism and leisure industries must take into account repercussions from a wide range of events. Some of these events are predictable, some less so – with the latter becoming more predominant. In planning, delivering and evaluating experiences, tourism and leisure industries need to take into account local, glocal, national and global environments. Such environments include, for example, substantive global conflicts, increasing occurrences of natural and human-induced disasters, localised social, cultural, political and economic unrest, growing divides between 'have' and 'have nots', safety and security issues, climate change imperatives, sustainability issues, increasing and decreasing mobility and migratory practices, intergenerational diversity, intra-, inter- and cross-cultural diversity, changes in generating markets and increasing connectivity. All these factors have contributed to the expansion of a 'knowledge economy', and the growth of emotion-based economies (Gobe *et al.*, 2001) and experience economies (Pine & Gilmore, 1998, 1999).

Given the preceding, a number of questions are germane for tourism and leisure industries. How can experience providers remain competitive? How can companies continue to hold their edge? How can companies 'weather' crises and still remain in the market? What are the implications and consequences of answers to these questions for long-term sustainability and corporate (social) responsibility? The underlying premise in this chapter is that research and 'quality' are key mechanisms to enable providers to gain and hold their competitive edges as well as for consumers to experience extraordinary experiences. Moreover, it is in the notion of 'quality' that providers, companies and consumers can distinguish experiences from each other. Albeit in the current global climate, those experiences which are deemed quality and sustainable will be the ones that will maintain market share. Purchasers of experiences (Dolnicar, 2004; Higham, 2007; Higham & Carr, 2002; Kim *et al.*, 2006; Zografos & Allcroft, 2007) and providers of experiences (Pohle & Hittner, 2008) are recognising a need for greening experience delivery as well as social responsibility and corporate social responsibility. By corporate social responsibility, I am referring to 'a collection of policies and practices linked to relationships with key stakeholders, values compliance with legal requirements, and respect for people, communities and the environment' (World Bank, 2005).

Given the preceding, the overall aims of this chapter are to:

(1) address the question – why research quality of experiences?
(2) reflect on past and current practices used to research experiences and quality;
(3) present a case study, which developed processes to evaluate the nature of quality of tourism experiences; and
(4) proffer a quality tourism and leisure experiences research agenda.

The first aim has been addressed in the opening to this chapter. Before progressing to the remaining aims, a point of nomenclature needs to be made. The title of this chapter used the term 'field(s)'. The term was deliberately chosen to represent both the fields of study, which include recreation, leisure, hospitality, entertainment, events, sport, travel and tourism as well as the research fields/settings in which quality experiences research has been and continues to be conducted.

Researching Experiences and Quality: Reflections on Past and Current Practices

The majority of studies undertaken of experiences and quality have utilised quantitative perspectives and have been informed by post/positivistic paradigms, especially critical realism or pragmatism. Such investigations draw on extant theories to build knowledge regarding, in this instance, experiences and quality. A number of writers have commented on the need for holistic and qualitative-based research informed by constructivism and interpretivsim, as a means to study tourism and leisure industries experiences and the quality of those experiences, in order to move beyond limited dimensional studies.

Others have specifically commented on the need for experience research to consider the multidimensional (Andereck *et al.*, 2006; Jennings, 1999; Jennings & Weiler, 2006; Lee *et al.*, 1994; Patterson & Pegg, 2009; Ritchie & Hudson, 2009; Volo, 2009) and the multiphase nature of experiences (Borrie & Roggenbuck, 2001; Clawson, 1963; Craig-Smith & French, 1994; Jennings, 1997; Killion, 1992; Ooi, 2005). Still others highlight the dynamic nature of experiences (Hull *et al.*, 1992; Jonas, 2007). Such dynamism, according to Nielson and Shelby (1977) and reported by Jonas, is a consequence of the resultant mix arising from the coalescing of experience settings, the protracted nature of experiences often over several days as well as the unpredictable nature of the interaction between the providers and the participants themselves. How then to study such dynamism? Again, qualitative studies are preferred as they enable researchers to achieve holistic and insider (emic) perspectives as well as 'capture' the multidimensional, multiphase and dynamic nature of experiences.

With regard to quality, much research is linked to service quality, and in particular, is based on Parasuraman *et al.*'s (1985, 1988) SERVQUAL measuring instrument. The model was developed through qualitative processes associated with executive (indepth) interviews and focus groups. SERVQUAL itself is based on questionnaire research design processes. In 1991, Parasuraman *et al.* refined SERVQUAL, and in their concluding statements they commented that 'SERVQUAL can fruitfully be supplemented with additional qualitative or quantitative research to uncover the causes underlying the key problem areas or gaps identified by a SERVQUAL study' (1991: 445). Here, Parasuraman and colleagues are inherently acknowledging that qualitative perspectives will enable researchers to move towards more holistic understandings of quality as opposed to fragmented, incomplete perspectives using more quantitative perspectives. Albeit Parasuraman *et al.* (1991) acknowledged that qualitative research might complement SERVQUAL findings; Jennings and Weiler (2006) still critique SERVQUAL and related tools for their objective rather than subjective research designs. Despite being popular as a tool, SERVQUAL has not been without other critics; for example, see Cronin and Taylor (1992). Yüksel and Yüksel (2001) have also critiqued the related service quality expectancy–disconfirmation paradigm with particular regard to experiential travel and tourism services. The edited work by Jennings and Nickerson (2006) provides alternate examples for studying 'quality' using qualitative and quantitative perspectives as well as mixed methods approaches. Additionally and similarly to 'experiences', a qualitative research design is advocated as being more suited to capture the multidimensional and complex nature of 'quality' (Jennings, 2006; Nickerson, 2006).

Researching Experiences and Quality: Interpreting Their Meanings

In experience-related literature, the framings of experiences have been 'described as organisational/business-based, individualistic, psychological and social in nature' (Jennings *et al.*, 2009: 300). Organisational-based framings focus on 'marketing, value and delivery'; individualistic framings relate to 'personal, affective, embodied... and memory'; psychological framings were associated with 'feelings, memory, intellect and behaviour'; social framings were noted as connected with 'lifestyle, and social context[s]' (Jennings *et al.*, 2009). Elsewhere, Ritchie and Hudson (2009) reviewed tourist experience literature and identified six broad categories or 'streams'. Ritchie and Hudson's (2009: 111–112) streams were framed as following, literature, which sought to (1) define the 'essence' of experiences; (2) 'understand...experience-seeking behaviour'; (3) explicate 'methodologies used in...experience research'; (4) 'explore and understand' different experience types; (5) assist with 'managerial issues'; and (6) distinguish 'an evolutionary trail of experience thinking'. Volo (2009: 113–115) categorises experience literature into three board areas: 'definitions'; 'complexity/nature'; and 'measurement'.

Just as there is diversity in interpreting experiences, various authors in the extant western literature have noted the difficulty in 'measuring' quality because of its nebulous, subjective and complex nature. Over time, quality has been interpreted as value for money, expectations being satisfied or exceeded, match between expectations and experience delivery (Jennings *et al.*, 2009). Additionally, related synonyms have been used to imply notions of 'quality'. These include, for example, the terms: 'extraordinary' (Arnould & Price, 1993; Arnould *et al.*, 1999; Jonas, 2007; Price *et al.*, 1995) and 'optimal' (Beck, 1987; Csikszentmihalyi, 1988; Iso-Ahola, 1980) albeit that these terms assume that quality is related to intrinsically motivating experiences. Ritchie and Hudson (2009: 119) have also noted the use of 'extraordinary' in relation to experiences as well as use of 'memorable'. Noteworthy here is the use of qualifiers to the term 'experience'. Such qualifiers serve to distinguish the experience beyond the 'ordinary' and enable the provider and experience-er (person engaged in the experience) to acknowledge and communicate the experience's distinction from other experiences. Similarly, the term 'quality' is applied to indicate distinction.

Researching Experiences and Quality: Western-Centric Framings

Embedded in each of the various framings and interpretations of experiences and quality, is a worldview founded on western and developed world individualistic societies' perspectives. What of collectivist value-based societies and cultures, such as China, Indonesia, Malaysia, India? Do they desire individualised tailorised tourism and leisure experiences? Do we as western researchers know? Dorfman (1998: 56) noted that '[t]he majority of the world's population is collectivist, and the [sic] roughly 70% often do not agree with Western views'. Similarly, Urry (1990, 2002) has commented, meanings differ between societies and cultures as well as across time.

In response to cultural value issues associated with SERVQUAL, a number of writers have questioned the assumption that SERVQUAL dimensions are homogenous across cultures (Furrer *et al.*, 2000; Raajpoot, 2004; Winstead, 1997). For example, Raajpoot (2004: 198) developed PAKSERV: 'a service encounter quality measurement, suited for use in a non-Western, Asian culture'. Raajpoot developed PAKSERV by drawing on the works of Hofstede (1980, 1984) as well as Hofstede and Bond (1988) and Schwartz's (1992) work on personal value measures. Raajpoot used a mixed methods approach including focus groups and mail out questionnaires in the process of modifying SERVQUAL into PAKSERV to determine the nature of the quality of experiences. More broadly, within related marketing literature, a number of other critiques have been made regarding the 'measurement' of 'quality' across cultures (Crotts & Erdmann, 2000; de Mooij, 1998; Donthu & Yoo, 1998; Dorfman & Howell, 1988).

Despite recognition of a lack of universality of concepts, and acknowledgment that 'although people are not the same, we tend to perceive them to be the same....This leads to cultural blindness: both perceptual and conceptual blindness' (de Mooij, 1998: 44). Due to this 'perceptual and conceptual blindness', we need to continually ask questions, such as is the use of the terms, 'quality' and 'experiences', part of standard vocabularies of global languages? Do the terms have established socio-cultural and taken-for-granted meanings in different cultures? For example, in South Korea, the term 'leisure' does not have a direct equivalent or a socio-cultural construct. As a result of globalisation, a new word, 'lei-port' was coined to accommodate the western developed world introduced notion of leisure and sport (Lee, 2001).

While as researchers, we may use strategies, such as translation and back translation processes in cross-cultural research, de Mooij (1998: 55) emphasises that although terms can be translated and back translated – 'the values included in the words can not be translated, and linguistic equivalence is thus not easily attained'. Earlier, social psychologists, Frijda and Jahoda (1966), also cautioned that cultural complexities make interpretations of research findings tenuous due to the diversity of alternate interpretations that may be generated, resulting in question-able findings. The same caution is worthy of attention in contemporary times within tourism and leisure experience industries research and quality research. Bearing these comments in mind, given the 'homo-genization of international markets and growing similarities in the tastes and habits of international consumers' (Mattila, 1999: 250), understanding the role of culture with regard to 'experiences' and 'quality' will provide 'competitive advantages' for experience providers. Subsequently, constructs need 'testing' in 'non-European countries' (Steenkamp *et al.*, 1999: 66). Overall, more research is required in these areas, particularly, intra-cultural, inter-cultural, cross-cultural and cross-national research. There is also a complementary need for collective, inclusive, multidisciplinary, multigenerational, multiresearcher agendas.

Researching Experiences and Quality: Changing Market Contexts

Within developed western world markets, rather than mass-delivered products and services, people are now expecting individualised and tailorised experiences (Gilmore & Pine, 2000; Jennings, 2001). In the 1990s, Lipscombe (1996: 40) forecast that future travel and tourism consumers will demonstrate 'sophistication' (Weiler & Hall, 1992), they will be choice-wise and lifestyle diverse (Martin & Mason, 1987) novel experience-focussed and co-decision makers (Fay *et al.*, 1987), as well as individuated and intent on personal development. The same remains true of western, developed travellers and tourists in the early stages of the 21st century. Binkhorst and Den Dekker (2009: 312) report that: '[t]oday we see [tourists and travellers] want context related, authentic experience[s]...and seek a balance between control by the experience stager and self determined activity with its spontaneity, freedom and self expression' as well as 'self development'.

Lipscombe (1996: 40) also cautioned that travel and tourism providers would need to be responsive and shift 'from...old products ([discon-nected], single activity, seasonal,...), mass markets, and traditional

destinations, towards new products (multiple activity, all seasons,...
integrated experiences), special markets, [as well as] new, emerging
destinations (Oelrichs, 1994)'. More recently, Binkhorst and Den Dekker
(2009: 313) argue that 'similar tourist product portfolios will not easily
distinguish one destination from another'. One of the challenges for
providers and destinations has been to avoid 'serial reproduction of
culture' (Richards & Wilson, 2006) and experiences! Similarly, like Fay
et al. (1987), Poon (1993) reiterated that the 'new tourist' also seeks to be
'in charge'. Binkhorst and Den Dekker (2009: 316) refer to this as co-
creation and suggest this is linked to travellers and tourists' quests for
'quality of life' [and quality of experiences]. Their suggestion supports
Lipscombe's earlier recommendation to change from mass to customer
direct marketing of their tourism and leisure experiences.

The global market place, however, is changing. The burgeoning
markets of numerous 'non-traditional' leisure and tourism-related
nations, such as India and China, Russia and former Eastern block
nations, are placing pressure on providers to supply these enormous
markets despite global economic crises. In the process of supporting
these rapidly increasing markets, as already noted, there are challenges
to western-based notions of what is a tourism/leisure experience and
what is a quality experience.

Researching Experiences and Quality: Sustainability, (Corporate) (Social) Responsibility and Business Ethics

At the outset of the 21st century, there are a number of issues that,
although they have long been issues, are only now gaining greater
currency in the discourses of tourism and leisure industries providers,
organisations and related businesses. Indeed, greater numbers of
stakeholders from both the demand and supply side of tourism and
leisure industries' economics are engaging in such discourses. These
discourses are associated with sustainability, (corporate) (social) responsibility and business ethics along with related issues of peak oil, climate
change, water and energy resources, as well as livelihoods including
quality of life. The commercial tourism and leisure industries literature
and media are punctuated with examples of experiences not being
sustainable, corporately (socially) responsible or ethical. For example,
Klein (2002) and the general media highlight a number of these practices
with regard to the cruise ship industry.

Sustainability, travel/leisure experiences and quality are inter-related.
Elsewhere, I have noted that, in practice, quality and sustainability are
not mutually inclusive terms (Jennings, 2006). In particular, stakeholders
need to reflect on whether the provision of quality tourism experiences
compromises 'development that meets the needs of the present without

compromising the ability of future generations to meet their own needs' (World Commission on Environment and Development, 1987); for the provision of quality tourism experiences is not always complementary to sustainable tourism experiences. '[S]ustainability, [(corporate) (social) responsibility], quality [and the nature of experiences] are [continuously being] constructed and reconstructed, interpreted and reinterpreted; [therefore] community and stakeholder involvement is vital; and... ethical standards of practice and codes of conduct are necessary' (Jennings, 2007a: 243). Reflective processes regarding quality, experiences, sustainability, (corporate) (social) responsibility and ethical practice should then be a continuous socio-cultural, economic, environmental and political negotiation.

The provision of quality experiences needs to be considered within a glocal/global context in an ever-changing world. For as noted at the World Summit on Sustainable Development – the 2002 Johannesburg Summit 'progress in implementing sustainable development has been extremely disappointing..., with poverty deepening and environmental degradation worsening' (United Nations Department of Economic and Social Affairs, 2002). In particular, climate change, peak oil, environmental degradation, and poverty continue to be challenges to offering 'quality tourism experiences' in a sustainable manner.

Consideration of quality tourism experiences within sustainable tourism principles is a responsible and necessary choice for sustaining market share and development (Jennings, 2007a, 2007b), especially bearing in mind the challenges of 21st century globally connected markets. Unless tourism and leisure industries' oriented research engages in successive cycles of monitoring and evaluating quality experiences delivery, sustainability of those experiences will be placed in jeopardy. The inextricable inter-relationship between sustainability and quality cannot be ignored. While the provision of 'quality' and simultaneously 'sustainable' tourism experiences may provide competitive edges, this needs to be informed by using knowledge-based platforms (Jafari, 1990) and ethics-based platforms (Macbeth, 2005). To reiterate, the provision of quality experiences needs to be considered within a holistic framework which includes and engages tourists, providers, governments, communities and the environment bearing in mind glocal and global contexts.

Researching Experiences and Quality: Reflections and a Way Forward

The preceding sections have presented a number of problematics associated with researching experiences and researching quality. These are summarised below:

- Predication towards post/positivistic, quantitative and western-centric research processes.
- Western-centric framings of experiences and quality.
- Predication towards developed world perspectives.
- The multidimensional, multiphase components of experiences and the nebulous, multidimensional and complex nature of quality.
- Diverse interpretations of experiences and quality.
- Need for more qualitatively framed perspectives to understand the nature of experiences and quality, especially holistically framed.
- Increasing markets of one within western-oriented cultures as opposed to collectivist-based cultures and their differing expectations of experience and quality and whether there are language and value equivalents for each of the terms.
- Experience and quality research may not be mutually supportive of sustainability, corporate (social) responsibility and business ethics agendas.

The next section overviews an example of praxis which aims to address a number of the problematics noted above.

Researching Quality Experiences: A Case Study From Tourism: Processes to Evaluate Quality Tourism Experiences

There is a burgeoning literature associated with understanding quality tourism experiences (Jennings *et al.*, 2009). In this section, one praxis example is provided to complement those presented elsewhere in this book. This example aims to demonstrate ways to gain insights towards understanding 'quality tourism experiences' and how to evaluate leisure and tourism industries delivery of experiences. The case study draws on the work of Jennings *et al.* (2007). This research team worked towards developing a quality tourism experience evaluation tool. The study focussed on one segment of the tourism industry: adventure travel and, in particular, the youth adventure travel market. The research processes were designed to achieve holistic, indepth understandings of quality tourism experiences from multiple perspectives drawn from the two primary stakeholders: adventure youth travellers and adventure tourism providers. In that study, the researchers identified the following as key elements of a quality tourism experience: combining experiences, experience delivery, personal connectivity, social connectivity and inter-connectivity of the entire adventure tourism experience. Table 5.1 provides interpretations of those terms and related research to monitor and evaluate the elements.

Table 5.1 Elements which filter the quality of youth adventure tourism experiences

Element	Interpretation	Related research for monitoring and evaluation
Combining experiences	Clustering of experiences to generate multiple connected experiences, assist accessibility, enable choice and balance between adventure, fun, challenge, relaxation and socialising opportunities	Action research (see Reason & Bradbury, 2006); benchmarking
Experience delivery	Delivering an experience instead of goods, products and services although the delivery may package the latter within the overall context of experiences	Reflexive journals, quasi-focus groups, i.e. conversation-based breakfast/lunch/evening-meals
Personal connectivity	Authentic individualised person to person interactions—connections between travellers and tourist providers	Self-reports, peer reviews, line manager assessment, experience-er feedback, action research
Social connectivity	Social interactions between a traveller and others, for example, variously other travellers, residents, experience providers	As above
Inter-connectivity of the entire adventure tourism experience	Experiences in different phases of adventure travel experiences impact on each other and are inter-related	Action research, reflexive journals, quasi-focus groups i.e. conversation-based breakfast/lunch/evening-meals, self-reports, peer reviews, line manager assessment, experience-er feedback

Source: Jennings *et al.* (2007)

How were these key elements and research strategies determined? The study used an interpretive social sciences paradigm to inform the overall research design. Such a paradigm recognises that there are multiple viewpoints of the world rather than a universal reality (positivism) or a reality which is improbablistically determined (postpositivism). The epistemological perspective was emically derived in that researchers were subjectively involved in the process of studying that which was to be known with those who knew (the youth travel market). Additionally, an interpretive social sciences paradigm recognises that knowledge is a sense-making process of meaning involving social interactions. The methodology of the interpretive social sciences is one that draws on qualitative methodologies. For this research, the study used the following empirical material gathering methods: semi-structured interviews, focus groups, travel diaries as well as short demographic questions. The empirical materials that these methods generated were (re)interpreted using grounded theory analysis based on a constructivist approach akin to Charmaz (2006) (see Jennings & Junek, 2007 for details regarding grounded theory in tourism and leisure studies). The process involved constant comparison of empirical materials as they were being collected. Successive approximation inductively sorted common themes which were then (re)interpreted into root concepts and thereafter into higher order concepts. Figure 5.1 presents the higher order concepts that emerged from the root concepts. The emergent theory was grounded through 'checks' with participants, an industry group as well as the researcher team.

To reiterate, the development of processes to evaluate quality tourism experiences were predicated on the use of an interpretive social sciences paradigm, a qualitative methodology as well as qualitative research methods for empirical material collection and interpretation. These processes due to their qualitative and intersubjective nature are 'implementable' within day-to-day functionings undertaken by experience providers. The processes enable experience providers to continually monitor changes in 'quality' interpretations as well as to continuously work towards improving the 'quality' of the delivery of experiences. Additionally, the processes operate as a mechanism to identify professional and staff development requirements.

Researching Quality Experiences: Management Implications and Research Agenda

To conclude this chapter, this section reflexively considers the preceding discourse and highlights the ramifications for management with regard to researching and understanding the nature of quality experiences. As noted at the start of this chapter, management needs to

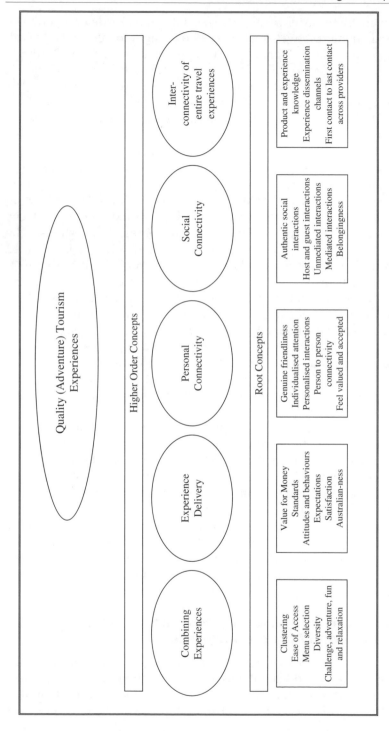

Figure 5.1 Root concepts and higher order concepts associated with quality adventure tourism experiences (*Source:* Jennings *et al.*, 2007)

use research and adopt 'quality' filters. Furthermore, management as well as tourism and leisure industries researchers need to:

- Continuously monitor and evaluate local, glocal, national and global environments and contexts.
- Question hegemonies with regard to knowledge and research practices.
- Work towards holistic perspectives and understandings of tourism and leisure experience industries phenomena.
- Engage in research which recognises differing cultural values, particularly individualistic and collective cultural framings and the consequences of these for tourism and leisure experience research.
- Contribute towards sustainable, corporate socially responsible and ethical business practices of tourism and leisure experiences.

Specifically, tourism and leisure industries research agendas need to:

- Embed reflexive practices.
- Incorporate research informed by evaluation literature and re-search processes.
- Develop emic and qualitative studies, which achieve holistic and insider perspectives as well as 'capture' the multidimensional and multiphase nature of experiences.
- Recognise and integrate other worldviews and perspectives via collective, inclusive, multidisciplinary, multigenerational, multi-researcher approaches.
- Frame research foci around intra-cultural, inter-cultural, cross-cultural and cross-national research.
- Research the provision of quality experiences within holistic frameworks, which include tourists, providers, governments, communities and the environment bearing mind glocal and global contexts.
- Challenge taken-for-granted assumptions, terminology, qualifiers and nomenclature.
- Model, demonstrate, and practice sustainability, corporate social responsibility and business ethics principles in research pro-cesses.

The above serves as one perspective of what constitutes a quality tourism and leisure experiences research agenda applicable for the 21st century. The agenda takes into account the multiplicity, diversity and complexity inherent in potential tourism and leisure experiences and that of experience-ers as well as providers. It recognises the role and influence of dominant research paradigms with regard to research processes and knowledge construction. It is a research agenda for use across global landscapes. As an agenda, it is founded on the premise that research and 'quality' are key mechanisms to enable providers to gain and hold their competitive edges as well as for experience-ers to 'experience' quality experiences.

References

Andereck, K., Bricker, K.S., Kerstetter, D. and Nickerson, N.P. (2006) Connecting experiences to quality: Understanding meanings behind visitors' experiences. In G.R. Jennings and N. Nickerson (eds) *Quality Tourism Experiences* (pp. 81–98). Burlington, MA: Elsevier.

Arnould, E.J. and Price, L.L. (1993) River magic: extraordinary experiences and the extended service encounter. *Journal of Consumer Research* 20 (1), 24–45.

Arnould, E., Price, L. and Otnes, C. (1999) Making consumption magic: A study of white-water rafting. *Journal of Contemporary Ethnography* 28 (1), 33–68.

Beck, L. (1987) The phenomenology of optimal experiences attained by white-water river recreationists in Canyonland National Park (Utah). PhD thesis, University of Minnesota.

Binkhorst, E. and Den Dekker, T. (2009) Agenda for co-creation tourism experience research. *Journal of Hospitality Marketing and Management* 18 (2–3), 311–327.

Borrie, B. and Roggenbuck, J. (2001) The dynamic, emergent, and multi-phasic nature of on-site wilderness experiences. *Journal of Leisure Research* 33 (2), 202–228.

Charmaz, K. (2006) *Constructing Grounded Theory: A Practical Guide Through Qualitative Analysis*. London: Sage.

Clawson, M. (1963) *Land and Water for Recreation: Opportunities, Problems and Policies*. Chicago, IL: Rand McNally.

Craig-Smith, S. and French, C. (1994) *Learning to Live with Tourism*. Melbourne: Pitman.

Cronin, J.J. and Taylor, S.A. (1992) Measuring service quality: A reexamination and extension. *Journal of Marketing* 56, 55–58.

Crotts, J. and Erdmann, R. (2000) Does national culture influence consumers' evaluation of travel services? A test of Hofstede's model of cross-cultural differences. *Managing Service Quality* 10 (6), 410–419.

Csikszentmihalyi, M. (1988) The future of flow. In M. Csikszentmihalyi and I. Csikszentmihalyi (eds) *Optimal Experience: Psychological Studies of Flow in Consciousness* (pp. 365–383). Cambridge: Cambridge University Press.

De Mooij, M. (1998) *Global Marketing and Advertising: Understanding Cultural Paradoxes*. Thousand Oaks, CA: Sage.

Dolnicar, S. (2004) Insights into sustainable tourism in Austria: A data-based a priori segmentation approach. *Journal of Sustainable Tourism* 12 (3), 209–218.

Donthu, N. and Yoo, B. (1998) Cultural influences on service quality expectations. *Journal of Service Research* 1 (2), 178–186.

Dorfman, P.W. (1998) Implications of vertical and horizontal individualism and collectivism for leadership effectiveness. *Advances in International Management* 12, 53–65.

Dorfman, P.W. and Howell, J.P. (1988) Dimensions of national culture and effective leadership patterns: Hofstede revisited. *Advances in International Management* 3, 127–150.

Fay, C.H., Mc Cure, J.T. and Begin, J.P. (1987) The setting for continuing education in the year 2000. *New Directions for Continuing Education* 36 (winter), 15–27.

Frijda, N. and Jahoda, G. (1966) On the scope and methods of cross-cultural research. *International Journal of Psychology* 1 (2), 109–127.

Furrer, O., Shaw-Ching Liu, B. and Sudharshan, D. (2000) The relationships between culture and service quality perceptions: Basis for cross-cultural market segmentation and resource allocation. *Journal of Service Research* 2 (4), 355–371.

Gilmore, J.H. and Pine, B.J. (2000) *Markets of One: Creating Customer-Unique Value through Mass Customization.* Boston, MA: Harvard Business School Press.

Gobe, M., Gob, M. and Zyman, S. (2001) *Emotional Branding: The New Paradigm for Connecting Brands to People.* New York, NY: Allworh Press.

Higham, J.E.S. (2007) *Critical Issues in Ecotourism: Understanding a Complex Tourism Phenomenon.* Amsterdam: Elsevier, Butterworth Heinemann.

Higham, J.E.S. and Carr, A. (2002) Ecotourism visitor experiences in Aotearoa/New Zealand: Challenging the environmental values of visitors in pursuit of pro-environmental behaviours. *Journal of Sustainable Tourism* 10 (4), 277–294.

Hofstede, G.H. (1980) *Culture's Consequences: International Differences in Work-related Values.* Beverley Hills, CA: Sage.

Hofstede, G.H. (1984) *Culture's Consequences: International Differences in Work-related Values (Abridged Edition).* Beverley Hills, CA: Sage.

Hofstede, G.H. and Bond, M.H. (1988) The Confucian-connection: From cultural roots to economic growth. *Organizational Dynamics* 16 (4), 4–21.

Hull, R., Stewart, W. and Yi, Y. (1992) Experience patterns: Capturing the dynamic nature of a recreation experience. *Journal of Leisure Research* 24 (3), 240–252.

Iso-Ahola, S. (1980) *The Social Psychology of Leisure and Recreation.* Dubuque, IO: Wm C. Brown.

Jafari, J. (1990) Research and scholarship: The basis of tourism education. *Journal of Tourism Studies* 1 (1), 33–41.

Jennings, G.R. (1997) The travel experience of cruisers. In M. Oppermann (ed.) *Pacific Rim 2000: Issues, Interrelations, Inhibitors* (pp. 94–105). London: CAB International.

Jennings, G.R. (1999) Voyages from the centre to the margins: An ethnography of long term ocean cruisers. PhD thesis, Murdoch University, Murdoch, Australia.

Jennings, G.R. (2001) 'Flow: Having the right skills for the challenge'. *2001: A Tourism Odyssey: TTRA 32nd Annual Conference Proceedings*, Fort Myers, Florida, 10–13 June, pp. 236–246.

Jennings, G.R. (2006) Quality tourism experiences – an introduction. In G.R. Jennings and N. Nickerson (eds) *Quality Tourism Experiences* (pp. 1–21). Burlington, MA: Elsevier.

Jennings, G.R. (2007a) Sustainability and future directions. In G. Jennings (ed.) *Water-based Tourism, Sport, Leisure, and Recreation Experiences* (pp. 223–251). Amsterdam: Elsevier.

Jennings, G.R. (2007b) *Sustaining Quality Tourism Experiences: Marketing and Management Research Implications for Tourism and Hospitality in Asia.* Tourism perspectives towards "Regional Development and Asia's Values". Dong-Eui University, 22–23 October, Busan, South Korea.

Jennings, G.R. and Junek, O. (2007) Grounded theory: Innovative methodology or a critical turning from hegemonic methodological praxis in tourism studies? In I. Ateljevic, N. Morgan and A. Pritchard (eds) *The Critical Turn in Tourism Studies: Innovative Research Methodologies* (pp. 197–210). Amsterdam: Elsevier.

Jennings, G.R., Lee, Y-S., Ayling, A., Ollenburg, C., Cater, C. and Lunny, B. (2007) *What Do Quality Adventure Tourism Experiences Mean for Adventure Travellers and Providers?* An Industry Report to the Gold Coast Adventure Travel Group. On WWW at http://businessgc.com.au/uploads/QTE%20 Summary.pdf. Accessed 20.2.09.

Jennings, G., Lee, Y-S., Ayling, A., Bunny, B., Cater, C. and Ollenburg, C. (2009) Quality tourism experiences: Reviews, reflections, research agendas. *Journal of Hospitality Marketing and Management* 18 (2–3), 294–310.

Jennings, G.R. and Nickerson, N. (eds) (2006) *Quality Tourism Experiences*. Burlington, MA: Elsevier.

Jennings, G.R. and Weiler, B. (2006) Mediating meaning: Perspectives on brokering quality tourism experiences. In G.R. Jennings and N. Nickerson (eds) *Quality Tourism Experiences* (pp. 57–78). Burlington, MA: Elsevier.

Jonas, L. (2007) Whitewater rafting. In G.R. Jennings (ed.) *Tourism, Sport, Leisure and Recreation Experiences* (pp. 153–170). Burlington, MA: Elsevier.

Killion, G.L. (1992) *Understanding Tourism*. Study guide. Rockhampton: Central Queensland University.

Kim, H., Borges, M.C. and Chon, J. (2006) Impacts of environmental values on tourism motivation: The case of FICA, Brazil. *Tourism Management* 27, 957–967.

Klein, R.A. (2002) *Cruise Ship Blues: The Underside of the Cruise Industry*. Gabriola Island, BC: New Society.

Lee, Y., Datillo, J. and Howard, D. (1994) The complex and dynamic nature of leisure experience. *Journal of Leisure Research* 26, 195–211.

Lee, Y.S. (2001) Tourist gaze: Universal concept? *Tourism, Culture and Communication* 3 (2), 93–99.

Lipscombe, N. (1996) The aged and adventure: A perfect match. *Australian Leisure* 7 (3), 38–41.

Macbeth, J. (2005) Towards an ethics platform for tourism. *Annals of Tourism Research* 32 (4), 962–984.

Martin, W.H. and Mason, S. (1987) Social trends and tourism futures. *Tourism Management* 8 (2), 112–114.

Mattila, A.S. (1999) The role of culture in the service evaluation process. *Journal of Service Research* 1 (3), 250–261.

Nickerson, N.P. (2006) Some reflections on quality tourism experiences. In G.R. Jennings and N. Nickerson (eds) *Quality Tourism Experiences* (pp. 227–235). Burlington, MA: Elsevier.

Nielson, J. and Shelby, B. (1977) River-running in the Grand Canyon: How much and what kind of use. *Proceedings of the River Recreation Management and Research Symposium*, Grand Canyon National Park, Colorado River Research Series, pp. 168–177. USDA Forest service, Washington, DC.

Oelrichs, I. (1994) Values tourism and endemic tourism planning: Sustainable tourism with a community focus. *Tourism Ecodollars. Conference Proceedings* Mackay, North Queensland, April.

Ooi, C.S. (2005) A theory of tourism experiences: The management of attention. In T. O'Dell and P. Billing (eds) *Experiencescapes: Tourism, Culture and Economy* (pp. 51–68). Copenhagen: Copenhagen Business School Press.

Parasuraman, A., Berry, L.L. and Zeithaml, V.A. (1991) Refinement and reassessment of the SERVQUAL scale. *Journal of Retailing* 67 (1), 39–48.

Parasuraman, A., Zeithaml, V.A. and Berry, L.L. (1985) A conceptual model of service quality and its implications for future research. *Journal of Marketing* 49, 41–50.

Parasuraman, A., Zeithaml, V.A. and Berry, L.L. (1988) SERVQUAL: A multi-item scale for measuring customer perceptions of service quality. *Journal of Retailing* 64 (1), 12–40.

Patterson, I. and Pegg, S. (2009) Marketing leisure to baby boomers and older tourists. *Journal of Hospitality Marketing and Management* 18 (2–3), 254–272.

Pine, J., and Gilmore, J. (1998) Welcome to the experience economy. *Harvard Business Review* 76 (4), 97–105.

Pine, J., and Gilmore, J. (1999) *The Experience Economy: Work is Theatre and Every Business is a Stage*. Boston, MA: Harvard Business School Press.

Pohle, G. and Hittner, J. (2008) Attaining sustainable growth through corporate social responsibility. *IBM Institute for Business Value*. Online document. On WWW at http://www-935.ibm.com/services/us/gbs/bus/pdf/gbe03019-usen-02.pdf. Accessed 03.06.10.

Poon, A. (1993) *Tourism Technology and Competitive Strategies*. Wallingford, UK: CAB International.

Price, L., Arnould, E., and Tierney, P. (1995) Going to extremes: Managing service encounters and assessing provider performance. *Journal of Marketing* 59, 83–97.

Raajpoot, N. (2004) Reconceptualizing service encounter quality in non-western contexts. *Journal of Service Research* 7 (2), 181–201.

Reason, P. and Bradbury, H. (2006) *Handbook of Action Research*. London: Sage.

Richards, G. and Wilson, J. (2006) Developing creativity in tourist experiences: A solution to serial reproduction of culture. *Tourism Management* 27, 1209–1223.

Ritchie, J.R.B. and Hudson, S. (2009) Understanding and meeting the challenges of consumer/tourist experience research. *International Journal of Tourism Research* 11, 111–126.

Schwartz, S.H. (1992) Universals in the construct and structure of values: Theoretical advances and empirical tests in 20 countries. In M.P. Zanna (ed.) *Advances in Experimental Social Psychology* (Vol. 25, pp. 1–65). San Diego, CA: Academic Press.

Steenkamp, J-B.E.M., ter Hofstede, F. and Wedel, M. (1999) A cross-national investigation into the individual and national cultural antecedents of consumer innovativeness. *Journal of Marketing* 63, 55–69.

United Nations Department of Economic and Social Affairs. (2002) *Johannesburg Summit 2002*. New York: United Nations Department of Economic and Social Affairs.

Urry, J. (1990) *The Tourist Gaze: Leisure and Travel in Contemporary Societies*. London: Sage.

Urry, J. (2002) *The Tourist Gaze* (2nd edn). London: Sage.

Volo, S. (2009) Conceptualizing experience. *Journal of Hospitality Marketing and Management* 18 (2–3), 111–126.

Weiler, B. and Hall, C.M. (1992) *Special Interest Tourism*. London: Belhaven.

Winstead, K.F. (1997) "The service experience in two cultures" a behavioural perspective. *Journal of Retailing* 73 (3), 337–360.

World Bank (2005) Corporate Social Responsibility. Online document. On WWW at http://www.info.worldbank.org/etools/library/latestversion_p.asp?objectID=139587&lprogram=11 Accessed. 15.05.05.

World Commission on Environment and Development, WCED (1987) *Our Common Future*. Oxford: Oxford University Press.

Yüksel, A. and Yüksel, F. (2001) The expectancy-disconfirmation paradigm: A critique. *Journal of Hospitality and Tourism Research* 25 (2), 107–131.

Zografos, C. and Allcroft, D. (2007) The environmental values of potential ecotourists: A segmentation study. *Journal of Sustainable Tourism* 15 (1), 44–66.

Chapter 6
Researching Visual Culture: Approaches for the Understanding of Tourism and Leisure Experiences

IAN GILHESPY and DAVID HARRIS

Introduction

Visual culture is a significant part of the experience economy, it is claimed (Schroeder, 2002). The analysis of this visual culture is likely to be of interest to academics and commercial practitioners alike if it leads to insights about the characteristics and pleasures of the experiences to be gained in this visual culture. This chapter reviews and evaluates a series of approaches to the study of visual culture in order to explore and explain the scope for these approaches for the understanding of tourism and leisure experiences. However, it is also argued that while an understanding of the visual aspects of tourism experiences is important, the emphasis on the visual needs to be tempered with the recognition of the ways in which tourists decode visuals, or 'embody' experiences that may challenge all of the senses.

The term 'visual culture' has been defined as 'the shared practices of a group, community or society through which meanings are made out of the visual, aural and the textual world of representations and the ways that looking practices are engaged in symbolic and communicative activities' (Sturken & Cartwright, 2009: 3). This is a definition with its basis in broadly anthropological approaches to 'culture' referring to whole ways of life and the communicative practices within it including, of course for our interests in this chapter, the everyday practices of consumers, not just in terms of the uses of advertising and marketing materials but any aspects of the touristic experience that involves forms of representation.

Addressing issues of consumer experience brings about an interesting convergence between academic and more conventional market research (Belk, 2006). The experience of knowledgeable and experienced customers generally, and leisure and tourism customers more specifically, seems to be complex enough to require a wide range of techniques including those that draw upon the qualitative techniques found in the

99

social sciences as well as the more conventional questionnaire-based methods that have characterised much market research. Increasingly, forms of research such as ethnography, autoethnography and biography are being utilised in the marketing literature alongside methods that make up the palette of visual methodologies, including compositional analysis (Schroeder, 2002), variants of semiotics and discourse analysis and types of elicitation methods. There is convergence too in the growing body of material explicitly concerned with utilising an understanding of visual culture for the creation and successful management of tourism and leisure experiences (Baerenholdt *et al.*, 2008).

Many of these approaches make significantly different assumptions at an epistemological level. Academic approaches are intended to address academic or political agendas in various combinations, while commercial approaches are more likely to be concerned with improving performance against a range of priorities. However, there continues to be great potential in the commercial application of much of academic work even though much of this critical work was not conceived for such purposes. The academic work we are about to review on realism, for example, is designed primarily to expose the narrative and visual devices that construct a passive subject, open to the main ideological mechanisms in modern capitalism. Such radical and critical approaches have been incorporated into commercial mainstream culture: surrealist imagery has been diverted from its critical purposes into making visually pleasing cigarette advertisements; avant-garde cinema has been pastiched in the music video. Brown's (2007) accounts of postmodern marketing high-light many examples.

Graduate entrants to the tourism and leisure businesses will probably have encountered critical theoretical work while at university, and should be capable of utilising the techniques whilst perhaps leaving behind some of the original critical intent. For critics, realist narratives deliver a passive and vulnerable viewer (Lapsley & Westlake, 2006), but for marketers, the capacity to bring about attitudinal and behavioural change is positively sought. Drawing upon the academic work designed to expose and criticise forms of representation may also lead to the ability to create absorbing images and involving narratives. Thus, just as academic commentators may take the cultural products of commercial activity as the objects of their study, so workers in the creative, tourism and leisure industries are likely to appropriate critical techniques for their own ends, a sort of reverse engineering. This chapter is concerned with the 'practices of looking', everyday social processes that most of us take for granted. The chapter examines a number of ways in which these practices of looking have been approached with the intentions that readers may gain a practical and critical understanding of the mechanisms involved and that they may improve their professional practice.

Researching Visual Culture

Visual ethnography

Ethnographic techniques originally used to understand social life in 'natural' settings are increasingly incorporating visual methods to record data (Banks, 2001; Pink, 2007a). Pink's (2008a) account of her 'slow tourism' experience of a day spent in the town of Mold, and her similar visit to Diss (Pink, 2008b), incorporate photography alongside her sensory and social experience. To achieve an embodied account of her visit, her methods include accounting for a range of sensory experiences as well as the social experiences she gains by engaging in a series of pre-arranged meetings with local people. It is through these means that Pink creates her experience of these towns: ethnography is presented as 'place-making' – an active, experiential process of construction – rather than visiting places and passive consumption. 'Place-making' might also be a commercially valuable concept to begin to grasp how tourists make sense actively of their visits and find pleasures of their own in the location.

Although Pink refers to the need for researchers to recognise their own role in the research process (Pink, 2008a: 182), she does not address any expectations she may have had of the town or its people ahead of the visit. Expectations of destinations are significant in some of the established tourism studies literature. It is the visual features of tourist expectations that form the starting point of Urry's (2002) hermeneutic circle in the tourist gaze: that tourists set out to consume sets of expectations of tourist sites based upon brochures and other media. Pink is more forthcoming about her political commitment to 'slow' politics which clearly governed her perceptions, choice of respondents and the themes she chose to illustrate, both on her visit to Mold (Pink, 2008a), to Diss (Pink, 2008b) and to the urban garden (Pink, 2007b). The extent to which tourist experiences are performed or preformed is a major issue for this chapter but it is intriguing that Pink's own photography is of a documentary or realist character (Pink, 2008a, 2008b). Pink's (2007b) video also reproduces the classic 'point of view' perspectives associated with documentary realism, a point we shall develop later.

The capacity of ethnographic methods to offer an understanding of natural settings links immediately to debates about tourism if we equate the 'natural setting' with the 'authentic'. As is well known, global visual media and the hyperreality (Eco, 1987; MacCannell, 1989) they produce make cultural contamination of the 'natural' an insuperable methodological problem as well as one for tourists seeking authenticity. Nor is this a particularly recent phenomenon: MacCannell (1989) talks about the constructed or mediated qualities of early tourism in Paris, even for the backstage elements of the tours, and the ways in which such constructions integrated work and leisure into some sort of inauthentic system of signs.

Modern ethnographic approaches have done much to uncover the particular meanings of tourist experiences in the midst of a sea of signification. The expectations of the tourists, created through a range of media using images and narratives are negotiated both by the tourists themselves and by the guides. To summarise some recent examples, in their participant-observation study of heli-kayaking, Kane and Tucker (2004) noted how the adventure tourists came to actively define themselves as genuine kayakers and adventurers, reducing any effects of the inevitably packaged and routine safety aspects of the trip; playing with reality and actively reinterpreting it becomes a major tourist accomplishment. Holyfield (1999) accompanied a river rafting expedition and noted the role of the company's guides in emphasising the romance of the experience and minimising its commercial aspects. Curtin (2005), in a similar vein, has written of the care taken by organisers of safari tours to ensure that tourists do not see fellow groups of tourists as they supposedly venture into the wild. Kelner (2001) also notes that modern pilgrimage tourists have to exercise selective perception as they visit Israel: the skilled narratives of the tour operatives help considerably in constantly managing the various kinds of 'authenticity' encountered. These findings may also be useful to the tour operators involved leading to training for tour guides and operatives in adding value to the experiences of the tourist or traveller as well as in the choice of images and text in promotional materials.

Methodological issues in practice

The techniques used to sort out and arrange meanings in ethnographic practice, to make them conform to an academic agenda have attracted considerable criticism from academics. Bourdieu (2000) argues that there is an inevitable element of symbolic violence involved in any attempt to take subjective meanings as mere data, as less than self-sufficient, and to subject them to what claims to be some higher order academic discourse. Advocates of autoethnography (such as Ellis & Bochner, 2006) make the same point. The data are typically subjected to a kind of dubious ordering and sorting by researchers occupying a superior status, as academics, and, quite frequently, as males. One consequence is an emotional coldness towards the events being described. A second is the systematic attempt to evade the author's own subjectivity. Instead, autoethnographers have suggested that texts be clearly authored, that the full subjectivity of the writer should appear in the text, even that the usually suppressed additional contributors to the text be credited with full authorship as well (see Chapter 7 for a further discussion of autoethnography). Denzin (2006) offers an account of a tourist trip to national parks in the USA, where he reflects on representations of Native American people. The different voices heard in the article include Denzin as a 10-year-old on a family trip, Denzin as a later writer, Denzin as an academic defending autoethnography and Denzin as a political activist, and none of these 'voices' occupy a position of authority or superiority over the others.

Ethnographic practice has also been subject to poststructuralist deconstruction (Clifford, 1988; Clough, 1992). Ethnographic practice, including the use of photography, can be seen to deliver its own effects: it does not just transparently describe reality but shapes or constructs it. In particular, ethnographic practice is responsible for delivering pleasurable effects for the reader/viewer, a feeling of 'being really there', of having understood at last a puzzling cultural practice, emotions and all. Clough (1992) argues that these 'realist' techniques are very similar to those used in commercial media, including soap operas.

Poststructuralist approaches have led to similar feminist work on both leisure and tourism, for example Aitchison (2000), deconstructing past work that relies on gendered concepts such as 'the gaze' (see below), or even 'the visit'. Wearing and Wearing (1996) argue that these concepts are inextricably rooted in male pleasures and male perceptions too. Predating Pink, they note that the flâneur, the exemplary practitioner of 'the gaze' could only be a gentleman of leisure. They also advocate seeing places as 'chora', that is unstructured places or spaces in which people meet rather than as destinations to visit with its attendant implications of power relations: 'spaces in which people interact, spaces that take their meaning from the people that occupy them, both the tourist and the host' (Wearing & Wearing, 1996: 234). They go on to argue that tourist businesses may benefit from offering 'the opportunity for relationality' (1996: 235), especially for those tourists wishing to 'perform' and explore their identities.

Similarly, Beezer (1995) criticises the 'male heroics' in (postmodern) adventure tourism. Instead, she suggests tourist companies offer a proper recognition of otherness as part of the pleasures of travel, including noting similarities in the problems faced by women in other countries, rather than stressing their exotic otherness. Fullagar (2002) also wants to break with male discourse, with its limited notions of otherness still couched in binary terms, in favour of 'possibilities of glimpsing other modes of desire and hence different ethical relations between self and other, self and world' (2002: 57). She keeps travel diaries to illustrate her full immersion in the present and contrasts those with more remote academic accounts. In an attempt to broaden the pleasures of escape offered by travel, she records how she enjoys the disturbing effects of otherness rather than trying to interpret or grasp it conceptually, feeling a 'desire to disappear' (2002: 68) rather than to master.

Such critiques have commercial implications in the creation of tourism experiences. The recognition of the gendered characteristics of promotional material and the incorporation of additional female pleasures could have the benefits of engaging a different audience. However, there is a real problem with alternative, feminist forms of representation and narrative. So deeply does gender penetrate culture and language that only unconventional forms of expression seem immune, and only highly skilled tourists could experience them. Such alternatives would certainly offer considerable challenges to the expectations, and possibly the cultural capacities of the conventional consumer.

Analysing tourist photographs

Studying actual tourists and their personal records, including tourist photographs, leads to different emphases again. In particular, as Bohnsack (2008) argues, the intentions of the actual tourist, and the meanings of the photographs he or she takes, might be expected to be partly unconscious, or pre-reflexive, emanating from an 'habitus'. To paraphrase the argument, tourists themselves might be able to describe *what* they have photographed but not *why*. As a result, the researcher needs to take into account much more the methodological problems of interrogating the amateur photographer.

Bohnsack (2008) suggests that we revisit ethnomethodological approaches to see how shared meanings are constructed in actual conversations. He cites, in particular, Garfinkel's admiration for the documentary method advocated by Mannheim. For Garfinkel (1972), Mannheim offered a description of the documentary method of interpretation as the search for '... an identical, homologous pattern underlying a vast variety of totally different realisations of meaning... treating an actual appearance as "the document of", as "pointing to", as "standing on behalf of" a presupposed underlying pattern' (358).

Garfinkel's (1972) article is famous for describing an experiment where subjects were invited to construct something meaningful from the apparent responses of a supposed counsellor but which was really a tape recorder behind a screen making random comments. The subjects of the experiment made every effort to interpret these answers in a way that made coherent sense to them, even when the answers provided an initial surprise. The subjects were also extremely forgiving of what appeared to be contradictions in the answers and seemed to find some genuine meaning in them. Garfinkel (1972) suggests that sociologists and ethnographers use similar techniques to make sense of their data, using unclarified and probably unscientific rules to turn data into 'documents'.

This production of 'documents' can be seen at work with visual data too as in attempts to use photographs for research. In a good example of the process, Johns and Clark (2001) invited tourists to take photographs and then analysed them. After claiming to focus analysis of tourist myths on actual tourist perceptions, however, Johns and Clark offer their own theoretically and politically informed reading of the results. This leads them to dismiss some tourist photographs as 'trite' or 'insincere', 'clichéd' or 'contrived', while others are rated as 'intensely personal'.

Garrod (2008) reviews a number of earlier approaches and opts for 'volunteer-employed photography' in which a sample of visitors and tourist are provided with cheap disposable cameras and invited to take snaps of the features of Aberystwyth that illustrate their perceptions, and then to comment on them in various ways. Garrod (2008: 384) knows that such snaps alone will not exhaust the meaning of the term 'destination image' since 'images are constructed not just from the visual look of a place but from its atmosphere and the emotions it evokes', but he thinks volunteer photographs will improve on the usual techniques of analysing commercial photographs. The photographs are then subjected to a coding process, and those of tourists and residents compared using statistical tests of significance (despite the very small sample). A subtheme is to use the data to test Urry's view about the importance of commercial photographs as influencing tourists' destination images. An inconsistent pattern of similarities and differences between the two groups is noted, and there is some similarity between volunteer photographs and the commercial postcards in sale in the town.

Garrod's approach also raises the issue about the undiscussed effects of the actual technology. He advocates using simple cheap disposable cameras as a way to cut down on the costs of lost equipment, and stresses the familiarity of the equipment for tourists. He also suggests that using a camera 'forces the individual to determine what is to be included in the shot and what is to be omitted' (2008: 386), but there is considerably more flexibility available in cameras with more facilities than the cheap disposable ones offer. The determinants of what is included in the shot might well include the technical characteristics of the lens and aperture: a volunteer might have chosen different views had they been provided with a telephoto lens capable of recording far-off details, or a wide-angle lens to include more context.

The point arises even more strongly in Garrod's (2009) follow-up study, which compares tourist photographs taken with simple disposable cameras with those depictions of the town in picture postcards (presumably taken by professional photographers with professional kit). The intention is again to provide some empirical test for Urry's 'hermeneutic circle' between commercial images and tourist's actual photographs. One difference is that picture postcards often feature 'panoramic views of the town taken from one of the hills overlooking . . . [the town] . . . whereas tourists' photographs did not' (Garrod, 2009: 356).

One reason for this could have been simply that disposable cameras do not take effective panoramic shots; however, tourists could have considered the shot but rejected it, perhaps unconsciously, as with many other possible shots, rather than never having thought of it, which is what Garrod infers. Garrod suggests that: 'The professional photographer is more likely to ascend [a hill]' (Garrod, 2009: 352), but that is an assumption working back from the shots themselves. The log books written by the tourists recorded only their (conscious) reasons for taking photographs, not the reasons for rejecting other shots, nor whether they actually did climb the hills or not.

In a more open procedure, Loeffler (2004) invites respondents to use their own photographs not so much as hard data, but as visual prompts to recall and discuss their own experiences in adventure tourism. He claims that photographs offer better stimuli for recollection and further that the recollections are less influenced by the researcher. Notwithstanding these claims the results are still coded in a conventional manner again.

In the most non-directive technique, Pike (2003) advocates a semi-structured elicitation technique to analyse a sample of destination images from the point of view of the tourist, using the repertory grid method associated with the work of Kelly. Although Pike uses professional images, the technique has also been used to analyse photographs taken by tourists, for example by Botterill (1989). The proposition is that people use various bi-polar constructs to order their worlds semantically.

Constructs are elicited and made explicit by presenting subjects with images and inviting them to construe what they take to be similarities and differences between the images (usually in sets of three). Coshall (2000: 86) gives an example: 'a tourist might apply the construct "good value for money" to potential destination A, whereas the contrast "too expensive" might be applied to destination B. Each construct–contrast pair constitutes one basic dimension of cognitive appraisal of the environment'. Constructs actually elicited in his study included 'snobbish – closer to my taste', 'high-status visitors – average' and 'for adults – children would love it' (Coshall, 2000: 87). It is important to remember that these constructs are how tourists themselves construe the matter, regardless of the researcher's theoretical or political values.

When subjects run out of constructs, the resulting set is thought of as a repertory. A particularly interesting claim for the technique is that once new respondents cease to add any constructs to the stock, the sample can be said to be adequate (Pike, 2003: 316). Pike claims that, beyond academic applications, the technique has obvious practical benefits for the tourism industry: 'Repertory grid offers the operational advantage of being a structured technique with economy of data for analysis... the method was as important to market research as the development of the questionnaire' (Pike, 2003: 316).

Finally for this section, it is interesting that it is still photographs that are commonly analysed rather than tourist videos or films. Films, in particular, can convey cognitive and affective content, Kim and Richardson (2003) argue, as they develop narratives over time. Affective content is important in encouraging a sense of familiarity with places and empathy with people living in them. It is possible that this is equivalent to the experience of shared time which emerges during performances. Their own study looks, rather unusually, at a commercially produced film which features definite locations, and they have a number of interesting ways to measure possible impacts on destination choice, including the use of an 'empathy scale', developed originally in advertising, to measure viewer identification with the characters being depicted. There seem to be immediate applications for the design of promotional tourist material.

Studies that use moving images seem to require the sort of analysis of representations and narratives that have been developed in the specialist field of film theory, we want to suggest. Of course, the specific of tourism will remain, but there are many interesting parallels between the two fields of study. For example, in our view, Kim and Richardson's (2003) notions of familiarity, engagement and empathy with the characters that develop over time are well discussed as aspects of what is referred to in film theory as 'realist narrative'. More practically, Silverstone (1989) noted some years ago that the techniques of display and narrative construction in heritage sites and museums were heavily influenced by those developed in film and television. It is also clear that some major tourist destinations – above all those in Orlando run by Disney or Universal Studios – unite the pleasures of watching popular film with those of visiting theme parks, and it is common to find analyses of Disney which combine critiques both of the films and the sites (such as Hebdige, 2003 or Smoodin, 1994). It would be difficult to progress very far with the analysis of virtual tourism without an understanding of media conventions, of course.

Semiotic analysis of tourist brochures

Semiotic analysis is an important aspect of the discussion of realism in cinema which we discuss below, and it might be worth beginning with some familiar examples from tourism. The most well-known work offers semiotic analysis of the images in tourist brochures, as in Dann (in Selwyn, 1996), or later, Nelson (2005). The main representations identified include classic exotic tourist locations like beaches and scenery, sometimes with various combinations of locals and tourists. The early analyses typically suggested that a highly misleading and commercialised discourse developed about the innocent delights of tourism. There is an implication that some kind of 'false consciousness' is responsible, but there are also specific commercial reasons for the persistence of these images. Photographs may need to be 'realistic' in one sense (not misleading) to conform to advertising codes, and realism offers pleasure to the reader in the early stages of making their tourism choices. Bourdieu's (1984) work on the popular aesthetic emphasised that realist images invite immediate participation and involvement, an easy identification with the people depicted, learnt from the familiarity of the types of photographs involved. It is unlikely that tourist brochures are going to offer up surprises or insight.

To illustrate the pervasiveness of realist techniques, it is worth considering alternatives. The ironic photograph emphasises deliberate visual contradictions which have to be resolved with humour or critique. Scott (2004: 33) offers one example where 'The strap-line at the top of the poster reads: "World's Highest Standard of Living", and the text on the ad reads: "There's no way like the American way". Beneath the billboard stands a breadline of cold and ragged-looking black Americans, queuing for handouts...'. More radical forms of photographs challenge the viewer to consider representations or significations themselves, putting visual conventions in the foreground, rather than making them invisible as in realism. For example, the photographs of Cindy Sherman offer a feminist example challenging patriarchal archetypes in the photography of women, often by using parody (Mulvey, 1991).

Early cinema rapidly exploited the potential of the movie camera to alter naturalistic time in the form of slow motion and time lapse, enabling new understandings of motion. As we have hinted before, developing technology also led to non-naturalistic perspectives such as the overhead shot, the zoom, and other unusual tracking shots and camera positions. There are also hand-held, lightweight or waterproof cameras, miniature cameras, low-light facilities, electronic in-camera editing or steadicam equipment. Even popular camcorders have important technological devices such as complex lenses, automatic focus, and aperture and shot stabilisers. These devices have framing, lighting, focusing and narrative effects that might pass unnoticed by the amateur who sees the results in modern cinema as simply a record of 'reality'.

Realism

Many of the issues we have been discussing can be traced to the issue of realism and how that which is realistic must be deliberately represented, or signified, in visual forms. Realism is both a popular and commercially successful genre, and one which has attracted much critical commentary (Hayward, 2000; Lapsley & Westlake, 2006). Reality is never simply recorded without representation or signification intervening. Television and film have long been dominated by representations that crystallised in the early 20th century creating the 'realist' dramas that have become commonplace but rest upon a whole series of conventions relating to lighting, editing, directing and certain forms of narrative, all of which serve to allow us to experience our viewing in such a way that the construction of the text is rendered invisible. The cinema also rapidly developed a series of conventional narratives or codes, summarised best, perhaps, in Barthes (1975). To take the simplest example, it has become conventional to take the actual atmosphere as a code to signify emotional atmosphere, thus, dark brooding skies announce the existence of dark brooding thoughts in the minds of the main actors.

The documentary tradition of film-making also rests particularly strongly on allowing viewers an insight into the 'real' whilst disguising the editorial and production processes involved in their creation, as a kind of cinematic objectivity. Early documentarists saw an opportunity for film to offer an objective account of the experiences of a range of communities. However, those film makers were often faced with the dilemmas of not being able to 'capture the moment' and having to recreate 'natural episodes' in studios (such as the recreation of some fishing scenes in Grierson's 1929 classic *Drifters*).

Critiques of realism can be applied to both ethnographic and 'aesthetic' photographs of the kind used in the professional advertising of tourism destinations, and they might also serve to help analyse the photographs taken by tourists themselves. Reality is never simply captured in the photograph but chosen, interpreted and framed, not always in conscious or intended ways. As we have seen, ethnographic approaches often generated photographic still images and used them as means of documenting social processes, in particular, the use of 'old' photographs (Banks, 2001; Emmison & Smith, 2002). The use of existing photographs for this purpose is particularly problematical, however. The similarity of the photograph to the reality it represents may be illusory. Nevertheless, as Emmison and Smith (2002) point out, this use of photographs may have considerable value. They suggest a conceptual dichotomy referring to the presentation of the familiar in contrast to the presentation of something surprising. This parallels the well-known claim that ethnographic work makes the strange familiar and vice versa.

Positioning the Viewer

A particular variant of semiotic analysis, called Screen Theory, emerged to dominate the academic analysis of popular media in the late 1970s and has persisted since (Lapsley & Westlake, 2006; Turner, 2002). This approach suggests that images and narratives may work in combination to heavily influence the viewer, which is to say that images draw us in and create something of a paradoxical experience in which, although we are aware that there are other viewers sharing our experience, the experience can feel unique and special to us as individuals. Applying this approach to popular forms of cinema initially led to analyses of the ways in which individuals are flattered into believing that they are gaining some sort of personal insight from film. This sense of personal insight underpins our viewing experiences and this is crucial to our pleasure.

Realist texts are the default genre of popular film and television drama as well as being the dominant literary form. The realist text positions the viewer to allow access to the range of competing voices in any one given text, but one narrative position is often fully knowledgeable, and this master narrative is frequently the only consistent and unchallenged one. Readers gain pleasure from being able to examine the characters in this omniscient way. They are led to agree with this narrative position, and to see this master narrative as the truthful or realistic one. Sturken and Cartwright (2009: 59) dismiss the view that there are sinister ideological forces necessarily at work here arguing that 'this aspect of the practices of looking is neither insidious nor fully controlled by external forces such as advertisers or the media industry'. They go on to argue that, although texts may hold dominant meanings, a critical understanding of the practices of symbolic communication is important for producers as well as consumers both for understanding and for the re-configuration of those meanings. This point is similar to the one we have made about reverse engineering and we shall return to this when discussing resistance later in the chapter.

Williams (1994) also suggests the whole approach is far too general and driven by theory rather than close analysis or examination of actual pleasures. Lovell (1991), for example, emphasised that different forms emphasise the gaining of emotional wisdom rather than cognitive understanding, 'emotional realism' of the kind we were discussing with Kim and Richardson (2003) above.

Controlling Gazes

The work of Mulvey (especially Mulvey, 1975) takes much from the theoretical insights offered above but emphasises the significant feature of gender identification in the process and in the pleasures offered by classic realist texts. She suggests that the cinematic gaze is a male gaze. Using Hollywood films for the source material, she argues that viewers enjoy the pleasures of looking – or peeping – at women on the screen.

The viewing position suggests that the women on screen are unaware of the presence of the viewers, and further, they act in a range of titillating and indiscreet ways. The film often confirms the power dimensions of voyeuristic pleasure by a vocabulary of camera shots that take the position of the male observer casting an eye over the female. The narrative structure of the film performs its role too in confirming women's status as objects of the 'male look'. These elements combine in a process that dominates and restricts women: 'their role in narrative is limited almost entirely to make the hero act' (Mulvey, 1975: 60) in the way he does. In this way, 'mainstream film coded the erotic into the language of the dominant patriarchal order' (Mulvey, 1975: 60).

Work on the gaze has become familiar in tourist theory with Urry's famous discussion of the various tourist gazes. Urry (2002) draws on Foucault (1980), and thus stresses the disciplining of the subject via the operation of discourses. This notion of discourse offers '...a particular knowledge about the world which shapes how the world is understood and how things are done in it' (Rose, 2006: 79).

The Active Viewer

It is not only the act of writing that needs analysis, however, but that of active reading as well. It is not really enough just to gather 'data' from individuals as conventional empirical research claims to be able to do, nor to point to purely abstract possible readings and interpretations. The issue is whether ordinary viewers can track these acts of constructing meaning as well as academics, and what cultural resources they might need to do so. It would also be rash to underestimate the skill of professional writers in anticipating, incorporating and forestalling popular readings.

Urry's work does attempt to reveal some of the devices used by tour companies to construct the various gazes, ranging from promotional material to the layout of sites and viewing positions. However, although the individual tourist, viewer, reader or listener can resist particular gazes to some extent, largely by swapping between them, it may require substantial amounts of cultural capital, including a good working knowledge of alternative gazes, to escape completely. MacCannell (2001) has criticised Urry for overlooking the possibility of individual tourist commentary as a source of critical reflection, but he chooses a rather unusual and highly culturally competent human individual as his inspiration: Stendhal, a prolific and romantic 19th century French travel writer. Stendhal is far from being a typical tourist: Liukkonen (2008) notes that Stendhal's response to visiting Florence was unusually poetic: 'His psychosomatic reaction to the overdose of beautiful art, disorientation, powerful emotions from confusion to hallucinations, is nowadays called "Stendhal syndrome"'.

Some critics have seen a useful critical resource for viewers in 'popular cultural capital' (Fiske, 1987), which includes the considerable knowledge of media traditions and of other, sometimes contradictory or incomplete, texts held by the experienced viewer. This can be used to resist the totalising tendencies of organised gazes. Additional hope for those wishing to resist corporate or other sinister gazes may lie in the capacity to escape, at least temporarily, all social constraints in various ecstatic or highly corporeal encounters and high-risk adventures such as 'edgework' (Lyng, 1990). These encounters, in Lyng's example free-fall parachuting, can overwhelm the reliance on the visual and produce for the tourists themselves an unmistakable awareness of the non-visual senses. However, it is doubtful even here that the participant can fully escape the influence of various media descriptions and activities surrounding the event. Ferrell *et al.* (2001) describe how a licensed BASE-jumping event is turned into a media spectacle, and how mediated meanings are used even by the participants themselves to describe their pleasures, and we have discussed the problems these mediated meanings cause in attempts to analyse tourist myths in Johns and Clark (2001).

The Performing Tourist

A major source of criticism of the dominance of the visual in analysis has arisen from the performative turn in qualitative research. This work involves a strong claim that the performance activity in which the researcher takes part offers a radical new way to generate empirical knowledge directly, without mediation or representation: 'Categorisations and unanimity must yield to an understanding of openness, reflexivity and recursiveness during the research process... Qualitative methodology, therefore, requires a change of perspective which can draw on the idea of performance to meet these requirements of complexity' (Dirksmeier & Helbrecht, 2008). We have seen something of the arguments when reviewing work like Wearing and Wearing (1996), or Pink (2008a, 2008b), and it is a theme in Franklin's (2003) influential text. The same point is made in Perkins and Thorns (2001: 186) criticism of Urry: 'the gaze metaphor is too passive to encapsulate the full range of the tourist experience... a better metaphorical approach to tourism is to talk about the tourist performance', the authors argue.

As in Pink's (2008a) work mentioned earlier, the concern here is to grasp the ways in which tourists enact their own experiences. 'Performances are socially negotiated not only between actors but also with a present or imagined audience' (Pink, 2008a: 179). As an example of the practical implications, the case studies reported by Baerenholdt *et al.*

(2008) examine the ways in which families enact their holidays – specifically visits to heritage sites – using the materials afforded to them in terms of the physical structure of the sites. Baerenholdt *et al.* (2008) are at pains to distance themselves from the determinist version of Urry's hermeneutic circle in which tourists seek out a set of photographic images based on their knowledge of tourism brochures and other media, especially television. Instead consumers, first, enact their intimacy and togetherness and, second, enact their relations to the past in what the authors refer to as the 'fantastic realism' of the touristic/leisure site: 'It is the global web of circulating signifiers mediated through films, images, objects and narratives that enables people to take possession of and identify with the past' (Baerenholdt *et al.*, 2008: 197).

Examining this relationship between signification and tourist performance may also have managerial applications in the experience economy. Returning to the theme of 'reverse engineering', it might be possible to use the conventions of realism identified by the critics to reproduce the type of consumer who sees their individual personality and subjectivity invested in consuming a particular tourist experience or negotiated with important social contacts. Realist promotional material might offer a suitably individualised knowledge effect, as in claims that tours will uncover the 'real America', or the 'real you' as tourists are offered suitable challenges with rival interpretations. However, it is important to remember that the design of tourist attractions may involve the scripting of tourist experiences, but this scripting is experienced by the no less concrete imaginations of the tourists themselves.

Concluding Remarks

Reviewing the uses of visual analysis in various research traditions reveals some interesting problems and possibilities. Although the specific terms of the debates have varied – objectivity in ethnographic research, authenticity in tourism, documentary objectivity in film studies – a central focus on realism seems useful. Realism is the most popular and possibly the most criticised form: it continues to generate academic criticisms and commercial practice simultaneously. And it also crucially offers a significant component of the pleasure to be gained in a variety of experiences. We have argued that the appreciation of authenticity in realist texts is based on a series of learned generic conventions even though the semblance of reality may be an artifice. Just as we enjoy a sense of authenticity in our media consumption – or truthfulness to use McGuigan's (1996) phrase or 'true-to-life' to use Frith's (1997) term in his discussion of the pleasures of music consumption – we enjoy the apparent insights to be gained from ethnographic writing, documentary, photography and from touristic experiences. Accounts of postmodernist culture (Connor, 1992; Strinati, 1995) report that contemporary life in Western cultures has become so saturated by media influences that authentic experience has become impossible. All of these accounts serve to deconstruct the appearance of reality in cultural forms. Our suggestion is that the challenge here is not only to understand how these 'realism-effects' operate in order to deconstruct them but also how to understand the pleasures to be gained in order to be able to create and manage them: to offer suitable narratives.

References

Aitchison, C. (2000) Poststructural feminist theories of representing others: Their response to the 'crisis' in leisure studies 'discourse'. *Leisure Studies* 19, 127–144.
Baerenholdt, J., Haldrup, M. and Larsen, J. (2008) Performing cultural attractions. In J. Sundbo and P. Darmer (eds) *Creating Experiences in the Experience Economy* (pp. 176–202). Cheltenham: Edward Elgar.
Banks, M. (2001) *Visual Methods in Social Research*. London: Sage.
Barthes, R. (1975) *S/Z*. London: Jonathan Cape.
Bourdieu, P. (1984) *Distinction: A Social Critique of the Judgement of Taste*. London: Routledge and Kegan Paul.
Bourdieu, P. (2000) *Pascalian Meditations*. Cambridge: Polity Press.
Beezer, A. (1995) Women and 'adventure travel' tourism. *New Formations* 21, 119–130.
Belk, R. (ed.) (2006) *Handbook of Qualitative Research Methods in Marketing*. Northampton: Edward Elgar.
Bohnsack, R. (2008) The interpretation of pictures and the documentary method. *Forum: Qualitative Social Research* 9 (3), Article 14 [online]. On WWW at http://www.qualitative-research.net/index.php/fqs/article/view/1171/2592.
Botterill, T. (1989) Humanistic tourism? Personal constructions of a tourist: Sam visits Japan. *Leisure Studies* 8, 281–293.
Brown, S. (2007) Postmodern marketing. In M. Baker and S. Hart (eds) *The Marketing Book* (6th edn). London: Butterworth-Heinemann.
Clifford, J. (1988) *The Predicament of Culture: Twentieth Century Ethnography, Literature and Art*. London: Harvard University Press.
Clough, P. (1992) *The End(s) of Ethnography: From Realism to Social Criticism*. London: Sage.
Connor, S. (1992) *Postmodernist Culture: An Introduction to Theories of the Contemporary*. Oxford: Butterworth-Heinemann.
Coshall, J. (2000) Measurement of tourist images: The repertory grid approach. *Journal of Travel Research* 39 (1), 85–89.
Curtin, S.C. (2005) Nature, wild animals and tourism: An experiential view. *Journal of Ecotourism* 4 (1), 1–15.
Denzin, N. (2006) Analytic autoethnography, or deja-vu all over again. *Journal of Contemporary Ethnography* 35 (4), 419–428.
Dirksmeier, P. and Helbrecht, I. (2008) Time, non-representational theory and the "performative turn" – Towards a new methodology in qualitative social Research. *Forum: Qualitative Social Research* 9 (2), Article 55 [online]. On WWW at http://www.qualitative-research.net/index.php/fqs/article/view/385/840.
Eco, U. (1987) *Travels in Hyperreality*. London: Picador.

Ellis, C. and Bochner, A. (2006) Analyzing analytic autoethnography: An autopsy. *Journal of Contemporary Ethnography* 35 (4), 429–449.

Emmison, M. and Smith, P. (2002) *Researching the Visual*. London: Sage.

Ferrell, J., Milovanavic, D. and Lyng, S. (2001) Edgework, media practices, and the elongation of meaning: A theoretical ethnography of the Bridge Day events. *Theoretical Criminology* 5 (2), 177–202.

Fiske, J. (1987) *Television Culture*. London and New York: Routledge.

Foucault, M. (1980) *Power/Knowledge: Selected Interviews and Other Writings*. Brighton: Harvester Press.

Franklin, A. (2003) *Tourism*. Thousand Oaks, CA: Sage.

Frith, S. (1997) *Performing Rites: On the Value of Popular Music*. Oxford: Oxford University Press.

Fullagar, S. (2002) Narratives of travel: Desire and the movement of feminine subjectivity. *Leisure Studies* 21 (1), 57–74.

Garfinkel, H. (1972) Common sense knowledge of social structures: The documentary method of interpretation. In J. Manis and B. Meltzer (eds) *Symbolic Interaction: A Reader in Social Psychology* (2nd edn) (pp. 201–208). Boston, MA: Allyn and Bacon.

Garrod, B. (2008) Exploring place perception: A photo-based analysis. *Annals of Tourism Research* 35 (2), 381–401.

Garrod, B. (2009) Understanding the relationship between tourism destination imagery and tourist photography. *Journal of Travel Research* 47 (3), 346–358.

Hayward, S. (2000) *Cinema Studies: Key Concepts*. Florence, KY: Routledge.

Hebdige, D. (2003) Dis-gnosis: Disney and the re-tooling of knowledge, art, culture, life, etc. *Cultural Studies* 17 (2), 150–167.

Holyfield, L. (1999) Manufacturing adventure: The buying and selling of emotions. *Journal of Contemporary Ethnography* 28 (1), 3–32.

Johns, N. and Clark, V. (2001) Mythological analysis of boating tourism. *Annals of Tourism Research* 28 (2), 339–359.

Kane, M. and Tucker, H. (2004) Adventure tourism. The freedom to play with reality. *Tourist Studies* 4 (3), 217–234.

Kelner, S. (2001) Narrative construction of authenticity in pilgrimage touring. *Proceedings of the 96th Annual Meeting of the American Sociological Association* [online], Anaheim, California, August. On WWW at http://brandeis.edu/cmjs/pdfs/ASA 2001.pdf. Accessed 03.06.10.

Kim, H. and Richardson, S. (2003) Motion picture impacts on destination images. *Annals of Tourism Research* 30 (1), 216–237.

Lapsley, R. and Westlake, M. (2006) *Film Theory: An Introduction* (2nd edn). Manchester: Manchester University Press.

Liukkonen, P. (2008) Stendhal (1783–1842) – pseudonym of Marie-Henri Beyle. Online document: On WWW at http://www.kirjasto.sci.fi/stendhal.htm. Accessed 03.06.10.

Loeffler, T. (2004) A photo elicitation study of the meanings of outdoor adventure experiences. *Journal of Leisure Research* 36 (4), 536–556.

Lovell, T. (ed.) (1991) *British Feminist Thought: A Reader*. Oxford: Blackwell.

Lyng, S. (1990) Edgework: A social psychological analysis of voluntary risk taking. *The American Journal of Sociology* 95 (4), 851–886.

MacCannell, D. (1989) *The Tourist: A New Theory of the Leisure Class*. New York: Schocken.

MacCannell, D. (2001) Tourist agency. *Tourist Studies* 1 (1), 23–37.

McGuigan, J. (1996) *Culture and the Public Sphere*. London: Routledge.

Mulvey, L. (1975) Visual pleasure and narrative cinema. *Screen* 16 (3), 6–18.

Mulvey, L. (1991) A phantasmagoria of the female body: The work of Cindy Sherman. *New Left Review* 1 (188), 148.

Nelson, V. (2005) Representation and images of people, place and nature in Grenada's tourism. *Geografiska Annaler* 87 (B), 131–143.

Perkins, H. and Thorns, D. (2001) Gazing or performing? Reflections on Urry's tourist gaze in the context of contemporary experience in the Antipodes. *International Sociology* 16 (2), 185–204.

Pike, S. (2003) The use of repertory grid analysis to elicit salient short-break holiday destination attributes in New Zealand. *Journal of Travel Research* 41, 315–319.

Pink, S. (2007a) *Doing Visual Ethnography* (2nd edn). London: Sage.

Pink, S. (2007b) Walking with video. *Visual Studies* 22 (3), 240–252.

Pink, S. (2008a) An urban tour. The sensory sociality of ethnographic place-making. *Ethnography* 9 (2), 175–196.

Pink, S. (2008b) Mobilising visual ethnography: Making places and making images. *Forum: Qualitative Social Research* 9 (3), Article 36 [online]. On WWW at http://www.qualitative-research.net/index.php/fqs/article/view/1166/2581.

Rose, G. (2006) Visual methodologies. In G. Griffin (ed.) *Research Methods for English Studies* (pp. 67–90). London: Routledge.

Schroeder, J. (2002) *Visual Consumption.* London: Routledge.

Scott, B. (2004) Picturing irony: The subversive power of photography. *Visual Communication* 3 (1), 31–59.

Selwyn, T. (ed.) (1996) *The Tourist Image: Myths and Myth-making in Tourism.* New York: John Wiley.

Silverstone, R. (1989) Heritage as media: Some implications for research. In D. Uzzel (ed.) *Heritage Interpretations: The Natural and Built Environment* (vol. 2) (pp. 138–148). London: Belhaven Press.

Smoodin, E. (ed.) (1994) *Disney Discourse: Producing the Magic Kingdom.* New York: Routledge.

Strinati, D. (1995) *Postmodern Culture.* London: Routledge.

Sturken, M. and Cartwright, L. (2009) *Practices of Looking: An Introduction to Visual Culture* (2nd edn). Oxford: Oxford University Press.

Turner, G. (ed.) (2002) *Film Cultures Reader.* Florence, KY: Routledge.

Urry, J. (2002) *The Tourist Gaze* (2nd edn). London: Sage.

Wearing, B. and Wearing, S. (1996) Refocusing the tourist experience: The flâneur and the chorister. *Leisure Studies* 15, 229–243.

Williams, C. (1994) After the classic, the classical and ideology: The differences of realism. *Screen* 35 (3), 275–292.

Chapter 7

'Been There, Done That': Embracing our Post-trip Experiential Recollections through the Social Construction and Subjective Consumption of Personal Narratives

RICHARD KEITH WRIGHT

(Re)Creating a Truly 'Unforgettable' Experience

> Memory is important for the tourism industry because future decisions are based on it. For the tourist, that memory is perhaps the single most important source of information he or she will use in making a decision about whether or not to revisit... For family, friends, co-workers, etc., assessments of that experience will be an important factor as they make their own travel arrangements. (Braun-La Tour *et al.*, 2006: 360)

In 1963, Marion Clawson suggested that leisure-based tourism was experienced in a complex 'multi-phased nature', which incorporated the anticipation (pre-trip), the journey ('away'), the activities (whilst at the destination), the return ('home') and, finally, the recollection (post-trip memories). Later that decade, Clawson and Jack Knetsch further complemented this notion, discussing the various contextualised events and encounters that helped shape each of these five stages of the complete 'holiday' experience (Clawson & Knetsch, 1966). In doing so, however, they duly noted a general lack of research or understanding on/about the personal meanings attached to the post-trip 'recollection'. Four decades later, and despite the rapid growth in leisure and tourism-related studies, it appears as though their observation is equally applicable today (Braasch, 2008; Richards & Wilson, 2006). A quick glance over the experiential-focused leisure and tourism literature, for example, suggests that very little has changed when it comes to our knowledge of producing and consuming memories of non-everyday 'lived' experiences (Berridge, 2007; Braun-La-Tour *et al.*, 2006; Chang, 2005).

According to C.K. Prahalad and Venkatram Ramaswarmy (2003), meaningful experiences are possible anywhere and visible everywhere. Ellen O' Sullivan and Kathy Spangler (1999: 1) have also suggested that our past experiences are integrated and infused into all aspects of our consumption and existence. Despite such observations, however, the gaze of most managers, and researchers alike, appears predominantly focused upon the impacts caused by tourism-based development and/or the behaviour of 'tourists' (i.e. at the venue/destination) (Morgan, 2006; Uriely, 2005). The motivational factors that influence the 'tourists' initial decision-making process has also proven a popular topic of academic enquiry (Braun-La Tour *et al.*, 2006; Richards & Wilson, 2006; Ryan, 2002).

The aim of this chapter is to acknowledge another way of exploring the 'everyday' consumption of past leisure and tourism experiences. Put another way, I wish to focus (y)our gaze upon the importance of Clawson's post-trip 'reflections' by looking specifically at how we attach personal meaning to our socially constructed memories. Though it is impossible to cover it all in one outing, I would like to highlight two reflexive 'memory-based' methodologies, both of which can be used to explore 'lived' experiences through the construction and consumption of personal narratives. The first, Memory-work, is a feminist-inspired framework created by German socialists during the early 1980s (Crawford *et al.*, 1992; Markula & Friend, 2005; Onyx & Small, 2001). The second, Autoethnography, is essentially a poststructuralist, literary-inspired method whose cultural anthropological origins are said to date back to the mid 1970s (Ellis, 2009; Reed-Danahay, 1997; Sparkes, 2002).

While neither of the social constructionist approaches discussed in this chapter are considered particularly 'new', both remain somewhat over-looked entities within the fields of leisure and tourism research. Despite the noticeable lack of Memory-workers and Autoethnographers currently situated outside the realms of sociology or anthropology (Sparkes, 2002), I hope to highlight the potential of both approaches in relation to the continued advancement of leisure and tourism-related experiential research. Both, for example, acknowledge the underlying importance of society on the construction and the 'everyday' consumption of self-identity and socially 'lived' experiences (Ellis, 1999; Reed-Danahay, 1997; Small, 2008). What's more, both essentially strive to systematically explore the meaningful relationships between who we are and how we act/behave. In keeping with the theme of this text, my chapter not only looks at those working *with* the memories of leisure and tourism consumers (i.e. through the use of the Memory-work framework), but also those attempting to extract meaning *from* their own memories of leisure and tourism experiences (i.e. through the use of Autoethnography). Before we go any further, however, I wish to set the scene and offer some context with regards to the uptake of personal narrative-based memory research.

Working *with* Memory

Narrative is generally perceived to be the primary way through which we organise our personal lived experiences into temporally meaningful episodes (Polkinghorne, 1988; Richardson, 2000). Lewis Hinchman and Sandra Hinchman (1997: xvi) consider it to be 'discourses with a clear sequential order that connect events in a meaningful way for a definite audience and thus offer insights about the world and/or people's experiences of it'. According to poststructuralists, our lives and personal identities are essentially plot-driven social stories (Elliott, 2005; Murray, 2003; Richardson, 1995). Despite the lack of Memory-based leisure and tourism literature (Braasch, 2008), the academy's fascination with the subject of narrating non-fictional accounts of past lived experiences is anything but under-developed, especially within the social sciences (Bloom, 1996; Bochner *et al.*, 1997; Crites, 1986; Duncan, 1998; Ellis & Bochner, 1992; Kiesinger, 1998; McAdams, 1993; Richardson, 1995; Ricoeur, 1991).

The (re)construction and (re)consumption of personal memories is seen as an expressive phenomena that, if interpreted correctly, can be used in the creation of 'meaningful' knowledge about the self and society (Bal, 1999; Bruner, 2005; Chang, 2005; Crang & Travlou, 2001; Crawford *et al.*, 1992; Edsenor, 1997; Golden, 1976; Haug, 1987; Said, 2000; Schudson, 1992; Shotter, 1984; Small, 2008). In 1976, Patricia Golden noted how storied reflections of past events could be used to express or explain the temporal process of meaningful experiences from a more emotional (human) perspective, including all the planned/unplanned, predictable/unpredictable encounters discovered along the way. John Shotter (1984) also stressed the importance of consuming personal narratives of past experiences, arguing that all human 'agency' is fundamentally based on our ability to reflect. What's more, none of us live in isolation (Ellis & Bochner, 2000). Our personal identities and actions are inevitably affected by those we have seen, heard or read about in our past.

Historian, Kerwin Klein (2000) links the recent upsurge in memory-based explorations to the 'dramatic change in linguistic practice' that occurred during the 1980s and 1990s. Despite the growth, however, there is still no universally accepted method of exploring the meanings attached to our personal recollections of the past (Elliott, 2005; Murray, 2003). Much like our multiple selves, and social identities, our memories present themselves in a number of guises, including personal, cultural, collective, spatial and autobiographical (Braasch, 2008; Kelley, 1999; Radstone, 2000). From a leisure and tourism perspective, a significant amount of 'knowledge' exists on the importance of both offering and experiencing an 'unforgettable' event, encounter or excursion (Berridge, 2007; Lee *et al.*, 1994; Lengkeek, 2000; Mannell & Iso-Ahola, 1987; Morgan, 2006; Ryan, 2002). Somewhat less, however, has been written on the emotional values and personal meanings attached to our recollections of past holiday experiences (Small, 2008).

Braun-La Tour *et al.* (2006) suggest that exploring our emotional retrospective can provide an unparalleled opportunity to (re)evaluate and (re)interpret the meanings attached to past tourist experiences. They also discuss the extent to which destination managers, and tourism marketers in particular, are known to target consumer's memories of past holidays and travel experiences, creating 'false memories' specifically designed to influence consumer behaviour (Loftus, 2003). That said, there remains a genuine lack of consensus regarding the most suitable direction from which our nostalgia-driven reflections should be accessed, analysed and articulated to either the industry or the academy (Chang, 2005). Arguably, much of the tourism focus on the experiential has focused on how our memories of events and encounters can go on to affect our future consumption and spending habits. Little has been produced on the affect these memories have on the 'everyday' or present construction of self-identity.

Edward Bruner's (2005) distinction between trips that's are 'lived', 'experienced' and 'told', highlights one of the most prominent difficulties facing those attempting to (re/de)construct personal memories. His anthropological gaze into the culture of the tourist acknowledges the unavoidable influence played by both time and space on the way we contextualise our past. He discusses the fact that, unlike you and me (or the tourist), our memories of past travel experiences never age. On the contrary, they are always consumed within the present day socially constructed context in which they are created. Those interested in understanding various aspects of the tourist experience, including travel behaviour and destination loyalty, note how the initial decision-making process is ultimately affected (to some degree) by comparison drawn from past events and excursions, whether it relates to a particular product, person or place (Pizam & Mansfield, 1999; Swarbrooke & Horner, 2007; Yoon & Uysal, 2005). Having provided some initial context, and introduced the subject of adopting a narrative approach to studying the post-trip recollection phase of leisure and tourism experiences, I will now focus on the first of the two memory-based methods to be introduced within this chapter.

Adopting and adapting memory-work

According to June Crawford *et al.* (1992: 37), the 'underlying theory' of Memory-work relates to the notion that 'the self is socially constructed through reflection'. Though not without its critics (see Reinharz, 1992), advocates of 'Memory-work' appear confident of its ability to offer an unparalleled framework in the exploration, examination and subsequent theorisation of the experiential (Crawford *et al.*, 1992; Haug, 1987; Stephenson *et al.*, 1996). Created by feminists as a means of overcoming the gap between feminist theory and the lived experience, Memory-work is said to offer more than just an interpretive method of collecting 'rich' and often 'sensitive' qualitative data (Farrar, 2001; Haug, 1987; Markula & Friend, 2005). Memory-work's methodological framework allows small groups, referred to as 'co-researchers', to narrate and relive past experiences, allowing them to revisit activities that have helped shape their self-identity. It also encourages those involved to share ideas, knowledge and, most importantly, the analysis process.

The creator of the original 'Memory-work' framework, Frigga Haug, argued that the self is dependent on how 'everyday' life is experienced (Haug, 1987). The first step of the method's data-collection process involves the development of an agreed theme/topic. Next, each 'co-researcher' is expected to go away and construct a personal narrative based on a memory related (in some way) to the chosen topic. The key is to be as detailed, yet distanced or detached, as possible. Unlike Autoethnography, the stories constructed are written in the third person and avoid the inclusion of interpretation, explanation or self-justification (Onyx & Small, 2001). Once done, the group comes together to discuss their newly created narratives, looking specifically for the gaps, absences, contradictions, inconsistencies, similarities and differences that may emerge in the memories being shared (Koutroulis, 1996). The fourth stage of the Memory-work process involves the personal experience being revisited, but allows the individual to incorporate issues and evaluate the meanings discussed amongst the collective. The final stage sees the updated narratives collectively (re)appraised (once again) within the group of 'co-researchers' (Markula & Friend, 2005).

While it's yet to fully establish itself within the realms of leisure and tourism research, the 'rules' of Memory-work have been adopted, and adapted, by researchers located around the world and operating within a number of academic disciplines (Onyx & Small, 2001). To date, the majority of existing 'memory-work' literature has concentrated on sensitive, gender-based, experiences that include mental and physical illness. That said, such topics have typically been framed within, or directly related to, everyday social phenomena, from education to employment (see, for example, Davies, 1994; Ingleton, 1994; Koutroulis,

1996, 2001). Though rare, its adoption by several leisure or tourism-situated researchers also reveals its potential as a valuable/viable method of studying, and allocating meaning to, less traumatic personal experiences (e.g. from retail to recreation).

Through their seminal study of the memories adults created on/around the subject of their childhood holidays, Crawford *et al.* (1992) found Haug's original Memory-work provided a strong methodological platform, which – with a little bit of adjustment – enabled the construction of an open, two-way dialogue with our memories of lived experiences. In 1994, Jeannie Douglas used her adaptation of the method to explore the memory-based narratives of 1950s Australian women travellers (Douglass, 1994). Likewise, Loraine Friend (1997), Coralie McCormack (1995, 1998) and Jenny Small (1999, 2001, 2002, 2003, 2008) have all utilised their own interpretation of the updated 'Memory-work' guidelines introduced by Crawford (*et al.*) to research the leisure and tourism experiences of female respondents. Lorraine Friend, for example, has utilised both phenomenology and hermeneutics within her various leisure-situated Memory-work projects to illustrate the importance of the lived experience and the holistic interactive construction of emotionally 'meaningful' knowledge (see also, Friend, 1997; Friend & Rummel, 1995; Friend & Thompson, 2000, 2003; Friend *et al.*, 2000; Grant & Friend, 1997; Markula & Friend, 2005).

In keeping with the feminist-inspired foundations, much of Friend's consumer behaviour-based research has focused on the meanings women shoppers attach to memories of past retail experiences, excursions and environments. In 1995, along with Amy Rummel, she noted how 'the social significance of an experience only becomes meaningful when there is "reflection" with one's self' (220). In 2003, this time with Sheena Thompson, she narrowed the focus to look specifically at the different ways in which two women (named *Sweetie* and *Deserie*) experienced and identified with 'nasty' retail encounters. Working alongside Pirko Markula, Friend's (2005) sports management-situated review not only touches upon her desire to tap into the 'real' subjectivity of how we remember the past, but also discusses how those involved in the production and consumption of personal narratives are able to utilise them to target 'that which is conscious to an individual'. They concluded that:

> ...through analysis of each memory, it ['memory-work'] seeks to obtain a heightened understanding of lived experiences, the pre-objective consciousness. 'Memory-work', therefore, documents experiences of past events that, one way or another, have been meaningful in the individual's life. In addition, the purpose is to

understand these meanings as collective meanings and, consequently, reach to the essence of phenomena beyond an individual
experience. (2005: 445)

While Friend's memory-work studies have largely focused on issues
of gender and ethnicity within the shopping experiences of New Zealand
women, Jenny Small's research on the tourist-related experiences of
Australian women, and her subsequent work on childhood memories,
has attempted to advance the field of tourism through the use of
innovative new qualitative methodologies (Small, 2008). While much of
her 1999 *Tourism Management* article focuses on explaining Memory-
work's link to both the social constructionist paradigm and feminist
theory, she also offers tourism academics a long-overdue introduction to
the philosophy and procedure of conducting this type of narrative-based
research (Small, 1999). Her doctoral research involved four groups of
white, urban, middle-classed women and girls from within the Sydney
area (Small, 1999). Each group consisted of either four or five participants, or 'co-researchers', and were designated by age. In keeping with
Haug's original framework, Small also placed herself within one of her
groups and willingly conducted the same tasks as everyone else (Small,
1999). Within her critique of the method, she justified her adoption and
adaptation of memory-work, claiming it 'seemed to fit comfortably with
the subject matter of the research – women's holidays' (1999: 30).

Small's aforementioned *Tourism Management* article effectively highlighted the importance of social interaction and pre-established relationships, as opposed to factors such as cost, distance and the destination, on
the memories generated from these women's tourist experiences (Small,
1999). Interestingly, it also acknowledged the 'complexity and contra-
diction' of her co-researchers' holiday experiences, noting how their
memories were largely focused on the desire to balance the feeling of
freedom and escape from their perceived, socially constructed, everyday
responsibilities (i.e. motherhood). Several of her 'co-researchers' were
said to have revealed feelings of fear and/or guilt related to their
perceived 'everyday' duty of care (i.e. towards their children) (Small,
1999). It also led to them directly comparing their memories of past
experiences with their perceptions of how others may experience similar
holidays, including those placed within the other age groups and various
members of their family (i.e. their husbands and parents) (Small, 1999).

As with the leisure-based research of Friend, Small's work on
memories of tourist experiences fully illustrates the value of a holistic
approach to the experiential, not to mention the hermeneutic relationship
that exists between the five phases identified by Marion Clawson (1963).
Small, along with several other memory-workers, also acknowledge

Glenda Koutroulis' (1993) argument that memory-works status as a theory (or method) is dependent upon the stance taken by the co-researchers, claiming it only to be feminist in its 'ideal' form (i.e. where everyone has the same degree of investment/involvement in the research). Clearly, this can prove problematic in academic studies where sole authorship/ownership is preferred or, in the case of most graduate research, expected. The assignment of joint responsibility and the 'collapsing of the subject and object of research' (Small, 1999: 28) certainly raises a number of questions regarding who is actually working for whom (Cadman *et al.*, 2001; Markula & Friend, 2005). Another issue that is questioned by some of the existing critiques of 'memory-work' is that of methodological transferability (Koutroulis, 1993; Onyx & Small, 2001).

The individual motivation of each and every 'co-researcher' is also a well documented concern to practicing memory-workers (Small, 2008). Cadman *et al.* (2001) discussed the issue of ownership and authorship in their informative and honest reflection of the power (or lack of it) held by memory-workers, especially those perceived to be in charge. Overall, the problems of empowerment appeared rife when it comes to the group settings and collective analysis of each narrative (Cadman *et al.*, 2001). The biggest problem surrounds the need to remain equal (i.e. true to the methodology) and avoid asserting control (i.e. power or identity) over the collective proceedings (Koutroulis, 2001). While memory-work allows the researcher to look into the past, those who use it are happy to acknowledge the unavoidably 'reality' that the memories shared will inevitably be distorted and influenced by the context in which they are created (Gillies *et al.*, 2004; Stratford, 1997). The personal experience may be the catalyst for the narrative created, but it is the content embodied within the memory itself that holds the real value (Haug, 1987). And, as Crawford *et al.* (1992: 51) duly notes, 'the memories are [always] true memories, that is, they are memories and not inventions or fantasies'.

According to Small (2004), the collective analysis of memories that takes place within the group settings created during the 'memory-work' process results in the creation of meanings that are neither objective nor subjective. On the contrary, in keeping with the desire to remove traditional academic dualisms, the knowledge outcomes of the 'memory-work' process are commonly referred to as being inter-subjective (i.e. systematically constructed through socially negotiated thoughts, feelings and emotions) (Crawford *et al.*, 1992; Schratz *et al.*, 1995). While 'memory-work' was initially developed as a means of discovering how women's social experiences could help to determine their self-identity (Haug, 1987), Markula and Friend (2005) saw no reason why it shouldn't be used to uncover previously excluded experiences of any other group in society. They also suggested the framework could easily be adapted to embrace the literary-inspired narrative turn.

Bronwyn Davies (1994, 2000), Barbara Kamler (1996) and Susanne Gannon (2001) have all adapted the method to create 'collective biographies', allowing those involved to (re)tell their stories from a first-person perspective. What's more, a number of Scandinavian, literary-inspired, sport scientists have gone one step further and dropped the collective approach to Memory-work, focusing their entire explorations on their own personal memories of past lived events, emotional experiences and unforgettable social encounters (see Innanen, 1999; Kosonen, 1993; Sironen, 1994; Tiihonen, 1994). Unlike those studied by Loraine Friend or Jenny Small, these memory-based narratives involve the author encouraging their readers to become the co-researcher (in their own time) and make/take their own multiple truths from the recollections being relived (i.e. via their own reflections and reinterpretations of the emotional lived experiences being addressed). As with the work of Friend and Small, however, the issues of gender and identity creation play a prominent role in the memories narrated, many of which are based on the author's insecurities during childhood.

The similarities between this approach to experiential research and Autoethnography are certainly more evident than the original memory-work concept adopted by Frigga Haug and/or the adapted guidelines developed by Crawford (*et al.*). They also provide this storyteller with a suitable bridge to the second part of his chapter. Having provided an introductory overview of the Memory-work method, including how it has been used to study both leisure and tourism experiences, I would now like to focus upon the potential of Autoethnography as a means to exploring and extracting meaning from our lived experiences. Rather than focus too much attention upon the comparisons between the two methods, I would rather concentrate on introducing where it has come from, how it works and who has used it within a leisure and/or tourism setting. I am happy to leave the majority of comparison-making to you (the reader).

Working *from* Memory

Our memories of past events, encounters and excursions are arguably one of the most important ways in which we understand or extract meaning from the experiences we produce and consume (past, present and future). While leisure and tourism activities are rarely categorised as either 'life-changing' or 'personal milestones' (especially when compared to subjects such as terminal illness and/or the loss of a loved one), it has been argued that leisure and tourism experiences can affect one's identity and a number of levels, including personal and cultural (Chang, 2005; see also Chapter 2). According to Carolyn Ellis (2004), it was anthropologist Karl Heider who first used the term 'Autoethnography' in 1975. That said, it is David Hayano who is largely credited as being the creator of this fully reflexive form of experiential research (Ellis, 2004; Reed-Danahay, 1997; Sparkes, 2002). Breaking from the traditional rules of 'going native', Hayano focused his anthropological gaze upon the experiences of his own culture. His 1979 study of professional poker players, for example, saw him become an 'insider' by virtue of being, as opposed to going, 'native' (Hayano, 1979). Being a professional poker player, he argued that he was able to achieve something that other cultural anthropologists had never. He suggested that it guaranteed him an intimate familiarity with the group (or full membership). And, as a result, the experiences and emotions he set out to (re)interpret were largely his own. He effectively became the subject and the object – the researched, as well as the researcher (see Coffey, 1999; Ellis, 1999; Hayano, 1979; Van Maanen, 1988).

Autoethnography connects the autobiographical (our past) with the ethnographic (our present) (Reed-Danahay, 1997). In doing so, it effectively challenges the traditional ways of both telling and knowing. In 1997, Art Bochner described how the ambiguities and messiness of Autoethnography challenges the rational actor model of social performance, stressing the importance of the journey, as opposed to the final destination. He also accredited Autoethnographers with eclipsing the scientific illusion of control and mastery found in traditional realism. Unlike adopters of Memory-work, Autoethnographers are concerned only with writing a first-person account through narrative-based systematic introspection (Ellis, 1991). Ellis and Bochner (2000: 733) refer to it as 'an autobiographical genre of writing and research that displays multiple layers of consciousness, connecting the personal to the cultural'. Ultimately, as a form of ethnography, it not only overlaps but incorporates elements of art and science-based academia (Ellis, 2009; Wolcott, 1995).

According to Amanda Coffey (1999: 125), auto-ethnographic writing 'locates the self as central' and 'gives analytical purchase to the autobiographical'. It also allows the narrator sufficient room to narrate a story based entirely upon their recollections of a particular lived experience. Crucially, however, it is not so much the detail of the memories that matter, but their articulation and the explanation of their significance (i.e. with regards to the meanings that can be associated with the lived experience being discussed) (Sparkes, 2002). According to Ellis (1997: 133), a story's validity should be judged by whether it evokes 'a feeling that the experience described is authentic and lifelike, believable and possible; the story's generalisability can be judged by whether it speaks to readers about their experiences'. All stories are partial and, as noted earlier in the chapter, our memories are always reinterpreted from our present circumstances (Bruner, 2005; Kelley, 1999; Small, 2008).

Andrew Sparkes (2002: 105) acknowledges the production of auto-ethnographic tales 'brings perils as well as pleasures, problems as well as possibilities and potentials'. Both he and Ellis have written detailed accounts of the inappropriate methods used to assess autoethnographical contributions to the academy, focusing particular attention on the claims of self-indulgence and navel gazing narcissism. As Kathryn Church (1995) duly points out, however, the self is a social phenomenon and, as a result, any memory-based study is also a study of the society (i.e. time and space) in which they have been created and are consumed/contextualised (Gergen & Gergen, 2003). Eric Mykhalovskiy (1996) also offered some of the staunchest, and subsequently well-documented, support to all of those keen to embrace the emotional subjectivity of the self. He challenged traditional reductive practices and argued that 'to write individual experience is, at the same time, to write social experience' (141). He dismissed calls of self-indulgence or narcissism, pointing to the belief that autoethnographies simply encourage an alternative way of telling/showing personal memories that are never directed towards a universal reader, with universal characteristics.

Much like the literary-inspired Memory-work produced by the Scandinavian sport scientists noted earlier, the crux of Autoethnography is the degree of emotional response generated (or evoked) from the reader. Ellis and Bochner (2000) acknowledge the ever-present connec-tions between personal and socio-cultural experiences, stipulating how Autoethnographers 'not only observe the world around them, but also examine their internal perceptions and feelings about their place in that world'. Unlike the Memory-work framework discussed earlier, Auto-ethnographers have complete control and authorship/ownership of the entire process (Sparkes, 2002). They are not 'co-researchers' looking at a particular social phenomenon. As noted in my introduction, locating examples of existing leisure and tourism-related Autoethnography is no simple task. In fact, to date, it appears to have been largely overlooked or ignored by most academics operating outside of the more contemporary subsets of cultural anthropology and/or sports-related sociology (Sparkes, 2000).

While times are certainly changing, the reluctance of tourism aca-demics to embrace a fully reflexive stance to narrative-based research has been noted on several occasions over the past decade (see Feighery, 2006; Hall, 2004; Hollinshead, 2004; Hollinshead & Jamal, 2001; Morgan & Pritchard, 2005; Noy, 2007; Tribe, 2004; Westwood, 2005, 2006). One of the few tourism academics to embrace the concept of Autoethnography, Chaim Noy (2007: 349) discusses how he has found himself approaching the tourist experience as being 'a state of mind' that is omnipresent in westernised societies. In his Autoethnography of a poetic tourist, he reveals his belief that 'when people recall and recount their tourist-related experiences, they take on the expression of re-calling a dream, a daydream or a (religious) vision. They seem to be focusing on a point that lies elsewhere, beyond or past the here-and-nows of everyday spaces and routine practices' (350). The similarities between this and the existence of a 'third space' discussed by memory-workers such as Small (2008) appear to emphasis the complexity of (re)interpreting the meanings attached to past lived experiences.

Noy (2007) notes how Autoethnography can allow the researcher to relive and reconstruct past events 'in ways that are not "purely academic or that result in an over-intellectualization of the *sense* of having an experience"' (350, emphasis in original). Much like my own study on my sport tourist experiences in Melbourne (Wright, 2009), Noy hoped that the adoption of an autoethnographical approach would prove more insightful and evoke a deeper sense of appreciation of the subject. Again, like Small, he also comments about the correspondence and increasing overlapping relationship between tourism and everyday life (Noy, 2007). He acknowledges and appears to support John Urry's view that people in modern society are tourists for much of the time, whether it is merely a case of recalling the past, experiencing the present or dreaming about the future (Urry, 2000).

The links to notions of self, identity, escapism and authenticity are certainly rife within Noy's adoption of Autoethnography and he quotes Dean MacCannell's (1989: 9) suggestion that 'by following the tourists, we may be able to arrive at a better understanding of ourselves'. Sheena Westwood (2006) also discusses the difficulty in studying the tourist experience, arguing that the subjectivity and inconsistency of post-trip recollections can be directly linked to the sheer diversity of intrinsic and extrinsic influences that affect our everyday decision-making. Her autoethnographic doctoral study addressed individual relationships between tourism products and consumers at a micro-level, looking specifically at how the participants' personalities, life experiences and aspirations combine to shape their expectations, perceptions and subsequent experiences. Her 'findings' illustrate the significance of tourist experiences on the construction of self-identity (Westwood, 2005, 2006).

Along with, and on occasion alongside, Westwood, Nigel Morgan and Annette Pritchard have also opted to embrace an autoethnographical approach to exploring the meanings generated by tourist memories (Morgan & Pritchard, 2005). Rather than looking at the language used to recall stories of past holidays, they look at the souvenirs and tangible reminders purchased whilst 'away' from 'home'. In keeping with the autoethnographical genre, they opted to write themselves 'into' their text, hoping to 'reveal the subjective meanings ascribed to tourism experiences, practices and performances' (Morgan & Pritchard, 2005). In their

2005 *Tourist Studies* article on the materiality of tourism reflections, Morgan and Pritchard attempt to look at how the tourism experience can influence our behaviour and identity (both self and social). On the subject of tourism as a part of everyday life, they note how:

> ...experience-based research in tourism studies should, where possible, attempt to reflect this discourse of transformation and the self-consciousness of 'the tourist moment' in the research process. There is also an opportunity here to use our own lived experience as a resource and to overcome that sense of artificial opaqueness in much tourism scholarship – since we can be sure that the same academics who strive to write 'objectively' about travel are, have been and will be tourists, travellers or post-tourist cynics. (2005: 35)

In terms of leisure and tourism-situated Autoethnography, I think it's accurate to say we've only just touched the surface of its raw potential. While there may be a host of aspiring storytellers located within tourism departments around the world, I would argue that too much of our 'everyday' self-identity remains conveniently hidden away behind closed doors (i.e. away from the academic spotlight). Attend any leisure and tourism conference and you will witness a number of enthusiastic academics passionately presenting past and present work that is clearly very close to their heart. Unfortunately, my own experience – at both leisure and tourism conferences – suggests that you are unlikely to see (or hear) these people openly recalling their personal travel and tourism-related research experiences, or the direct influence their past had on their research. Having introduced Autoethnography and illustrated the surprising lack of tourism-related personal narratives, I would like to draw this chapter to its conclusion by offering some thoughts for the future.

Conclusion

To date, neither Memory-work nor Autoethnography has been widely utilised within the realms of leisure or tourism research, despite the increased awareness and attention being paid on the production and consumption of unique, subjective, lived experiences. Sadly, the likes of Jenny Small, Lorraine Friend, Chaim Noy, Sheena Westwood, Nigel Morgan and Annette Pritchard remain the exception when it comes to researching the holistic nature of the tourist experience. This noticeable lack of memory-based research is surprising considering the vital and unmistakable role it clearly plays in the production and consumption of both leisure and tourism events, encounters and excursions. The sheer growth of tourism studies over the past two decades has made it increasingly difficult to locate an area, or event, that has not been researched by someone (at some point in time). To me, the adoption of Autoethnography offered the opportunity to look at the tourist experience from a completely different direction. And, as you may have guessed, I am certainly keen to see more leisure and tourism researchers adopting memory-based methodologies (i.e. as a means of exploring the personal meanings we attach to our past holiday experiences).

Our socially constructed memories not only affect our future experiences, but also how we approach the present day. To its advocates, 'Memory-work' certainly represents more than just a technique for data collection and narrative comparison. While written recollections are the main data source of Memory-work, the process allows for the inclusion of the uncensored, and first-person, 'stories' that emerge within the group during their time together. And this is, arguably, where the similarities between this method and Autoethnography are most noticeable. Though Memory-work focuses on the empowerment of others, through the creation of 'co-researchers', the reflexive nature of autoethnographic exploration is much more self-orientated. Autoethnographers place their emphasis on the creation of evocative narratives that encourage the audience to 'experience the experience' being recalled. Ultimately, narrating non-fictional stories of past events, encounters and excursions is seen as being just one way in which we can extract authentic meaning from our 'everyday' lives, including our numerous leisure and tourism experiences. More importantly, it also allows us to document and discuss the comparisons we all construct when classifying those located around us. We cannot completely exclude ourselves, or our past, from our present day research. And yet, most leisure and tourism academics still appear to try and do exactly that.

I'm not claiming Memory-work or Autoethnography represent a better way of exploring the experiential (only different). While travel/tourism has traditionally been seen as a means of escaping the everyday (see, for example, Chapter 2), our post-trip recollections are inadvertently situated within our daily lived environment. Rather than leave you with a set of recommendations to consider, I would rather use this final section to ask the following three questions. First, why are we afraid of talking to, and/or writing about, the identities we see in the bathroom mirror each morning? Second, do you think our own leisure and tourism memories are any less valid, or worthy of exploration, than those of the 'tourists' we observe, interview and (re)interpret? Third, and finally, why do we still place so much emphasis/importance upon the need to understand the consumer behaviour witnessed at the destination and/or the motivations of those looking to produce 'unforgettable' leisure experiences?

The academics introduced within my chapter were largely responsible for opening my eyes to the possibility and potential of exploring how my past has affected, and was affecting, my present day research. They encouraged me to embrace self-introspection and extract meaning from my personal narrative(s). They also led me to temporarily drop my 'realist' ethnography of trans-Tasman sport tourists and construct an Autoethnography about my emotional experiences as a sport tourist researcher. While time and space constraints have meant that I've only been able to brush the surface when it comes to the potential of utilising memories to explore leisure and tourism experiences (through personal narrative), I hope I have provided enough to increase your curiosity. My primary objective was to offer something that got you thinking about Memory-work and Autoethnography as two alternative ways of looking at leisure and tourism experiences. And, as a result, it has taken me several attempts to find the right balance between talking *at* and talking *to* the intended audience of this publication.

As noted on several occasions already, the two approaches addressed within this chapter have been seriously overlooked in terms of the leisure and tourism experience. But their potential is arguably unmistakable, and I am confident that both methods can play a prominent role in the expansion of the experiential paradigm, particularly Autoethnography. I wanted to offer something that leaves you wanting more information and unable to ignore the references found at the end. I wanted to offer a taste of the evocative nature of Autoethnography, as well as provide a 'memorable' contribution to the consumption of leisure and tourism-based experiential research. I want you asking questions about the applicability and authenticity of constructing personal narratives to explore the meanings attached to our recollections of the past. This may be the final sentence, but I hope it represents the start of your own journey into the emotional world of memory-based narrative enquiry.

References

Bal, M. (1999) Introduction. In M. Bal, J. Crewe and L. Spitzer (eds) *Acts of Memory: Cultural Recall in the Present* (pp. vii–xvii). Hanover: University Press of New England.

Berridge, G. (2007) *Event Design and Experience*. Oxford: Butterworth-Heinemann.

Bloom, L.R. (1996) Stories of one's own: Non-unitary subjectivity in narrative representation. *Qualitative Inquiry* 2 (2), 176–197.

Bochner, A.P. (1997) It's about time: Narrative and the divided self. *Qualitative Inquiry* 3, 418–438.

Bochner, A.P, Ellis, C. and Tillmann-Healy, L. (1997) Relationships as stories. In S. Duck (ed.) *Handbook of Personal Relationships* (2nd edn, pp. 307–324). New York: Wiley.

Braasch, B. (2008) *Major Concepts in Tourism Research – Memory*. Centre for Tourism and Cultural Change (CTCC). Research Paper, August 2008. Leeds: Leeds Metropolitan University.

Braun-La Tour, K.A., Grinley, M.J. and Loftus, E.F. (2006) Tourist memory distortion. *Journal of Travel Research* 44, 360–367.

Bruner, E. (2005) *Culture on Tour.* Chicago: The University of Chicago.

Cadman, K., Friend, L., Gannon, S., Ingleton, C., Koutroulis, G., McCormack, C., Mitchell, P., Onyx, J., O'Regan, K., Rocco, S. and Small, J. (2001) Memory-workers doing memory-work on memory-work: Exploring unresolved power. In J. Small and J. Onyx (eds) *Memory-work: A Critique* (Working Paper Series, 20/01). School of Management, University of Technology, Sydney, Australia.

Chang, T.C. (2005) Place, memory and identity: Imagining 'New Asia'. *Asia Pacific Viewpoint* 46 (3), 247–253.

Church, K. (1995) *Forbidden Narratives.* London: Gordon & Breach.

Clawson, M. (1963) *Land and Water for Recreation: Opportunities, Policies and Problems.* New York: Rand McNally.

Clawson, M. and Knetsch, J. (1966) *Economics of Outdoor Recreation.* Baltimore: John Hopkins.

Coffey, A. (1999) *The Ethnographic Self: Fieldwork and the Representation of Identity.* London: Sage.

Crang, M. and Travlou, P.S. (2001) The city and topologies of memory. *Environment and Planning D: Society and Space* 19, 161–177.

Crawford, J., Kippax, S., Onyx, J., Gault, U. and Benton, P. (1992) *Emotion and Gender: Constructing Meaning from Memory.* London: Sage.

Crites, S. (1986) Storytime: Recollecting the past and projecting the future. In T. Sarbin (ed.) *Narrative Psychology: The Storied Nature of Human Conduct* (pp. 153–173). New York: Praeger.

Davies, B. (1994) *Poststructuralist Theory and Classroom Practice.* Geelong, VIC: Deakin University Press.

Davies, B. (2000) *(In)scribing Body/landscape Relations.* Walnut Creek, CA: Alta-Mira Press.

Douglass, J. (1994) Woman's travel narratives of the 1950s. In K. Darian-Smith and P. Hamilton (eds) *Memory and History in Twentieth-Century Australia* (pp. 229–242). Melbourne: Oxford University Press.

Duncan, M.C. (1998) Stories we tell ourselves about ourselves. *Sociology of Sport Journal* 15, 95–108.

Edsenor, T. (1997) National identity and the politics of memory: Remembering Bruce and Wallace in symbolic space. *Environment and Planning D: Society and Space* 15, 175–194.

Elliott, J. (2005) *Using Narrative in Social Research: Qualitative and Quantitative Approaches.* London: Sage.

Ellis, C. (1991) Sociological introspection and emotional experience. *Symbolic Interaction* 14, 23–50.

Ellis, C. (1997) Evocative autoethnography: Writing emotionally about our lives. In W. Tierney and Y. Lincoln (eds) *Representation and the Text* (pp. 115–139). New York: State University of New York Press.

Ellis, C. (1999) Heartful autoethnography. *Qualitative Health Research* 9, 669–683.

Ellis, C. (2004) *The Ethnographic I: A Methodological Novel about Autoethnography.* Walnut Creek, CA: AltaMira Press.

Ellis, C. (2009) *'Revision'.* Walnut Creek, CA: AltaMira Press.

Ellis, C. and Bochner, A.P. (1992) Telling and performing personal stories. In C. Ellis and M. Flaherty (eds) *Investigating Subjectivity: Research on Lived Experience* (pp. 79–101). London: Sage.

Ellis, C. and Bochner, A.P. (2000) Autoethnography, personal narrative, reflexivity: Researcher as subject. In N.K. Denzin and Y.S. Lincoln (eds) *Handbook of Qualitative Research* (2nd edn, pp. 733–768). London: Sage.

Farrar, P.D. (2001) Too painful to remember: Memory-work as a method to expose sensitive research topics. In J. Small and J. Onyx (eds) *Memory-work: A Critique* (Working Paper Series, 20/01). School of Management, University of Technology, Sydney, Australia.

Feighery, W. (2006) Reflexivity and tourism research: Telling an (other) story. *Current Issues in Tourism* 9 (3), 269–282.

Friend, L.A. (1997) Memory-work: Understanding consumer satisfaction and dissatisfaction of clothing retail encounters. PhD thesis, University of Otago, Dunedin, NZ.

Friend, L.A. and Rummel, A. (1995) Memory-work: An alternative approach to investigating consumer satisfaction and dissatisfaction of clothing retail encounters. *Journal of Consumer Satisfaction, Dissatisfaction and Complaining Behavior* 8, 214–222.

Friend, L.A. and Thompson, S.M. (2000) Using memory-work to give feminist voice to marketing research. In M. Catterall, P. Maclaran and L. Stevens (eds) *Marketing and Feminism: Current Issues and Research* (pp. 94–111). London: Routledge.

Friend, L.A. and Thompson, S.M. (2003) Identity, ethnicity and gender: Using narratives to understand their meaning in retail shopping encounters. *Consumption, Markets and Culture* 6 (1), 23–41.

Friend, L.A., Grant, B.C. and Gunson, L. (2000) Memories. *Australian Leisure Management* 20, 24–25.

Gannon, S. (2001) (Re)presenting the collective girl: A poetic approach to a methodological dilemma. *Qualitative Inquiry* 7, 787–800.

Gergen, M. and Gergen, K. (eds) (2003) *Social Construction: A Reader.* Thousand Oaks, CA: Sage.

Gillies, V., Harden, A., Johnson, K., Reavey, P., Strange, V. and Willig, C. (2004) Women's collective constructions of embodied practices through memory work: Cartesian dualism in memories of sweating and pain. *British Journal of Social Psychology* 43, 99–112.

Golden, P.M. (1976) *The Research Experience.* Itasca, IL: F.E. Peacock.

Grant, B.C. and Friend, L.A. (1997) Analysing leisure experiences through memory-work. In D. Rowe and P. Brown (eds) *Proceedings of the 1997 Australian & New Zealand Association for Leisure Studies Conference* (pp. 65–70), Newcastle, Australia: Australian and New Zealand Association for Leisure Studies and the Department of Leisure and Tourism Studies, The University of Newcastle, 9–11 July.

Hall, M. (2004) Reflexivity and tourism research: Situating myself and/with others. In J. Phillimore and L. Goodson (eds) *Qualitative Research in Tourism* (pp. 137–154). London: Routledge.

Haug, F. (1987) *Female Sexualisation: A Collective Work of Memory* (E. Carter, trans.). London: Verso.

Hayano, D.M. (1979) Auto-ethnography: Paradigms, problems, and prospects. *Human Organisation* 38 (1), 99–104.

Hinchman, L.P. and Hinchman, S.K. (eds) (1997) *Memory, Identity, Community: The Idea of Narrative in the Human Sciences.* Albany: SUNY Press.

Hollinshead, K. (2004) Ontological craft in tourism studies: The productive mapping of identity and image in tourism settings. In J. Phillimore and L. Goodson (eds) *Qualitative Research in Tourism: Ontologies: Epistemologies and Methodologies* (pp. 83–101). London: Routledge.

Hollinshead, K. and Jamal, T. (2001) Delving into discourse: Excavating the inbuilt power-logic(s) of tourism. *Tourism Analysis* 6 (1), 61–72.

Ingleton, C. (1994) The use of memory-work to explore the role of emotions in learning. *Research and Development in Higher Education* 16, 265–271.

Innanen, M. (1999) Secret life in the culture of thinness. In A.C. Sparkes and M. Silvennoinen (eds) *Talking Bodies: Men's Narratives of the Body and Sport* (pp. 120–134). So Phi, Finland: University of Jyvaskyla.

Kamler, B. (1996) From autobiography to collective biography: Stories of aging and loss. *Women and Language* 19, 21–26.

Kelley, M. (1999) Making memory: Design of the present on the past. In M. Bal, J. Crewe and L. Spitzer (eds) *Acts of Memory: Cultural Recall in the Present* (pp. 218–230). Hanover: University Press of New England.

Kiesinger, C. (1998) From interview to story: Writing "Abbies life". *Qualitative Inquiry* 4 (1), 71–95.

Klein, K.L. (2000) On the emergence of memory in historical discourse. *Representations* 69, 127–150.

Kosonen, U. (1993) A running girl. In L. Laine (ed.) *On the Fringes of Sport* (pp. 16–25). St Augustin, Germany: Academia Verlag.

Koutroulis, G. (1993) Memory-work: A critique. *Annual Review of Health Social Science: Methodological Issues in Health* Research (pp. 76–96). Geelong: Centre for the Study of the Body and Society, Deakin University.

Koutroulis, G. (1996) Memory-work: Process, practice and pitfalls. In D. Colquhoun and A. Kellehear (eds) *Health Research in Practice: Volume 2* (pp. 95–113). London: Chapman and Hall.

Koutroulis, G. (2001) Soiled identity: Memory-work narratives of menstruation. *Health* 5 (2), 187–205.

Lee, Y., Dattilo, J. and Howard, D. (1994) The complex and dynamic nature of leisure experience and leisure services. *Journal of Leisure Research* 26 (3), 195–211.

Lengkeek, J. (2000) Imagination and differences in tourist experience. *World Leisure Journal* 42 (3), 11–17.

Loftus, E.F. (2003) Make believe memories. *American Psychologist* 58 (11), 867–873.

MacCannell, D. (1989) *The Tourist: A New Theory of the Leisured Class*. New York: Schocken Books.

Mannell, R. and Iso-Ahola, S. (1987) Psychological nature of leisure and tourist experiences. *Annals of Tourism Research* 14, 314–331.

Markula, P. and Friend, L.A. (2005) Remember when... Memory-work as an interpretive methodology for sport management. *Journal of Sport Management* 19, 442–463.

McAdams, D. (1993) *The Stories We Live by: Personal Myths and the Making of the Self*. New York: Morrow.

McCormack, C. (1995) My heart is singing: Women giving meaning to leisure. MEd thesis, University of Canberra, Canberra.

McCormack, C. (1998) Memories bridge the gap between theory and practice in women's leisure. *Annals of Leisure Research* 1, 7–49.

Morgan, M. (2006) Making space for experiences. *Journal of Retail and Leisure Property* 5 (4), 305–313.

Morgan, N. and Pritchard, A. (2005) On souvenirs and metonymy: Narratives of memory, metaphor and materiality. *Tourist Studies* 5 (1), 29–53.

Murray, M. (2003) Narrative psychology and narrative analysis. In P.M. Camic, J.E. Rhodes and L. Yardley (eds) *Qualitative Research in Psychology: Expanding Perspectives in Methodology and Design* (pp. 111–131). Washington, DC: American Psychological Association.

Mykhalovskiy, E. (1996) Reconsidering table talk: Critical thoughts on the relationship between sociology, anthropology and self-indulgence. *Qualitative Sociology* 19, 131–152.

Noy, C. (2007) The language(s) of the tourist exeprience: An autoethnography of the poetic tourist. In I. Ateljevic, A. Pritchard and N. Morgan (eds) *A Critical Turn in Tourism Studies: Innovative Research Methodologies* (pp. 349–370). Amsterdam, The Netherlands: Elsevier.

O'Sullivan, E. and Spangler, K. (1999) *Experience Marketing: Strategies for the New Millennium.* State College, PA: Venture.

Onyx, J. and Small, J. (2001) Memory-work: The method. *Qualitative Inquiry* 7 (6), 773–786.

Pizam, A. and Mansfield, Y. (1999) *Consumer Behaviour in Travel and Tourism.* New York: Haworth Hospitality Press.

Polkinghorne, D.E. (1988) *Narrative Knowing and the Human Sciences.* Albany: State University of New York Press.

Prahalad, C.K. and Ramaswarmy, V. (2003) The new frontier of experience innovation. *MIT Sloan Management Review* 44 (4), 12–18.

Radstone, S. (2000) Working with memory: An introduction. In S. Radstone (ed.) *Memory and Methodology* (pp. 1–24). Oxford: Berg.

Reed-Danahay, D. (ed.) (1997) *Auto/ethnography: Rewriting the Self and the Social.* Oxford: Berg.

Reinharz, S. (1992) *Feminist Methods in Social Research.* Oxford: Oxford University Press.

Richards, G. and Wilson, J. (2006) Developing creativity in tourist experiences: A solution to the serial reproduction of culture? *Tourism Management* 27 (6), 1209–1223.

Richardson, L. (1995) Writing-stories: Co-authoring 'the sea monster,' a writing story. *Qualitative Inquiry,* 1, 189–203.

Richardson, L. (2000) Writing: A method of inquiry. In N.K. Denzin and Y.S. Lincoln (eds) *Handbook of Qualitative Research* (pp. 923–948). Thousand Oaks, CA: Sage.

Ricoeur, P. (1991) Life: A story in search of a narrator. In M.J. Valdes (ed.) *A Ricoeur Reader: Reflection and Imagination* (pp. 137–155). Toronto: University of Toronto Press.

Ryan, C. (2002) *The Tourist Experiencee* (2nd edn). London: Continuum.

Said, E.W. (2000) Invention, memory, and place. *Critical Inquiry* 26, 175–192.

Schratz, M., Walker, R. and Schratz-Hadwich, B. (1995) Collective memory-work: The self as a re/source for re/search. In M. Schratz and R. Walker (eds) *Research as Social Change: New Opportunities for Qualitative Research* (pp. 39–64). London: Routledge.

Schudson, M. (1992) *Watergate in American Memory: How We Remember, Forget, and Reconstruct the Past.* New York: Basic Books.

Shotter, J. (1984) *Social Accountability and Selfhood.* Oxford: Basil Blackwell.

Sironen, E. (1994) On memory-work in the theory of body culture. *International Review for the Sociology of Sport* 29 (1), 5–13.

Small, J. (1999) Memory-work: A method for researching women's tourist experiences. *Tourism Management* 20, 25–35.

Small, J. (2001) Memory-work: An introduction. In J. Small and J. Onyx (eds) *Memory-work: A Critique* (Working Paper Series, 20/01). School of Management, University of Technology, Sydney, Australia.

Small, J. (2002) Good and bad holiday experiences: Women's and girls' perspectives. In M. Swain and J. Momsen (eds) *Gender, Tourism, Fun(?)* (pp. 24–38). Elmsford, NY: Cognizant Communications.

Small, J. (2003) The voices of older women tourists. *Tourism Recreation Research* 28, 31–39.

Small, J. (2004) 'Memory-work'. In J. Phillimore and L. Goodson (eds) *Qualitative Research in Tourism: Ontologies, Epistemologies and Methodologies* (pp. 255–272). London: Routledge.

Small, J. (2008) The absence of childhood in tourism studies. *Annals of Tourism Research* 35 (3), 772–789.

Sparkes, A.C. (2000) Autoethnography and narratives of self: Reflections on criteria in action. *Sociology of Sport Journal* 17, 21–43.

Sparkes, A.C. (2002) *Telling Tales in Sport and Physical Activity: A Qualitative Journey.* Champaign, IL: Human Kinetics.

Stephenson, N., Kippax, S. and Crawford, J. (1996) You and I and she: Memory-work, moral conflict and the construction of self. In S. Wilkinson (ed.) *Feminist Social Psychologies: International Perspectives* (pp. 182–200). Buckingham: Open University Press.

Stratford, E. (1997) 'Memory-work', geography and environmental studies: Some suggestions for teaching and research. *Australian Geographical Studies* 35, 206–219.

Swarbrooke, J. and Horner, S. (2007) *Consumer Behaviour in Tourism.* Amsterdam: Butterworth-Heinemann.

Tiihonen, A. (1994) Asthma. *International Review for the Sociology of Sport* 29 (1), 51–62.

Tribe, J. (2004) Knowing about tourism: Epistemological issues. In J. Phillimore and L. Goodson (eds) *Qualitative Research in Tourism: Ontologies, Epistemologies and Methodologies* (pp. 46–62). London: Routledge.

Uriely, N. (2005) The tourist experience: Conceptual developments. *Annals of Tourism Research* 32 (1), 199–216.

Urry, J. (2000) *Sociology Beyond Societies: Mobilities for the Twenty-First Century.* London: Routledge.

Van Maanen, J. (1988) *Tales from the Field: On Writing Ethnography.* Chicago, IL: University of Chicago Press.

Westwood, S. (2005) Out of the comfort zone: Situation, participation and narrative interpretation in tourism research. Paper Presented at 'The First International Congress of Qualitative Inquiry, University of Illinois at Urbana-Champaign', 5–7 May 2005.

Westwood, S. (2006) Shopping in sanitised and un-sanitised spaces: Adding value to tourist experiences. *Journal of Retail and Leisure Property* 5, 281–291.

Wolcott, H.F. (1995) *The Art of Fieldwork.* Walnut Creek, CA: Altamira.

Wright, R.K. (2009) From the abbey to the academy: The heartful autoethnography of a lost and lonely-looking, self indulgent, sport tourist. PhD thesis, University of Otago, Dunedin, NZ.

Yoon, Y. and Uysal, M. (2005) An examination of the effects of motivation and satisfaction on destination loyalty: A structural model. *Tourism Management* 26, 45–56.

Chapter 8

Capturing Sensory Experiences Through Semi-Structured Elicitation Questions

ULRIKE GRETZEL and DANIEL R. FESENMAIER

Introduction

Tapping into the consumers' mind is essential when designing tourism and leisure experiences and creating effective marketing tools to promote them. However, capturing perceptions and/or memories of experiences is far from easy. Much of consumers' thinking occurs in their unconscious and only surfaces through metaphors and stories; yet, most research practices wrongly assume that consumers have easy access to memories or attitudes and can readily explain their thinking and behaviours (Zaltman, 2003). The challenge of capturing perceptions and memories of experiences is especially apparent for sensory aspects of experiences, as a lot of sensory information is unconsciously processed. Sensory descriptions or depictions of experiences are critical in the context of experiential marketing but are difficult to formulate if the sensory essence of experiences as perceived by the consumers is unknown and cannot be easily captured through traditional research approaches.

Tourism experiences have been extensively studied in terms of motivations and activity patterns, with respect to authenticity, relationships to places, aesthetics, or in terms of outcome-related concepts such as benefits, evaluations, sentiments and satisfaction, using both quantitative and qualitative approaches (Cohen, 1979; Cutler & Carmichael, this volume; Jackson *et al.*, 1996; Li, 2000; Pearce & Caltabiano, 1983; Ryan, 2002; Wang, 1999; Woodside *et al.*, 2007, to name just a few). Recently, Oh *et al.* (2007) proposed a structural measure of tourism experiences based on the four realms of experiences described by Pine and Gilmore (1999) as involving Education, Escape, Esthetics and Entertainment. While measuring these four realms of experience can indeed provide some insights regarding the dimensions of the experience offering (a bed and breakfast experience in the case of Oh *et al.*'s study), personal meanings and feelings are lost. In addition, sensory components of tourism experiences have been largely neglected in past research (Quan & Wang, 2004). As far as the measurement of experiences is concerned,

137

approaches vary greatly and mostly involve either highly structured, quantitative measures or qualitative methodologies aimed at eliciting deeper meanings. While the first are typically unable to tap into concepts that are not easily accessible in the consumer's mind, such as sensory experiences, the others cannot be used for larger scale studies to extract dominant experience dimensions. To close these gaps in the current literature on tourism experiences, this chapter proposes a mixed methods approach to studying the sensory components of tourism experiences. The chapter is organised as follows: First, it discusses the importance of sensory dimensions of tourism experiences. Then, it provides an over-view of elicitation techniques and their potential in making sensory aspects of experiences accessible in the minds of consumers. Next, an elicitation technique specifically designed to capture the sensory aspects of tourism experiences is presented. This technique is then illustrated in the context of a specific case study. The chapter concludes with a discussion of the advantages and limitations of the elicitation technique and the implications of its results for experiential tourism marketing.

Background

Sensory experiences

Engaging experiences are the central value proposition in an experi-ence-based economy (Pine & Gilmore, 1999). As such, experiences need to be carefully designed, produced, organised, foreseen, calculated and priced in order to provide new strategic opportunities for destinations and tourism providers (Stamboulis & Skayannis, 2003). This requires a thorough understanding of what constitutes experiences, what consu-mers desire or associate with extraordinary and meaningful experiences, and what the role of marketers is in creating such experiences. Schmitt (1999) describes new consumption experiences as providing sensory, emotional, cognitive, behavioural and relational values that replace functional values. Marketers provide the stimuli that result in customer experiences. Thus, experiential marketing needs to not only appeal to the heart and the mind of a consumer but also his or her senses. Successful brands stimulate and create connections based on sensory synergy communicated through multiple sensory touchpoints (Lindstrom, 2005).

Tuan states very eloquently, 'the senses, under the aegis and direction of the mind, give us a world' (1993: 35). Consumption involves seeing, hearing, tasting, feeling and smelling (Holbrook & Hirschman, 1982). Sensory experiences are immediate, powerful and capable of changing our lives profoundly, yet they are typically not used to their full potential in marketing (Gobe, 2001). Tourism experiences have been mostly defined based on visual experiences, as expressed in the notion of the 'tourist gaze', while other senses have been widely neglected (Urry, 2002). Sensory experiences can be both supporting and central to the overall tourism experience (Quan & Wang, 2004). Therefore, they play an important role in structuring tourism experiences. Yet, the sensory dimensions of tourism experiences remain largely unrecognised and under-researched.

While no two experiences are exactly the same, experiences can be classified in terms of their generic emerging properties (Schmitt, 1999). This applies to not only the cognitive, behavioural, relational and emotional aspects but also to the sensory dimensions of experiences. This means that even the sensory dimensions of experiences can and should be measured. Unfortunately, it seems that existing measurement approaches are extremely limited in their ability to capture sensory aspects of experiences as not only tourism marketers but also the consumers themselves are often unaware of the role of sensory stimuli in the construction of their overall consumption experiences. Thus, eliciting responses with respect to sensory dimensions of experiences requires deep engagement and careful probing typically only possible through qualitative research (Arnould & Epp, 2006). And, while these approaches can greatly inform our understanding of the nature and structure of sensory experiences, they cannot provide information regarding the desired, imagined or experienced sensory appeals of a larger sample of tourists necessary to design sensory experience offerings or experiential marketing communication strategies. Consequently, a methodology is needed that can effectively elicit implicit and embedded knowledge, but can be applied to a larger sample of respondents.

Elicitation techniques

Elicitation techniques aim at eliciting knowledge about a domain rather than information about a person. Elicitation techniques have been identified as important for researching salient concepts (Middlestadt *et al.*, 1996). The goal is to uncover feelings, beliefs and attitudes with respect to the domain, which many consumers find difficult to articulate (Webb, 1992). Thus, elicitation techniques seek to transcend communication barriers. The core premise of elicitation techniques is that deep thoughts can be encouraged by applying probing techniques. Thus, similar to projective techniques like Rorschach inkplot tests and sentence completion exercises (Donoghue, 2000), elicitation techniques often rely on stimuli which can be either concrete or ambiguous. The most commonly used elicitation techniques are pile sorts, triad tasks and free lists (Borgatti, 1998). The free-list technique involves asking respondents to list all the elements related to the domain they can think of, pile sorts typically involve cards that subjects have to sort according to similarities or dissimilarities followed by an articulation of how the judgement was made, and triad tests expose respondents to three concepts at a time, from which they have to eliminate the one they judge to be most different. These elicitation techniques are often used to determine which product attributes influence product choices (Bech-Larsen & Nielsen, 1999). Responses elicited from the subjects are then content-analysed depending on the specific goals of the research.

A more recently developed elicitation technique is metaphor elicitation (Zaltman, 2003). The initial probe in the metaphor elicitation process is typically an image that represents a visual metaphor. Respondents are asked to describe it and to explain what it stands for in relation to the domain in question. Based on their responses, they are then probed again to produce additional thoughts and feelings. One issue is of course the selection of the metaphor and probes, which can greatly direct the answers. It is important to select pictures or metaphor statements that are ambiguous enough to allow for a multitude of responses. This considered, metaphor elicitation seems to provide an especially effective avenue to bring less accessible thoughts and feelings to a level of awareness at which they can be further explored and communicated in the context of marketing research. Zaltman (2003) also acknowledges the important role of imagination and vivid mental imagery in enabling consumers to engage in deep thoughts. Metaphors can encourage such imaginative thinking. While elicitation is mostly used in the context of qualitative research, more recent studies suggest that it can also be a useful concept for quantitative research endeavours.

Laddering is a specific type of elicitation technique aimed at under-standing cognitive structures in the mind of the consumer (Grunert & Grunert, 1995). It is typically implemented as an in-depth, one-on-one interviewing technique based on a series of directed probes (Reynolds & Gutman, 2001). The goal is to derive association networks, so-called ladders, which represent perceptual orientations of consumers and illustrate meaningful associations made by the consumers at different levels of abstraction. Thus, laddering is based on asking respondents for word associations with the probes. The probes are usually employed in a strict sequential manner leading consumers to think from the more concrete to more abstract concepts. One of the important elements of laddering is evoking a situational context. According to Reynolds and Gutman (2001: 34), 'laddering works best when respondents are provid-ing associations while thinking of a realistic occasion in which they would use the product'. The analysis of data from such laddering interviews is focused on determining the structural relationships among constructs mentioned in the interview. Thus, one of the main advantages of laddering is that it can lead to quantitative results through means of rigorous coding. Also, it allows for emotional and unconscious factors to be captured (Grunert *et al.*, 2001). And, since each respondent provides a large number of data points as part of the stepwise elicitation procedure, a relatively small sample size can provide considerable insight regarding consumer choice and brand distinctions (Reynolds *et al.*, 2001). A laddering interview begins with warm-up questions and then moves the respondent up the levels of abstraction. An important part of this first process is to create brand distinctions so that the rest of the interview can be focused on a specific brand. 'Top of Mind Imaging' has been proposed as a valuable technique in laddering to identify the most conspicuous characteristics of a brand (Reynolds *et al.*, 2001). It involves asking respondents to give one or more first-thought associations for the brand. Data analysis of laddering responses requires content analysis and coding of the data as a first step, followed by a hierarchical analysis of the relationships between the coded concepts (Gengler & Reynolds, 2001).

Laddering interviews have been extensively used in leisure and tourism research in the context of means-end chain theory to extract consumer values and motivations (McDonald *et al.*, 2008). For example, Klenosky *et al.* (1993) used it to study ski destination choice, Klenosky (2002) applied it to examine relationships between push and pull factors in guiding Spring break travel behaviours and McIntosh and Prentice (2000) applied it to visitation of museums and heritage sites. McIntosh and Thyne (2005) stress the importance of laddering specifically in understanding the subtleties of tourist behaviour and the salient dimensions in the thinking of tourism consumers. One of the problems with laddering techniques is that they aim at re-producing the cognitive structure that presumably exists in the mind of the consumer. This involves a rather simplistic view of the human mind and does not acknowledge the influence of the methodology on the hierarchy of concepts which results from the procedure. However, hierarchies set aside, they can tap into associations that are not necessarily 'top of mind'. Thus, both metaphor elicitation and laddering seem to be suitable methodologies to capture the sensory aspects of tourism experiences. However, the question is whether they can be successfully combined and implemented in the context of a larger scale study.

The Sensory Experience Elicitation Protocol

Combining the advantages of metaphor elicitation and of laddering, Gretzel and Fesenmaier (2003) developed an elicitation technique specifically geared at eliciting sensory association networks present in the minds of consumers. The technique is referred to as Sensory Experience Elicitation Protocol (SEEP), with reference to the trickling down of laddering questions to ever-deeper levels of the consumer mind, tapping into concepts of ever-greater abstraction. In the original study, the methodology was applied to a sample of 1436 respondents who were asked to describe the associations they had with travel destinations in the Midwest United States. Accordingly, SEEP is currently geared towards eliciting sensory associations with respect to vacations at specific destinations but can certainly be modified to fit other tourism experiences. For instance, it could be applied to elicit what sensory experiences would be desired in a luxury city hotel room, to probe for sensory experiences and emotions encountered when visiting a dark tourism site like a concentration camp, or to test the brand image of a restaurant chain.

In contrast to both laddering and metaphor elicitation, SEEP is implemented as part of a survey questionnaire rather than a personal interview. The specific SEEP questions are illustrated in Figure 8.1. SEEP is based on direct elicitation (Bech-Larsen & Nielsen, 1999), asking the respondents to come up with sensory attributes most relevant to the product/destination. Drawing upon existing laddering techniques, the protocol starts with a top of mind imaging task as a warm-up. It is assumed that this first question elicits concepts that are more concrete, easily accessible in memory and readily communicated. To probe for the less accessible and more abstract sensory experience associations, the technique further involves narrative transportation (Green & Brock, 2002) through the use of a metaphor and the encouragement of vivid mental imagery by asking the survey respondents to imagine that they had just arrived at a destination and that they were looking out through

---

We would like to learn about the way you <u>think</u> and <u>feel</u> about pleasure trips to Destination X

When you think about Destination X, what are the **three things or feelings** that **first come to your mind**?

1. [_____]   2. [_____]   3. [_____]

Imagine that you have just arrived at Destination X. You walk inside your hotel room, and you open the window…what do you see?
[_____]

Now imagine that you have finished unpacking. What are you going to do next?
[_____]

You are ready for dinner. The waitress comes to your table to take your order. What are you going to order?
[_____]

Close your eyes and think about a vacation to Destination X. What color dominates your mental image?
[_____]

What kinds of scents do you smell during this pleasure trip to Destination X?
[_____]

What sounds do you hear?
[_____]

Figure 8.1 SEEP questions

their hotel room window. Thus, rather than relying on an actual image, SEEP relies on a story fragment as the stimulus. This is then followed by a series of semi-structured questions tapping into different sensory qualities of the imaginary experience. These questions serve as the additional probes as proposed by Zaltman (2003). The questions start with easily accessible activities and visual attributes, while later moving to more salient sensory concepts such as taste, specific colours dominating the mental imagery, smell and sound. Therefore, in accordance with laddering techniques, the level of abstraction increases with each question. SEEP currently includes six additional probing questions, which could of course be easily expanded if, for example, touch is a key sensory dimension to be captured or social dimensions of the experience are of importance to the research. The goal of SEEP is to produce responses that can then be coded based on content analyses and further analysed with respect to structural properties.

Case Study: Capturing Experiences Associated with Elkhart County, Indiana

The case study presented in this chapter concerns a small, rural destination in northern Indiana, in the Midwest United States. Elkhart County, Indiana is predominantly known for the large Amish community who calls the area its home. The landscape provides views not only of Amish farms and small country roads on which Amish people ride in horse-drawn buggies, but also of quaint towns with flea markets, antique stores and museums. Many visitors come to Elkhart County to buy crafts made by the Amish or to savor one of their famous family-style meals. At the same time, the area offers opportunities for outdoor activities such as biking, golfing, kayaking, fishing and hiking. Elkhart County is also known as a centre for the production of recreational vehicles (RVs). Many of the manufacturers offer tours, there is a large RV museum in the community, and campgrounds and RV rallies attract many RVers every year. The destination brands itself as both 'AmishCountry' and as 'RV Capital of the World'. While these two brands are defined based on amenities, the experiences the destination offers are manifold, involve all senses and are not easy to describe in functional terms.

As part of their overall strategic branding effort, the Elkhart County Convention and Visitors Bureau wanted to better understand the sensory experiences that travellers associate with vacations at the destination. The goal was to inform both online and offline sensory marketing campaigns through concepts elicited from consumers rather than supply-driven descriptions. Specifically, commonly held associations were to be captured so that they could be integrated into advertising texts as well as imagery.

Methodology

Data were collected using an online survey methodology. The study was conducted in December 2007, with invitations sent to 2275 individuals who had requested travel information from the Elkhart County Convention and Visitors Bureau that year. No incentives were offered for participation in the survey. A reminder email was sent in January 2008. The effort led to 141 responses, with a response rate of 6.2%. To investigate possible non-response biases, the demographic characteristics of the respondents were compared with those of respondents to previous surveys for the destination. The results indicated that the sample reflected the typical visitor to the area as identified in previous studies, with respondents being older (43.6% were 55 years or older), mostly (61.1%) without children living in their household and household incomes of $75,001 or more (55.4%). The respondents were pre-dominantly female (63.6%), which was also the case in previous studies and is typical given the role of females in travel planning and decision-making processes (Kim *et al.*, 2007; Zalatan, 1998; Austria National Tourist Office, 2006). A majority (75.9%) had visited Elkhart County within the previous five years and almost all (89.8%) had at least some familiarity with the area. Only three of the respondents who were not familiar with Elkhart County provided answers to the experience questions. Since the goal of the research was to elicit the image of the destination rather than actual experiences, their responses were retained in the data set.

The online questionnaire included the SEEP elicitation methodology described above, which was modified to fit the context of the study: sensory experiences associated with destinations located within Elkhart County, Indiana. A majority of the respondents completed the semi-structured questions; however, of the 103 respondents who started the process, only 88 provided answers for all questions. Yet, the answers they provided were quite elaborate. The top of mind question elicited 589 words, the visual question 519 words, the activity question 615 words, the taste question 573 words, the colour question 372 words, the scent question 460 words and the sound question 560 words. The survey respondents used a variety of words to describe the different sensory inputs they expect from a vacation in the area. In an effort to identify common themes and make the classification process more efficient, a preliminary analysis of the text data was conducted using CATPAC II (Woelfel & Stoyanoff, 1993). CATPAC is a text analysis software that, based on a neural network algorithm, derives frequencies of words included in a text. It eliminates so-called stop words (words like 'the' and 'or' with no meaning for the study) based on a list that can be modified by the researcher and then, by parsing the text, it counts and identifies unique words. It also identifies the words that most frequently co-occur in the text; however, given the short answers elicited in this study, this specific function was not deemed useful. Instead, the resulting output was only used to identify the words that were most frequently mentioned to portray the various dominant sensory associations. A frequency of 4 was determined as the most suitable cut-off point as opinions of four people are usually seen as constituting a group opinion (Asch, 1955). The text data was then dummy-coded into these common sensory dimensions (assigned the value 1 if the sensory dimension was present in the response and coded as 0 if it was not).

Chi-square tests were conducted to examine potential differences in the experience dimensions mentioned with respect to several respondent characteristics as well as preferred travel activities. Finally, assuming that experience is a function of the combination of certain sensory inputs, cluster analysis was used to investigate the relationships among the different sense categories and to explore if and how respondents combined sensory experiences into coherent bundles that could be used as direct inputs for marketing-related communication materials.

Results

Experience funnel questions

The word Amish clearly dominated the responses to the first question in the elicitation protocol. Table 8.1 provides a complete listing of words that were mentioned at least four times. The words provide a very interesting representation of the overall destination image, which is consistent with the branding effort of the destination. The results also show that both the Amish and the RV experience are represented. Shopping and food are identified as important aspects of the destination. In addition, the sentiment is overwhelmingly positive, expressed through words such as good, friendly, interesting, fun and peaceful.

The mental imagery question also provided interesting results (Table 8.2). Most respondents described seeing a 'countryside' setting with fields and Amish buggies. The words used were more diverse than in the first question but still very much related to the same imagery. Only a small portion of words referred to urban settings (buildings, parking lots). Interestingly, RV is again mentioned several times. Those respondents remarked that they would be looking out of their RV rather than a hotel room window. While this information could not be derived from the frequency analysis alone, the CATPAC results drew attention to the word and triggered the need to follow up given the word's obvious mismatch with the rest of the frequently mentioned concepts.

Table 8.1 Top of mind thoughts and feelings about the destination

Term	*Frequency*
Amish	63
Country	21
RV	18
Shopping	18
Food	15
Good	15
Friendly	14
Peaceful	13
People	12
Market	11
Flea	9
Relaxing	7
Area	6
Beautiful	6
Quiet	6
Countryside	5
Home	5
Interesting	5
Laidback	5
Antiques	4
Fun	4
Quaint	4
Slow	4

The next question asked respondents about their activities upon arrival at the destination. Table 8.3 shows that respondents envisioned a rather active experience that involved going for a walk, driving around, shopping, eating out, using the hotel pool and finding travel information or brochures (information and brochures are not listed in the table as they only occurred three times each). Relaxation did appear as a concept but was not as prominent as the others.

Table 8.2 Mental imagery descriptions

Term	Frequency
Amish	17
Buggy	12
Countryside	11
Country	9
Farmland	7
RV	7
Trees	7
Beautiful	6
Fields	6
Green	6
Horses	6
Lots	6
Grass	5
Open	5
Stay	5
Buildings	4
Flowers	4
People	4
Quiet	4
Rural	4
Small	4

Sensory experience domains

Table 8.4 lists the sensory words most frequently used to describe the tastes, colours, scents and sounds associated with the destination. Chicken and homemade Amish food, pie and mashed potatoes as well as family-style dinner were most frequently used to describe the dining experiences associated with the destination. These dishes reflect the offerings of the Amish restaurants in the area. While some mentioned eating a local speciality as the experience associated with a visit to Elkhart County, others referred to more generic food items such as steak and roast pork.

Table 8.3 Activity descriptions

Term	Frequency
Go	23
Walk	17
Visit	12
Around	11
Drive	11
Eat	11
Shop	11
Amish	9
Shops	8
Area	7
Look	7
Town	6
Hotel	5
Pool	5
Country	4
Countryside	4
Find	4
Relax	4
Travel	4

The colour Green associated with fields and grass was the most prominently mentioned colour. Blue was also mentioned frequently. The Reds and Whites of barns and farm buildings were also included in the mental images of many of the respondents, followed by the Black of Amish buggies, Yellow, fall colours and the Brown of Amish horses. The colour domain was definitely the most uniform in terms of the words used, which is not surprising.

Freshness and fresh air were frequently mentioned as scents associated with the Elkhart County experience. Smells related to baking and cooking were also associated with a vacation at the destination. The smell of cut grass or hay was described by several respondents, as was the smell of flowers. Interestingly, less pleasant smells such as horse manure

Table 8.4 Sensory domain descriptions

Taste		Colour		Scent		Sound	
Term	Frequency	Term	Frequency	Term	Frequency	Term	Frequency
Chicken	27	Green	56	Fresh	48	Horses	41
Food	15	Blue	20	Farm	32	Birds	35
Amish	14	Red	12	Cut	24	Clip-clop	24
Homemade	14	Colours	11	Smells	23	Hooves	19
Pie	12	Fields	11	Air	17	Buggy	16
Potatoes	12	White	11	Baking	16	Traffic	11
Mashed	11	Grass	10	Hay	15	Children	10
Dinner	10	Black	9	Grass	13	People	9
Familystyle	9	Yellow	9	Flowers	8	Roads	9
Local	9	Fall	7	Horses	7	Amish	8
Fried	6	Amish	6	Bread	6	Quiet	7
Good	6	Brown	6	Apple	5	Laughing	6
Meal	6	Sky	6	Breeze	5	Music	6
Steak	6	Bright	5	Cinnamon	5	Pull	6
Vegetables	6	Horses	4	Cooking	5	Sounds	6

Table 8.4 (*Continued*)

Taste		Colour		Scent		Sound	
Term	*Frequency*	*Term*	*Frequency*	*Term*	*Frequency*	*Term*	*Frequency*
Restaurant	5	Light	4	Country	5	Firewood	5
Apple	4	Orange	4	Leaves	5	Talking	5
Country	4			Manure	5	Wind	5
Meat	4			Pie	5	Cracking	4
Pork	4			Lake	4	Down	4
Probably	4			Popcorn	4	Playing	4
Roast	4						
Speciality	4						

and farm animal smells were also mentioned. They clearly fit with the overall country atmosphere that seems to dominate the experience in Elkhart County.

As far as sounds were concerned, the 'clip-clop' of horse hooves and buggies being pulled down country roads was the most frequently mentioned dimension, followed by birds. However, children and people-related sounds such as laughing and talking as well as music and firewood cracking were also listed by the respondents. In addition, wind sounds and no sounds (quietness) were used to describe the experience. Interestingly, some respondents also mentioned traffic sounds. This dimension does not fit with the idyllic country-experience with which the other dimensions seem to be related.

The sensory words for each domain were then further purified. Words like sounds and words that were used to describe the sensory experience but did not have a meaning on their own as 'pull' and 'down' in 'the sound of horses pulling a buggy down the road', were eliminated. Words that described the same sensory concept were combined, e.g. 'mashed' and 'potatoes' or 'baking' and 'bread'. The goal was to extract up to 10 dimensions for each domain; however, in the case of the scents domain, 11 dimensions were extracted. The specific dimensions extracted for the taste domain are described in Table 8.5.

Relationships with demographics and activity-based experience measures

It is important to understand whether certain dimensions within the four sensory experience domains are more likely associated with the destination by certain groups of respondents. As far as the influences of demographic variables on the experiential descriptions were concerned, differences in terms of gender, age and income were investigated using Chi-square tests. No significant relationships were found regarding age, suggesting that these experience dimensions are independent of the age of the respondent. In the case of gender and income, only three significant differences were found; thus, it can be concluded that the dimensions are generally not dependent on the demographic character-istics of the respondent. The three differences referred to traffic sounds (with males being more likely to mention it: 21.9% Male, 5.4% Female; $p = 0.019$; $\chi^2 = 5.5$), firewood cracking sounds (with females being more likely to mention it: 10.7% Female, 0% Male; $p = 0.055$; $\chi^2 = 3.7$) and horse smells (with wealthy respondents more likely to mention it: 18.2% for $\$ > 100,001$, 0% for $\$50,001–100,000$ and 0% for $\$ < 50,000$; $p = 0.005$; $\chi^2 = 10.5$). Those who had visited Elkhart in the past five years were more likely to mention horse sounds (52.6% compared to 18.8%; $p = 0.015$; $\chi^2 = 6.1$), and less likely to mention bird sounds (30.3% compared to 68.8%; $p = 0.008$; $\chi^2 = 8.4$).

Table 8.5 Dimensions under each sensory domain

Taste	Colour	Scent	Sound
Chicken	Green	Farm/manure	Horses
Pie	Blue	Fresh air	Birds
Mashed potatoes	Red	Baking	Traffic
Local	White	Grass/hay	Children
Steak	Black	Flowers	People
Vegetables	Yellow	Horses	Quiet
Amish	Fall Colours	Apple	Music
Familystyle	Brown	Lake	Firewood cracking
Homemade		Leaves	Wind
Pork		Popcorn	
		Cooking	

Relationships were also tested with respect to activities, as many market segmentation efforts as well as experience measures are based on questions related to activities undertaken when on vacation. As part of the survey, the respondents were asked to select up to three activities they typically participated in during vacations in the Midwest United States. They were presented with a list of 24 activities that reflected a diverse range of common vacation activities for the region (e.g. visiting a historic site, birdwatching, gambling, etc.). However, seven activities had counts of five or less and were excluded from further analysis. The selected 17 activity choices were cross-tabulated with the 38 sensory dimensions. Only 38 out of the 646 possible combinations (5.9%) were significant. This suggests that there is very little overlap between the activity-based measure and the sensory experience based measure. The significant relationships could be due to chance alone; however, at closer inspection they do not appear to be completely random.

Colours and activities.   As far as colours are concerned, significant ($p < 0.05$) positive relationships were found for the colour white and participating in outdoor activities (40% as opposed to 9.4%; $p = 0.034$; $\chi^2 = 4.5$), attending a boat or auto show (50% as opposed to 8.3%; $p = 0.002$; $\chi^2 = 9.8$) and participating in a tour (30.8% as opposed to 7.8%; $p = 0.015$; $\chi^2 = 6.0$). This means that respondents who said they engaged in these activities during Midwest vacations were significantly more likely to mention white as a colour they associate with a vacation in

Elkhart County. Significant positive relationships were also found between black and watching sports events (42.9% as opposed to 7.2%; $p = 0.003$; $\chi^2 = 9.1$) and going shopping/antiquing (17.5% as opposed to 4%; $p = 0.034$; $\chi^2 = 4.5$) as well as for blue and shopping/antiquing (30% as opposed to 12%; $p = 0.034$; $\chi^2 = 4.5$). Positive associations further occurred between yellow and visiting a beach or waterfront (26.1% as opposed to 9%; $p = 0.037$; $\chi^2 = 4.3$), while there was a negative relationship between yellow and visiting a national or state park (3.1% as opposed to 19%; $p = 0.034$; $\chi^2 = 4.5$).

Smells and activities.　　With respect to smells, positive relations were found between the smell of horses and going for a walk (20% as opposed to 5.5%; $p = 0.054$; $\chi^2 = 3.6$) as well as attending a boat/auto show (33.3% as opposed to 6.1%; $p = 0.017$; $\chi^2 = 5.7$), baking smells and gambling (60% as opposed to 20.5%; $p = 0.041$; $\chi^2 = 4.2$) as well as shopping/antiquing (35% as opposed to 12.5%; $p = 0.012$; $\chi^2 = 6.3$), apple smells and visiting friends and family (11.1% as opposed to 1.4%; $p = 0.043$; $\chi^2 = 4.1$), lake smells and dining at a good restaurant (11.1% as opposed to 0%; $p = 0.014$; $\chi^2 = 6.1$) and flower smells and visiting a theme park (30% as opposed to 6.4%; $p = 0.015$; $\chi^2 = 6$). Negative relationships were found between baking smells and participating in a tour (0% as opposed to 28.2%; $p = 0.013$; $\chi^2 = 6.2$), and farm smells and visiting family and friends (16.7% as opposed to 42.9%; $p = 0.041$; $\chi^2 = 4.2$).

Sounds and activities.　　Concerning sounds, a positive relationship occurred between traffic noise and hiking/biking (50% as opposed to 9.2%; $p = 0.003$; $\chi^2 = 9$). Positive associations were also found between bird sounds and participating in outdoor activities (80% as opposed to 35.2%; $p = 0.044$; $\chi^2 = 4$), music and gambling (33.3% as opposed to 4.6%; $p = 0.006$; $\chi^2 = 7.7$), shopping/antiquing (11.9% as opposed to 2%; $p = 0.052$; $\chi^2 = 3.8$) as well as dining at a good restaurant (12.8% as opposed to 1.9%; $p - 0.034$; $\chi^2 = 4.5$), horse sounds and attending festivals/events (63.0% as opposed to 39.4%; $p = 0.039$; $\chi^2 = 4.3$), quiet and hiking/biking (33.3% as opposed to 6.9%; $p = 0.026$; $\chi^2 = 5$) and wind sounds and visiting a beach/waterfront (21.7% as opposed to 4.3%; $p = 0.010$; $\chi^2 = 6.7$). Negative relationships were found between music and visiting historic sites (0% as opposed to 10.2%; $p = 0.054$; $\chi^2 = 3.7$), children sounds and attending festivals/events (0% as opposed to 13.6%; $p = 0.043$; $\chi^2 = 4.1$) and people sounds and visiting a beach/waterfront (0% as opposed to 20%; $p = 0.020$; $\chi^2 = 5.4$). This means that travellers who visit historic sites are less likely to associate a visit to the destination with music, those who attend festivals/events did not think of children sounds and those who enjoy beaches or waterfronts do not have associations with people sounds.

Tastes and activities.　　Some relationships were also found between activities and tastes. Those who take scenic drives are less likely to mention chicken as a desired meal than those who do not engage in this activity (15.4% as opposed to 35%; $p = 0.032$; $\chi^2 = 4.6$), while those who go for walks are more likely to mention Amish food (31.3% as opposed to 10.8%; $p = 0.032$; $\chi^2 = 4.6$) and vegetables (18.8% as opposed to 4.8%; $p = 0.047$; $\chi^2 = 4.0$). Respondents who travel to Elkhart to visit family and friends are less likely to mention Amish food (0% as opposed to 17.7%; $p = 0.042$; $\chi^2 = 4.1$). Those who attend festivals and events are more likely to associate the destination with eating pork (10% as opposed to 1.4%; $p = 0.047$; $\chi^2 = 3.9$) and those who hike and bike associate it more with steak than those who do not (33.3% as opposed to 4.3%; $p = 0.004$; $\chi^2 = 8.3$). Those who visit historic sites are less likely to mention vegetables (0% as opposed to 11.5%; $p = 0.030$; $\chi^2 = 4.7$).

Overall, the findings suggest that the sensory experience dimensions capture aspects of experiences that cannot be represented through other variables such as activity patterns or demographic characteristics. They were also found to be largely independent of recent travel to the destination. Thus, eliciting and analysing the sensory aspects that consumers associate with a destination are important steps in the process of designing experiential offerings for a destination or marketing available experiences. The results also call for experience-based segmentation as opposed to the traditional demographic or activity-based approaches in order to identify different visitor segments.

Sensory experience bundles

The sensory domains have so far been treated in isolation. However, travel experiences are complex combinations of a variety of sensory inputs (Gretzel & Fesenmaier, 2003). To test this assumption and provide useful sensory combinations on which product development and marketing efforts can be based, a hierarchical cluster analysis (Hair *et al.*, 1998) of variables rather than respondents was performed in an effort to classify the 38 sensory dimensions into coherent experience bundles. This involved clustering the variables using Ward's method, a hierarchical clustering method aimed at minimising the variance within clusters, and the Lance and Williams distance measure, since the variables were binary and the Lance and Williams measure is a robust measure for dissimilarity (Faith *et al.*, 1987; Punj & Stewart, 1983). Specifically, it allowed for classification based on the presence of sensory association rather than both presence and absence. For the purpose of this research, an absence of the association in any combination of the variables should not be interpreted as similarity.

The dendrogram, resulting from the cluster analysis of the sensory domains is presented in Figure 8.2. A dendrogram visualises which elements were joined first into a cluster, indicating their similarity. The resulting dendrogram shows seven rather distinct clusters which do not join until late in the agglomeration effort. This means that the concepts within the cluster were often mentioned together, while concepts across clusters were not. Cluster 1 includes horse and bird sounds, grass and farm smells and the colour green. It seems to describe a farm-related sensory experience. Cluster 2 only consists of foods, namely chicken, mashed potatoes and pie. These three tastes were so strongly bundled together that they do not overlap with any other sensory dimensions. They describe a typical country meal. Of all the clusters, Cluster 2 is most closely related to Cluster 1, supporting the rural experience described in Cluster 1. Cluster 3 involves a very romantic autumn experience. It includes the smell of leaves, fall colours and brown, as well as the sounds

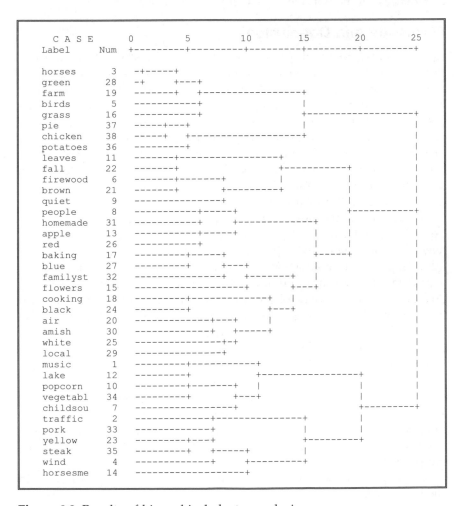

Figure 8.2 Results of hierarchical cluster analysis

of firewood cracking and quietness. Cluster 4 comprises of people sounds, homemade food, apple smells and the colour red. It seems to have almost nostalgic undertones. Cluster 5 appears to capture the Amish/country living experience: baking and cooking smells, fresh air, local foods, Amish family-style meals, and the smell of flowers set in a landscape with blue skies, white farm buildings and black Amish buggies. Cluster 6 is a fun experience: music, lake smells, popcorn smells, vegetables and children sounds. Cluster 7 is somewhat harder to interpret. It seems to describe a rather generic experience bundle with traffic and wind sounds, the smell of horses, pork and steak and the colour yellow. Overall, the clusters make sense and prove that sensory experiences can be bundled across the four sensory domains.

Discussion and Conclusion

The results provide important insights into the structure of tourism experiences as far as sensory domains are concerned. Although a multitude of words was used by the respondents to describe their imaginary experiences at the destination, it was fairly easy to extract dominant sensory dimensions under each domain. This suggests that while tourism experiences associated with a destination are personal, they are not completely idiosyncratic. Further, the sensory experiences that were elicited from the respondents were largely independent from socio-demographic characteristics and also showed only minimal rela-tionships with activity-based measures. Thus, it can be concluded that these sensory dimensions capture an important aspect of tourism experiences not covered by other measures, and that they provide a new way of potentially segmenting the market for the purpose of marketing the destination. Most importantly, the sensory dimensions could be grouped into bundles that span across multiple sensory domains. These experience bundles make intuitive sense and can form the basis of understanding experiences from a multi-sensory perspective. Overall, the findings highlight the importance of conceptualising tourism experiences from a sensory point-of-view. This is not only important for theory development in tourism but also for tourism management practice. While tourism product development is currently still mostly focused on providing and bundling activities, the results of the study suggest that tourism experiences encompass multiple sensory dimen-sions that need to be reflected and actively stimulated. SEEP can help identify what these sensory stimuli should be if used to elicit desirable sensory experiences.

The results also suggest that the methodology was rather successful in eliciting sensory responses in the context of an online survey. The fact that respondents were able to articulate sensory associations with the destination in terms of tastes, sounds, colors and scents proves that sensory concepts are salient but accessible if one probes carefully for them, even if the probe is impersonal and embedded in an online survey questionnaire. The importance of the warm-up questions is apparent in that they elicited largely functional destination attributes and general sentiments. The 'arrival' and 'hotel room' metaphors worked fairly well, except for those travellers who visit Elkhart County in their RVs and had a hard time relating to the hotel experience. This stresses the importance of selecting the right metaphor. Other metaphors should be explored to expand the validity of SEEP. Also, one of the limitations of the current version is that it does not include a question for the sense of touch as it was difficult to fit that into the hotel room context. Future studies applying SEEP as a methodology should certainly investigate if and how it could be included. Moreover, like most of the other elicitation techniques, SEEP still requires respondents to articulate feelings and sensory experiences in words alone as it relies on survey methodology. It is also not immune to the probes (especially the examples given to explain the concepts) leading the answers in certain directions.

The advantage of SEEP clearly lies in being applicable to large-scale studies. However, although facilitated by the content analysis, it still requires the coding of textual data into frequently mentioned sensory dimensions. Further, while most laddering studies aim at deriving hierarchical structures, the methodology presented in this chapter applies laddering in a looser sense and does not allow for detection of hierarchies regarding the different sensory domains within the experience bundles. This is somewhat of a limitation in that it treats all sensory domains as equal, while this might not be how consumers perceive them. On the other hand, it does not make a priori assumptions about specific links between concepts existing in the mind of the individual consumer. Another limitation is that SEEP does not ask for the evaluation of the concepts and, thus, cannot make assumptions about whether the sensory experiences are liked or disliked. What is possible is for the destination marketers to compare their current marketing efforts with the associations that consumers make and identify differences. The important question is whether a particular sensory experience is something that the destination wants to portray and actively communicate to consumers. Overall, the application of SEEP in the case of the study presented in this chapter was successful and led to interesting results based on which the destination marketing organisation has started to redesign its marketing communication efforts.

In an ever-more crowded marketplace it becomes increasingly difficult to communicate tourism experiences to consumers in engaging and noticeable ways. Experiential marketing that immerses consumers on multiple sensory levels is necessary to stand out. Emerging technologies offer a growing potential to implement such experiential marketing campaigns and even current website applications can be used to provide rather rich sensory descriptions supported by pictures and sounds. The information derived in this study can be implemented by the marketers of Elkhart County in terms of specific advertising appeals used (e.g. horse and buggy sounds in TV commercials or the use of fall colours and Amish food pictures on the website). Evoking senses has the potential to evoke rather strong emotions as our sensory systems, especially our sense of smell, and our emotional system are closely linked (Lindstrom, 2005). This is, of course, especially effective when these sensory cues match with the associations that the consumer already has. Thus, sensory-rich communication based on consumer research is also important with respect to encouraging brand attachment. Consequently, in order to design sensory-based destination marketing campaigns, a thorough understanding of the sensory appeals of the destination is needed. As a methodology, SEEP provides a starting point for more quantitative studies on sensory experiences in tourism. However, it certainly needs to be further explored and validated.

References

Arnould, E.J. and Epp, A. (2006) Deep engagement with consumer experience. In R. Grover and M. Vriens (eds) *The Handbook of Marketing Research* (pp. 51–82). Thousand Oaks, CA: Sage.

Asch, S.E. (1955) Opinions and social pressure. *Scientific American* 193, 31–35.

Austria National Tourist Office (2006) *Frauen im touristischen Kaufentscheidungsprozess* [Role of women in travel choice processes–in German]. Online document, October, 31. On WWW at http://www.austriatourism.com/xxl/_site/int-de/_area/465217/_subArea/628725/_id/628735/index.html. Accessed 16.11.06.

Bech-Larsen, T. and Nielsen, N.A. (1999) A comparison of five elicitation techniques for elicitation of attributes of low involvement products. *Journal of Economic Psychology* 20, 315–341.

Borgatti, S.P. (1998) Elicitation techniques for cultural domain analysis. In J. Schensul and M. LeCompte (eds) *The Ethnographer's Toolkit* (Vol. 3) (pp. 1–26). Walnut Creek, CA: Altimira Press.

Cohen, E. (1979) A phenomenology of tourist experiences. *Sociology* 13 (2), 179–201.

Donoghue, S. (2000) Projective techniques in consumer research. *Journal of Family Ecology and Consumer Sciences* 28, 47–53.

Faith, D.P., Minchin, P.R. and Belbin, L. (1987) Compositional dissimilarity as a robust measure of ecological distance: A theoretical model and computer simulations. *Vegetatio* 69, 57–68.

Gengler, C.E. and Reynolds, T.J. (2001) Consumer understanding and advertising strategy: Analysis and strategic translation of laddering data. In T.J. Reynolds and J.C. Olson (eds) *Understanding Consumer Decision-Making: The Means-End Approach to Marketing and Advertising Strategy* (pp. 119–141). Mahwah, NJ: Lawrence Erlbaum.

Gobe, M. (2001) *Emotional Branding: The New Paradigm for Connecting Brands to People*. New York: Allworth Press.

Green, M.C. and Brock, T.C. (2002) In the mind's eye: Transportation-imagery model of narrative persuasion. In M.C. Green, J.J. Strange and T.C. Brock (eds) *Narrative Impact: Social and Cognitive Foundations* (pp. 315–341). Mahwah, NJ: Lawrence Erlbaum.

Gretzel, U. and Fesenmaier, D.R. (2003) Experience-based internet marketing: An exploratory study of sensory experiences associated with pleasure travel to the midwest United States. In A. Frew, M. Hitz and P. O'Connor (eds) *Information and Communication Technologies in Tourism 2003* (pp. 49–57). Vienna: Springer Verlag.

Grunert, K.G., Beckmann, S.C. and Sørensen, E. (2001) Means-end chains and laddering: An inventory of problems and an agenda for research. In T.J. Reynolds and J.C. Olson (eds) *Understanding Consumer Decision-Making: The Means-End Approach to Marketing and Advertising Strategy* (pp. 63–90). Mahwah, NJ: Lawrence Erlbaum.

Grunert, K.G. and Grunert, S. (1995) Measuring subjective meaning structures by the laddering method: Theoretical considerations and methodological problems. *International Journal of Research in Marketing* 12, 209–225.

Hair, J.F., Anderson, R.E., Tatham, R.L. and Black, W.C. (1998) *Multivariate Data Analysis* (5th edn). Upper Saddle River, NJ: Prentice Hall.

Holbrook, M.B. and Hirschman, E.C. (1982) The experiential aspects of consumption: Consumer fantasies, feelings, and fun. *Journal of Consumer Research* 9 (September), 132–140.

Jackson, M.S., White, G.N. and Schmierer, C.L. (1996) Tourism experiences within an attributional framework. *Annals of Tourism Research* 23 (4), 798–810.

Kim, D-Y., Lehto, X. and Morrison, A. (2007) Gender differences in online travel information search: Implications for marketing communications on the Internet. *Tourism Management* 28 (2), 423–433.

Klenosky, D. (2002) The "pull" of tourism destinations: A means-end investigation. *Journal of Travel Research* 40 (May), 385–395.

Klenosky, D, Gengler, C. and Mulvey, M. (1993) Understanding the factors influencing ski destination choice: A means analytic approach. *Journal of Leisure Research* 25, 362–379.

Li, Y. (2000) Geographical consciousness and tourism experience. *Annals of Tourism Research* 27 (4), 863–883.

Lindstrom, M. (2005) *Brand Sense: Build Powerful Brands through Touch, Taste, Smell, Sight and Sound*. New York: Free Press.

McDonald, S., Thyne, M. and McMorland, L-A. (2008) Means-end theory in tourism research. *Annals of Tourism Research* 35 (2), 596–599.

McIntosh, A.J. and Prentice, R. (2000) Affirming authenticity consuming cultural heritage. *Annals of Tourism Research* 26, 589–612.

McIntosh, A.J. and Thyne, M.A. (2005) Understanding tourist behavior using means-end chain theory. *Annals of Tourism Research* 32 (1), 259–262.

Middlestadt, S.E., Bhattacharyya, K., Rosenbaum, J., Fishbein, M. and Shepherd, M. (1996) The use of theory based semistructured elicitation questionnaires: Formative research for CDC's prevention marketing initiative. *Public Health Reports* 111 (supplement 1), 18–27.

Oh, H., Fiore, A.M. and Jeoung, M. (2007) Measuring experience economy concepts: Tourism applications. *Journal of Travel Research* 46 (November), 119–132.

Pearce, P.L. and Caltabiano, M.L. (1983) Inferring travel motivation from travelers' experiences. *Journal of Travel Research* 22 (2), 16–20.

Pine, B.J. and Gilmore, J.H. (1999) *The Experience Economy.* Boston, MA: Harvard Business School Press.

Punj, G. and Stewart, D.W. (1983) Cluster analysis in marketing research: Review and suggestions for application. *Journal of Marketing Research* 20 (2), 134–148.

Quan, S. and Wang, N. (2004) Towards a structural model of the tourist experience: An illustration from food experiences in tourism. *Tourism Management* 25, 297–305.

Reynolds, T.J., Dethloff, C. and Westberg, S.J. (2001) Advancements in laddering. In T.J. Reynolds and J.C. Olson (eds) *Understanding Consumer Decision-Making: The Means-End Approach to Marketing and Advertising Strategy* (pp. 91–118). Mahwah, NJ: Lawrence Erlbaum.

Reynolds, T.J. and Gutman, J. (2001) Laddering theory, method, analysis, and interpretation. In T.J. Reynolds and J.C. Olson (eds) *Understanding Consumer Decision-Making: The Means-End Approach to Marketing and Advertising Strategy* (pp. 25–62). Mahwah, NJ: Lawrence Erlbaum.

Ryan, C. (2002) Motives, behaviours, body and mind. In C. Ryan (ed.) *The Tourist Experience* (2nd edn) (pp. 27–57). New York: Continuum.

Schmitt, B.H. (1999) *Experiential Marketing: How to get Customers to Sense, Feel, Think, Act and Relate to Your Company and Brands.* New York: The Free Press.

Stamboulis, Y. and Skayannis, P. (2003) Innovation strategies and technology for experience-based tourism. *Tourism Management* 24, 35–43.

Tuan, Y-F. (1993) *Passing Strange and Wonderful – Aesthetics, Nature and Culture.* Washington, DC: Island Press.

Urry, J. (2002) *The Tourist Gaze: Leisure and Travel in Contemporary Societies* (2nd edn). London: Sage.

Wang, N. (1999) Rethinking authenticity in tourism experience. *Annals of Tourism Research* 26 (2), 349–370.

Webb, J.R. (1992) *Understanding and Designing Marketing Research.* London: Academic Press.

Woelfel, J. and Stoyanoff, N.J. (1993) CATPAC: A Neural Network for Qualitative Analysis of Text. Working Paper. Buffalo, NY: University of New York at Buffalo.

Woodside, A.G., Cruickshang, B.F. and Dehuang, N. (2007) Stories visitors tell about Italian cities as destination icons. *Tourism Management* 28, 162–174.

Zalatan, A. (1998) Wives' involvement in tourism decision processes. *Annals of Tourism Research* 25 (4), 890–903.

Zaltman, G. (2003) *How Customers Think-Essential Insights into the Mind of the Market.* Boston, MA: Harvard Business School Press.

Part 3
Managing the Experience

Chapter 9

Delivering Quality Experiences for Sustainable Tourism Development: Harnessing a Sense of Place in Monmouthshire

CLAIRE HAVEN-TANG and ELERI JONES

Introduction

Despite the premium that high-quality tourism products command, core tourism products are very similar, particularly in rural areas. Innovative and creative augmentation of core products can make destinations and individual businesses within destinations more distinctive and establish a unique selling proposition. According to Ooi (2004: 112) 'destinations are becoming more globalised and alike in their offerings', whilst Ritzer (1998: 135) suggests that 'tourism is growing increasingly McDonaldized'. Successful rural regeneration programmes can create homogenised rural tourism destinations with similar comparative advantage (Ritchie & Crouch, 2003) that are difficult to differentiate. As a result, rural tourism destinations are competing in a very crowded marketplace. Consequently, many rural destinations seek to intelligently and effectively utilise destination resources to create high-quality visitor experiences and ensure sustainable competitive advantage.

Inimitable visitation experiences can be developed through a Sense of Place (SoP), immersing visitors in the local atmosphere and enabling them to sample local produce and participate in local events. The SoP concept, which can be selectively customised by individual businesses, adopts a more resource-orientated approach that focuses on the natural, physical and socio-cultural capital of a rural destination. Various SoP frameworks have been developed based on alternative packaging of the core attractors of a destination – people, culture, landscapes, history, food, e.g. Scotland (Durie *et al.*, 2006) and Wales (Wales Tourist Board, nd). The Wales Tourist Board's (WTB) framework comprises six themes: *Wales and its People; Working with the Welsh Language; Working with Buildings; Food and Drink; Using Creativity and the Arts;* and *The Great Outdoors.* This chapter applies the WTB framework to the case of Monmouthshire and explores how SoP can deliver high-quality unique and memorable rural tourism experiences whilst enhancing sustainable rural development.

Literature Review

Tourism markets are becoming increasingly sophisticated, as tourists migrate from mass consumption towards more authentic products and personal experiences for new meaning and self-actualisation (Cooper & Hall, 2008; LaSalle & Britton, 2003). The tourism industry's response has been to develop experience-based products, whereby experiences become the product and provide tourists with an interactive, holistic experience as an integral feature of the destination. Pine and Gilmore (1999: x) coined the term 'the experience economy' and suggest that recognition of 'experiences as a distinct economic offering provides the key to future economic growth'. However, experiences must be available to match the expectations of different visitor markets, which are heterogeneous, unpredictable and voluntary. Herein lies the dilemma – visitor experiences are personal, emotional responses to the destination and its people. Therefore, positive destination-level experiences depend on destination managers understanding visitor motivations.

Destination-level experiences are complex – they may be positive or negative and may evolve over time. To deliver such experiences, destinations need experience-oriented strategies, utilising destination resources, e.g. food, drink, language, arts, culture, to enhance the experience, link to sustainability and add value. Authenticity must be a common thread. 'Plain space must become a distinctive place for staging an experience' (Pine & Gilmore, 1999: 43). Experiencescapes (Cooper & Hall, 2008: 115) 'are landscapes of produced experience... physical spaces of market production and consumption in which experiences are staged and consumed'. Destination development and promotion can transform existing communities/places into packaged experiencescapes, for example: themed waterfronts, former industrial areas and restaurant or conference quarters. Such areas provide clear zones of interpretation – for visitors and local communities. Ritchie and Crouch (2003: 213) state that:

> The implication of the search for experiences is that each and every destination manager must attempt to view his or her destination not simply as a place to visit and a place to do things, but, more importantly, as the provider of visitor experiences – preferably enjoyable, memorable experiences – that will generate high levels of visitor satisfaction and the subsequent favourable word-of-mouth advertising that is essential to both competitiveness and sustainability.

Local residents in host communities are an integral part of these experiences and influence the quality of the experience. Indeed, local people and lifestyles are a fundamental resource in the rural tourism product and success is often dependent on their active engagement (Kneafsey, 1998), for example, many people have specialist skills, local knowledge and interests which are distinct and can be shared with their community in the form of social capital. Yet, local communities and businesses often forget that qualities comprising their everyday life add value and enrich the visitor experience. Schouten (2007: 36) proposes that:

> The tourist, the culture and the community are dependent on one another. The tourists need, for their authentic experience, the living culture and the maintenance and improvement of the resources, which in their turn depend on the spiritual and economic development of the local community.

Whilst packaged experiencescapes enhance destination branding for urban destinations, this approach is less easily applied to rural destinations. Rural topography and product portfolios are very different and rural areas are often difficult to distinctively differentiate because their core resources and attractors (e.g. landscape) are often very similar. Unlike urban destinations, rural areas tend to lack the iconic features which can be zoned into packaged experiencescapes. The decline of agriculture has stimulated tourism as an entrepreneurial activity and popular rural development/farm diversification strategy (Williams & Ferguson, 2005; Wilson *et al.*, 2001). Although rural areas have always attracted tourists, Sharpley (2007: 126) argues that 'rural tourism remained, until the mid 20th century, a relatively small scale, passive activity'. Changes to traditional rural economies and increasing interest in rural areas have contributed to the rapid development of rural tourism, which encompasses a wide range of activities, including farm-based holidays (Alexander & McKenna, 1998). Many rural communities have resorted to tourism for regeneration following the decline of more traditional industries. Consequently, the nature and scale of rural tourism has been transformed and assumed a more significant role as a vehicle for economic and social regeneration that directly or indirectly supports a range of industries and businesses. 'Many rural areas have re-defined themselves as consumption spaces in which history and rural tradition take over from modern agricultural production as the key elements of identification' (Cloke, 1993 cited in Richards & Wilson, 2006: 1209).

However, the loss of traditional industries may see the loss of indigenous community culture and identity, which has implications for social capital. The Office for National Statistics (2003: online) describes social capital as 'the pattern and intensity of networks among people and the shared values which arise from those networks. Greater interaction between people generates a greater sense of community spirit'. From a tourism perspective, this is important as local people and their lifestyles combine to provide social capital within the destination hence are fundamental to the success of rural tourism as they contribute to the visitor experience. Furthermore, local community engagement in the tourism product can provide a vehicle for regenerating rural community identity as local communities reflect on working collectively for the benefit of the community, as well as visitors. Additionally, community involvement in the rural tourism product can enhance the entertainment value of interpretation, especially in terms of bringing life to interpretation through storytelling activities, re-enactments and themed displays and festivals. Indeed, grass root festivals can aid heritage conservation, local pride and identity, employment and economic development. However, the chances of success and acceptance amongst member of the community are more likely if the local community take the initiative and drive these processes forward. Sustaining local values, culture and quality of life are key objectives in most tourism policies (Williams *et al.*, 1995). However, successful rural tourism policies must address changes within community life, as well as the local environment – hence are dependent upon the cooperation of local communities. Changes in the economic structure of rural economies impact on community identity and, ultimately, survival. Building social capital can ensure sustainable (long-term) competitive advantage for rural destinations, as well as integrating local communities into the experience. 'Increasingly...communities are realising that collectively, the sum of their cultural assets has greater tourism appeal than the individual assets within a community' (McKercher & du Cros, 2002: 113).

A major issue for rural tourism destinations is the dominance of small and medium-sized tourism businesses (SMTBs) which pose challenges for destination managers due to their special characteristics – notably low engagement with wider destination development strategies and hence implications for quality tourism experiences (Jones & Haven-Tang, 2005). SMTBs undoubtedly provide more interesting and challenging employment opportunities coupled with the ability to be more flexible in responding to visitor needs. However, whilst there are many entrepreneurially motivated SMTBs, competitive and sustainable destination management is often impeded by SMTBs with no desire to pursue commercial objectives, such as business growth, and who may have weak business strategies, exacerbated by a lack of business and management skills, negative attitudes towards training and ease of entry to the tourism industry. Furthermore, the tendency for some SMTB operators to compete on price rather than value ignores visitor expectations of quality, reduces competitiveness, restricts profitability and limits reinvestment potential (Jones & Haven-Tang, 2005). Thus, SMTBs can impact negatively on competitive and sustainable rural destination development and visitor experiences. Andereck *et al.* (2006: 95) suggest that:

> Tangible clues provided by visitors through the meanings they attach to their experiences can help improve or create a quality tourism experience. The clues vary from the simple to the complex... On the simple side; experiences are affected by bad service providers – front-line people who do not respond politely to a visitor. Poor service brings out negative comments and taints the quality of an experience.

This reinforces Pine and Gilmore's (1999: 69) belief that 'the easiest way to turn a service into an experience is to provide poor service, thus creating a memorable encounter of the most unpleasant kind'. In the rural setting, SMTBs are critical to drive the industry forward through innovative practices and bottom-up approaches to tourism development, which encourage local community participation, utilise social capital and limit external dependency. Examples of such approaches might include destination marketing consortia drawn from local tourism businesses and community-led tourism projects.

The other challenge for rural destination managers is identifying the best strategy for destination differentiation and competitiveness. Ritchie and Crouch (2003: 2) believe that:

> What makes a tourism destination truly competitive is its ability to increase tourism expenditure, to increasingly attract visitors while providing them with satisfying memorable experiences, and to do so in a profitable way, while enhancing the well-being of destination residents and preserving the natural capital of the destination for future generations.

Holloway (1994: 30) claims that many tourism destinations adopt a 'user-orientated' rather than a 'resource-orientated' approach leading to identikit destinations with few distinctive features – placelessness (Relph, 1976). Placelessness is synonymous with Ritzer's (1998) McDisneyisation proposition, in that 'what is supposed to be a human vacation turns for at least some into a non-human or even dehumanising experience' (Ritzer, 1998: 135) – essentially, applicable to any destination which takes a user-orientated approach. Ritchie and Crouch (2003) advocate destination strategies which turn comparative into competitive advantage and actively engage local communities providing social capital, promoting quality of life, preserving destination assets and creating a bottom-up approach to tourism development to sustain competitive advantage. However, this is not always easy to achieve in rural areas as the following case study illustrates.

Using a Sense of Place (SoP) to Deliver Quality Experiences

As we have seen, visitors are seeking distinctive experiences derived from the unique attributes of a destination, those which differentiate it from competitors. Such experiences arise from a holistic sense of being in a special distinctive place. SoP can have meanings at several levels embracing everything that is unique and distinctive about a place – special and memorable qualities that resonate with local people and visitors, personal, family or community stories, history, legends, geography, geology, flora and fauna, non-material characteristics which create the 'soul' or 'spirit' of a place (see also Chapter 4). Cooper and Hall (2008: 116) suggest that SoP 'is usually applied in the context of people who live in a location on a permanent basis and reflects how they feel about the physical and social dimensions of their community'. Hay (1998: 5) states that:

> Sense of place differs from place attachments by considering the social and geographical context of place bonds and the sensing of places, such as aesthetics and a feeling of dwelling. Insider status and local ancestry are important toward the development of a more rooted sense of place.

Stokowski (2002: 368) suggests that the concept of SoP is generally 'used to refer to an individual's ability to develop feelings of attachment to particular settings based on combinations of use, attentiveness and emotion'. Whilst Stewart *et al.* (1998) note that SoP can vary for individuals and that visitors can develop a SoP even after a short visit. Vanclay (2008: 7) uses the term 'spirit of place' to refer to the qualities that make a place special and proposes that people with a strong SoP have high levels of community connectedness, which he suggests is similar to social capital.

SoP can be used to exploit the unique attributes of a destination and differentiate it creatively from competitor destinations. Jamal and Hill (2004: 359) maintain that SoP requires space and place to be enacted through the 'identity, heritage and lived experience of both tourists and residents'. This requires a shift from heritage being a balance sheet of significant events and facts to being a vehicle that helps make sense of the present. Stokowski (2002: 372) suggests that creating SoP is a social task – much of what individuals know, feel or do in a destination is 'mediated by others...people actively create meaningful places through conversation and interaction with others'. Likewise, Vanclay (2008: 9) states that SoP 'is the contemporary everyday connection individuals have with their local spaces that gives their life meaning in the present'. McLean and Cooke (2003) emphasise that representation of heritage is created through co-consumption, illustrating the importance of community engagement (McKercher & du Cros, 2002; Schouten, 2007) in generating a SoP identity, particularly in rural areas, through reflection on their surroundings and how they benefit the community and visitors.

Indeed, Relph (1976: 55) stresses the importance of local residents in creating SoP – in terms of 'knowing implicitly this is where you belong'. Nickerson (2006: 232) supports these views and claims that 'communities that work together for a common good are more prepared to provide an atmosphere for quality experiences for residents and visitors'. Active engagement of local communities in developing SoP promotes quality of life and can help preserve the social and natural capital of a destination for future generations. Furthermore, it provides tourists with an interactive holistic experience (Pine & Gilmore, 1998) as an integral feature within the destination. In this context, two types of SoP are important – residents' attachment to their locality and tourists' sense of being in a distinctive place. For quality tourism experiences, these types are interrelated as SoP considers the physical and social dimensions of the community which are influenced by unique socio-cultural, natural and political environments. Interaction and engagement with the local community can provide tourists with a SoP. Therefore, quality tourism experiences depend on maintaining local residents' SoP, because, if local residents have a negative SoP, the quality of the tourist experience and the unique characteristics of the place – which attract tourists – may be negatively affected.

The SoP concept has been embraced by numerous UK tourism destinations (e.g. Birmingham City Council, 2004; Placebook Scotland, 2008). Using four SoP themes, Durie *et al.* (2006) demonstrate how the history of Scotland creates its SoP emphasising the inseparability of tourism and national identity:

> Destinations without any myths and legends have no interesting stories to tell their tourists. A destination without a past is bland... Destinations without history have no culture or character... Therefore, it is history that gives a destination its colourful past in which a sense of place is created. (Durie *et al.*, 2006: 43)

WTB (2003: 11) emphasise the 'importance of the culture of Wales in establishing a Sense of Place and arousing the curiosity and sense of adventure of visitors cannot be overstated'. Moreover, 'the uniqueness of Wales' history, language, culture and way of life are distinctive assets essential to sustaining a well-balanced tourism industry' (WTB, 2000: 80). WTB's tourism strategy emphasises the importance of creating 'a positive, distinctive and motivating identity for Wales as an attractive tourism destination in target UK and overseas markets' (WTB, 2000: 7). This aspiration demonstrates the need to identify core resources and attractors that underpin destination visitation and experiences. Cultural identity and history were identified as main motivators for visits to Wales (WTB, nd) but visitor expectations were rarely achieved. Although cultural understandings and expectations vary across time, geography and experience, visitors to Wales had certain expectations, such as hearing the Welsh language and discovering the history of an area, which were unfulfilled.

WTB-commissioned research resulted in a Cultural Tourism Strategy for Wales (WTB, 2003) committing to SoP development through a toolkit (WTB, nd) recognising destination's natural, physical and socio-cultural assets through six themes. 'Wales and its People' emphasises the importance of people in destinations focussing on social history, literary figures, popular entertainers and sports personalities. 'Working with the Welsh Language' highlights the Welsh language as a unique selling proposition for SMTBs in Wales. 'Working with Buildings' promotes buildings with industrial links through to medieval castles and more contemporary buildings. 'Food and Drink' stresses the importance of food and drink in the Welsh economy and visitor experiences – exploiting the local tourism multiplier effect, reducing food miles and enhancing sustainability. It also emphasises the need for distinctive dishes based on local produce. 'Using Creativity and the Arts' highlights how Wales's culture and creativity can be used to economic advantage, drawing on historic and contemporary influences and linking to festivals and events. 'The Great Outdoors' capitalises on Wales's natural assets – rural and coastal landscapes, habitats and wildlife and high- and low-impact outdoor activities on offer. These themes are similar to Scotland SoP theme – literature, food, landscape, music and film; different tastes, differing country; literature and place, nation and religion; heritage, authenticity and the appeal of Scotland (Durie *et al.*, 2006).

The SoP toolkit (WTB, nd) aims to: improve quality and enhance the tourism product across Wales; boost business and enhance status in a competitive market; promote the immediate and far-ranging benefits of working with distinctly local products. For SMTBs it adds value, improves competitiveness and profitability, whilst contributing to the tourism multiplier effect within the wider community. WTB asserts that visitors are seeking experiences, not just a destination, and expect authenticity and SMTBs should introduce a customised SoP into their businesses. However, WTB's SoP toolkit is generic and talks about what needs to be done; it does not explain how SoP can be achieved by SMTBs. SoP needs to be customised to meet the needs of different regions and counties in Wales to create an individual SoP. Customisation of SoP has been undertaken in several counties in Wales, notably Pembrokeshire and Monmouthshire.

Sense of Monmouthshire

Monmouthshire is one of 10 unitary authorities in South-east Wales and is located at the English-Welsh border on the West bank of the River Wye and includes parts of the Wye Valley Area of Outstanding Natural Beauty (AONB). It is unquestionably representative of a rural tourism destination. It has been shaped by invasions and other historical events. However, apart from a somewhat controversial relationship with the Welsh language, there is little to differentiate it from similar rural tourism destinations in England, such as Herefordshire.

In 2005, Monmouthshire's tourism generated just under £118 million (Monmouthshire County Council, 2006). Adventa, a local partnership of public, private and voluntary/community organisations (funded by the European Agriculture and Guidance Fund, Welsh Assembly Government and Monmouthshire County Council [MCC]), was formed to develop Monmouthshire as a strong, vibrant, self-reliant and entrepreneurial rural county that sensitively capitalises on its cultural, natural and social assets and delivers high-quality value-added products effectively, sustainably and profitably.

Adventa commissioned the research study that underpins this chapter to design and develop a Sense of Monmouthshire toolkit aimed at SMTBs in Monmouthshire and enhancing the experiences of the visitors to these businesses. A destination audit involving stakeholder interviews and participant observations sought to identify the natural, physical and socio-cultural attributes of Monmouthshire which could be used to enhance visitor experiences and to help SMTBs capitalise on these unique attributes and creatively differentiate themselves from competitors. Comments from interviewees illustrate the importance of this differentiation:

> We often forget that Monmouthshire is as exotic to foreigners as the Far East is to us.
> We have unique heritage skills, by networking with local history groups in the area, providers can build up a wealth of knowledge to impart with [sic] visitors.
> Any sense of place is about thinking 'outside the box' and adding personal touches to a localised product.

The toolkit is based on the generic themes outlined in WTB's SoP toolkit. SMTB experiences of the SoP toolkit are that it does not explain how to develop the SoP concept and is a challenge to implement. *Sense of Monmouthshire* was designed to facilitate implementation by providing pragmatic examples of how to develop SoP through an exploration of Monmouthshire's resources, including: The People of Monmouthshire; Working with the Welsh Language; Buildings of Monmouthshire; Dining at Monmouthshire's Great Table; Creative and Visual Monmouthshire and Monmouthshire's Great Outdoors. The themes aim to: enhance visitor experiences in Monmouthshire; raise SMTB awareness of what is happening within Monmouthshire and sustain rural SMTB survival rates. Each theme is discussed individually.

The People of Monmouthshire

People of Monmouthshire focuses on famous names, literary characters, saints and martyrs, scholars, royal connections, local stories and myths, and the interpretation of local heritage and culture. It encourages SMTBs to find out about people associated with their part of Monmouthshire and consider how they might weave these characters into the visitor experience. As interviewees said:

> We could exploit our people connections a lot more than we do, for example: Charles Rolls and Henry V...
> Monmouthshire has some very famous sons and daughters – these are a useful platform for attracting special interest groups...

An important way that people can be woven into a SoP is through exhibitions; trails; storytelling; interpretation panels; festivals and events. 'Stories represent patterns and express the meanings of place across society...The social and cultural values of place then become sustained in the language, culture and history collectively experienced, imagined and remembered' (Stokowski, 2002: 373). One interviewee providing costumed interpretation at Monmouthshire sites said:

> We use local legends to illustrate social history rather than national examples. This creates a link to the locality and a unique Sense of Place. For example, Monmouthshire was regarded as having the best archers... Local legends give a peephole to the past – a sense of time and place – things happened right here – so people look at familiar places with a different eye.

Working with the Welsh language: Being seen and heard in Monmouthshire

Language is central to creating a SoP (Stokowski, 2002) and *Working with the Welsh Language* suggests how SMTBs can incorporate the Welsh language into their activities. Welsh is one of the oldest languages in Europe and 'provides a unique differentiator with countries of the UK... Wales has a rich folklore and mythology associated with the language' (WTB, 2003: 41). The county of Monmouth emerged from the 1536 Act of Union (Michael, 1985) which referred to Monmouthshire as if it were not in Wales. Yet, Welsh was the dominant language in Monmouthshire until the latter half of the 18th century, when it was replaced by English with the increasing immigrant population (Howell, 1985). Monmouthshire's identity crisis continues to this day despite many Welsh place-names surviving in Monmouthshire. One interviewee commented that '*Monmouthshire is very distinctive because of the Wales–England meeting point; we should emphasise and exploit this distinctiveness more, because it makes us unique*'. Bilingual road signs and unpronounceable place-names add to the mystique of the destination. SMTBs can help visitors pronounce and understand Welsh place-names – adding to the visitor experience. Welsh-labelled produce, bilingual websites and signage, Welsh menus are all vehicles for promoting the Welsh language in SMTBs and developing the destination identity and brand. 'Lady Llanover [Monmouthshire resident and ardent Welsh language supporter] left an unexpected legacy to posterity. It was her advocacy that firmly fixed the female Welsh costume into tall black steeple hats, flannel shawls and skirts – the tourist symbol of Wales!' (Vaughan-Thomas, 1985 cited in Barber, 2004: 4). Monmouthshire's unique history and association with the Welsh language sets it apart from other Welsh (and English) counties and reinforces its distinctiveness – as Bond *et al.* (2003: 384) said 'in Wales, linguistic distinctiveness enables a strategic move away from a more traditional mass domestic tourism market…into "higher value", cultural tourism'.

Exploring inside and out: Buildings of Monmouthshire

Built heritage and other destination architecture play an important role in SoP and can be used as destination marketing tools providing a destination identity and offering memorable experiences (Klingmann, 2007). Built heritage is often safeguarded by legislation, and recognised as a form of cultural heritage. *Exploring Inside and Out* attempts to raise SMTB awareness of local buildings of historical and architectural significance. It also suggests how SMTBs can bring a Sense of Monmouthshire to their interior design and provides advice on researching the history of buildings. Reconstructing the past in the present through interpretation is the foremost challenge in linking heritage and tourism. The *Guide to the Great Churches in the Diocese of Monmouth* launched in June 2005 recognised the architectural, social and spiritual significance of 25 churches including two important medieval buildings – Tintern Abbey, reputedly the best-preserved medieval abbey in Wales, and Llanthony Priory. *Monmouthshire Discovery Tours* reconstruct the past through costumed interpretation (a Cistercian monk at Tintern Abbey and Gerald of Wales (discussing his journey around Wales) at Llanthony Priory). One interviewee commented that '*living history initiatives can raise awareness amongst local communities in terms of what they have to offer, such as: castles, walks, wildlife and food producers and how these can be linked together and interpreted to attract visitors'.*

Dining at Monmouthshire's Great Table: Food and drink

Food is 'an expression of the region, it is produced from local ingredients that are suited to regional soil and climate and transformed through the specific skills of local people' (Mason & Brown, 1999 cited in Groves, 2001: 246). Thus, explaining where SMTBs (and visitors) can find local produce and develop menus that give a flavour of Monmouthshire cannot be underestimated. Farmers' markets, for example, bring together producers and customers to create connectedness and traceability, as well as reducing food miles and enhancing the tourism multiplier effect. Asimov (2004) suggests that SoP in the wine business refers to wines which convey the special combination of soil, climate and human touch. Hence, to have a SoP, wines must be true to their origins. Monmouth-shire's wine-producing roots allegedly date back to Roman times with monasteries monopolising viniculture during the medieval period until their dissolution in the 16th century (Adventa, 2005). *Vine to Wine – a wine trail through the heart of Monmouthshire* celebrates Monmouthshire's food and drink resources. Gastronomy tourism is particularly significant for Monmouthshire spurred on by various food festivals including the annual Abergavenny Food Festival which celebrated its 10th anniversary in 2008. One interviewee commented that *'the* [Abergavenny] *Food Festival has put Monmouthshire on the "foodie" map; providers can take advantage of this by incorporating local produce in their menus and remembering to tell visitors that it is local. Traceability is increasingly important'.*

Creative and visual Monmouthshire: Arts and crafts

Local arts and crafts provide opportunities to showcase Monmouth-shire's culture and raise SMTB awareness of crafts, art, music, events and festivals. Working craft centres are visitor attractions in their own right where visitors can purchase locally produced, high-quality, authentic crafts (WTB, 2003), as well as possibly participating in art and craft experiences. Monmouthshire has a strong arts and crafts culture, including galleries, craft centres, potteries and workshops, which play an important role in the community by providing a link to the past, sustaining rural traditions, keeping people in touch with the natural environment and shaping Monmouthshire's future. A number of local craft centres, such as the Court Cupboard Craft Gallery in Llantilio Pertholey near Abergavenny, take a cooperative approach to developing SoP by promoting local artists and craftspeople using local produce and materials, as illustrated by one interviewee *'we should not just sell a product, but also its provenance'.* Provenance authenticates arts and crafts, often increasing the value and desirability of work and ensuring quality. *Made in Monmouthshire* is a local certificate of provenance identifying high-quality items produced locally from sustainable resources in an environmentally responsible way. At the destination-level *Made in Monmouthshire* is used as a vehicle for enhancing destination identity and sustainable competitive advantage. Public art is another powerful mechanism for developing a SoP, promoting civic pride and interpreting heritage and culture. The Chepstow High Street Regeneration Scheme, *Through the Arch – Poetry Bands in Paving* is one example promoting distinctiveness.

Monmouthshire's Great Outdoors

Monmouthshire's Great Outdoors capitalises on Monmouthshire's natural assets and outdoor activities. It suggests how SMTBs can develop walking or cycling trails and the benefits of visitor fact-files/bedroom browsers detailing local outdoors activities. Monmouthshire has a long history in terms of travel, as many Celtic saints from Monmouthshire and South-east Wales travelled inside and outside the county in the 5th and 6th centuries, attracting other missionaries to Wales and Monmouthshire. The Wye Valley – an AONB – is allegedly the birthplace of British tourism, as 1745 saw the first boat chartered for a visitor excursion on the River Wye. In 1782, William Gilpin published the first British tour guide *Observations on the River Wye and Several Parts of South Wales* creating interest in the area and attracting tourists, including artists, writers and poets, e.g. Wordsworth who wrote one of his best-known poems, *Tintern Abbey*, about the area (Bentley-Taylor, 2001). By the late 18th century there were numerous boats operating commercial excursions in response to tourist demand (Adventa, 2006).

Discussion

Ritchie and Crouch (2003) contend that in order to ensure destination competitive advantage, destination stakeholders must share a common destination vision and an appreciation of how to effectively utilise destination resources in order that rural landscapes are transformed into experiencescapes (Cooper & Hall, 2008). It is critical that all stakeholders, including SMTBs, unite over the bigger picture – the benefits for the destination as a whole through enhancing the visitor experience chain, working collectively (McKercher & du Cros, 2002) and acknowledging that the active engagement of local residents can promote quality of life in local communities and help to preserve the socio-cultural, physical and natural assets of a destination for future generations.

Through an integrated and holistic approach to tourism development incorporating cultural distinctiveness within a wider economic development, SoP should help to enhance the visitor experience; extend the tourism season by spreading the volume and value of tourism; promote quality and competitiveness; encourage innovation; develop a sense of community pride and preserve a rural destination's identity and distinct cultural and natural assets. The challenge for rural destination managers is identifying distinctive rural products in a very crowded marketplace by capitalising on endemic destination resources and transforming rural landscapes into experiencescapes (Cooper & Hall, 2008). Whether this has been achieved or not in Monmouthshire, despite the ongoing efforts of WTB, MCC and Adventa is highly debatable.

The SoP concept provides rural tourism destinations with a unique opportunity to creatively and sustainably exploit their natural, physical and socio-cultural capital in order to differentiate. Emphasising and exploiting 'difference' through SoP can counteract standardisation amongst places of consumption and provide destinations with a vehicle to integrate cultural distinctiveness with economic development and community identity. Thus SoP enables SMTBs to create unique quality visitor experiences which aid sustainable tourism development. Local communities and businesses often forget that qualities which make up their everyday life are part of the visitor experience and can add value and enrich that visitor experience. Berry's (Stenger, 1992: online) belief that 'If you don't know where you are; you don't know who you are' is not based on map-grid references but on senses, memories and social history. SoP can be used to exploit unique destination attributes and creatively differentiate a destination from its competitors, particularly in terms of the visitor experience. However, SoP needs to be selectively customised to exploit destination-distinctive social capital and attract visitors by providing unique visitation experiences, enabling them to absorb the atmosphere, sample local produce and participate in local events. Ultimately, to ensure sustainable competitive advantage and quality visitation experiences any SoP needs to evolve, as 'a destination's sense of place is not one that is static and objective, but is one that is constructed, contested and lived within a performative space' (Jamal & Hill, 2004: 359).

Rural destinations invariably have numerous examples of community events which have become visitor attractions, providing benefits for local communities as well as visitors. The involvement of visitors in the destination through the celebration of local food and drink, arts and crafts products ensures that visitors are not observers – outside the performance of culture – but actively help to develop sustainable competitive advantage harnessing the tripartite dependency of tourist, culture and community (Schouten, 2007). Jamal and Hill (2004: 368) assert that 'cultural and heritage areas come into being through the meaning-making activities of people interacting with objects, events and activities within historically, politically and culturally defined destination areas'. In addition to enhancing visitor experiences, events can be very attractive to communities and rural destinations seeking to address issues of civic and local pride, identity, inward investment, economic development, employment creation and regeneration (Derret, 2004). Furthermore, developing events anchored in the locality helps to strengthen tourism multiplier effect and promote cultural identity as well as enhancing SoP. To develop sustainable competitive advantage and enhance the visitor experience, links with food and drink, arts and crafts must be authentic and culturally embedded. The importance of provenance is not lost in Monmouthshire and the locally developed Abergavenny Food Festival celebrates Monmouthshire's food and drink products, whilst the *Made in Monmouthshire* initiative promotes local arts and crafts. This is incorporated in Adventa's Sense of Monmouthshire toolkit, which encourages SMTBs to use and promote local produce.

Any SoP must be selectively customised by individual businesses to exploit the distinctive natural, physical and socio-cultural assets of a destination and to provide a unique visitation experience. Developing a Sense of Monmouthshire would enable SMTBs to engage, explore and explain Monmouthshire's socio-cultural, physical and natural assets to visitors through extending these assets into their businesses and transforming plain space into distinctive space for staging experiences (Pine & Gilmore, 1999). The intention of the Sense of Monmouthshire toolkit was to combat destination homogeneity and build on the distinctive features within Monmouthshire, adding to the rural tourism portfolio and enhancing the visitor experience to create sustainable competitive advantage through effective utilisation of the destination resources. Developing a Sense of Monmouthshire is an ongoing challenge for SMTBs and must be a dynamic process to ensure it stays fresh and topical.

One of the major challenges for destination managers is getting SMTB managers or their staff to engage in training and development initiatives (Jones & Haven-Tang, 2005). The extent to which a Sense of Monmouthshire can be imposed by external organisations is debatable – even with the grass-roots approach adopted by Adventa. In line with many other destination-led initiatives, the widely noted (Jones & Haven-Tang, 2005; Lynch, 2000) lack of engagement by SMTBs has resulted in a low uptake of Sense of Monmouthshire modules by SMTBs despite very high module evaluation ratings by SMTBs who have completed the training. This lack of engagement may have negative implications for competitive and sustainable destination development and visitor experiences in Monmouthshire, as SMTBs may lack the understanding required to engage their visitors in order to provide memorable experiences.

One notable exception to Welsh SMTB non-engagement with destination initiatives has been the one-day customer care programme *Welcome Host* developed originally by the then WTB which achieved remarkable participation by SMTBs probably as a result of them being able to recognise such participation in their marketing activities through the Welcome Host Business Awards which reward an SMTB for its proportion of trained staff (gold 90%, silver 75% and bronze 50%) and can be used in marketing initiatives thus impacting on a business's bottom line. SoP is a less tangible concept and, post-training, SMTB operators would need to actually research, interpret and integrate SoP into their individual businesses. Clearly more tangible bottom-line benefits are needed to encourage participation in SoP training and implementation.

Building on high participation in *Welcome Host*, the *Croeso Cynnes Cymreig* (A Warm Welsh Welcome) training programme (launched by Visit Wales [previously WTB] in November 2008) is a broader programme to 'help all businesses strengthen skills, distinctiveness and flair in how we welcome visitors to Wales' (Welsh Assembly Government, 2008). It comprises three modules: Using Welsh in your Business; Providing a Warm Welcome; and Developing your Sense of Place. This may encourage SMTBs to engage with the SoP concept and help to address issues which impede coherent, competitive and sustainable destination development and negative impacts on the quality of the visitor experience (Andereck *et al.*, 2006; Jones & Haven-Tang, 2005; Nickerson, 2006). In Wales, it is hoped that this new programme will encourage businesses to develop their SoP and add value, improve competitiveness and highlight distinctiveness thereby enhancing visitor experiences and ensuring sustainable competitive advantage for destinations. Clearly, systematic evaluation of the achievement of the aims of *Croeso Cynnes Cymreig* is crucial. To date, evaluation by Adventa has been fairly cursory.

Conclusion

Various SoP frameworks have been developed based on alternative packaging of the core attractors of a destination – people, culture, landscapes, history, food – to enhance the visitor experience, link to sustainability and add value. Additionally, resource-orientated approaches (Holloway, 1994) help tourism destinations avoid becoming identikit destinations with few distinctive features. Different destinations, e.g. Birmingham, Scotland, Suffolk, Pembrokeshire, Monmouthshire, have used SoP with varying degrees of success. However, determining SoP success is questionable as SoP is a very intangible concept for visitors and locals. Furthermore, it is difficult to see short-term bottom-line benefits and SoP can be interpreted very differently by different stakeholders. Whilst destination leadership is important in providing a SoP framework and guidance for SMTBs about how to develop SoP, implementation needs to be driven by individual businesses and aligned to their business objectives, which pay attention to the wider destination strategy. A key challenge for a SoP initiative is providing motivation to SMTB managers through appropriately recognising their efforts to provide unique visitor experiences and impacting positively on an SMTB's bottom line.

References

Adventa (2005) *From Vine to Wine: A Wine Trail Through the Heart of Monmouthshire.* Abergavenny: Adventa.

Adventa (2006) *The Picturesque Wye Tours: Inspirational Valley – The Birthplace of British Tourism.* Abergavenny: Adventa.

Alexander, N. and McKenna, A. (1998) Rural tourism in the heart of England. *International Journal of Contemporary Hospitality Management* 10 (5), 203–207.

Andereck, K., Bricker, K.S., Kerstetter, D. and Nickerson, N.P. (2006) Connecting experiences to quality: Understanding the meanings behind visitors' experiences. In G. Jennings and N.P. Nickerson (eds) *Quality Tourism Experiences* (pp. 81–98). Burlington: Elsevier.

Asimov, E. (2004) Distinct tastes of the Northern Rhone. *New York Times.* Online document, September 1. On WWW at http://www.nytimes.com/2004/09/01/dining/01WINE.html?ei=5070&en=d3a3126e274610b9&ex=1125201600&pagewanted=print&position. Accessed 03.06.10.

Barber, C. (2004) *Llanover Country.* Abergavenny: Blorenge Books.

Bentley-Taylor, D. (2001) *Wordsworth in the Wye Valley.* Herefordshire: Logaston Press.

Birmingham City Council (2004) *A Sense of Place Project.* Online document. On WWW at http://www.digitalmidlands.org.uk. Accessed 03.06.10.

Bond, R., McCrone, D. and Brown, A. (2003) National identity and economic development: Reiteration, recapture, reinterpretation and repudiation. *Nations and Nationalism* 9 (3), 371–391.

Cooper, C. and Hall, C.M. (2008) *Contemporary Tourism – An International Approach.* Oxford: Butterworth-Heinemann.

Derret, R. (2004) Festivals, events and the destination. In I. Yeoman, M. Robertson, J. Ali-Knight, S. Drummond and U. McMahon-Beattie (eds) *Festival and Events Management: An International Arts and Culture Perspective* (pp. 32–50). Oxford: Butterworth-Heinemann.

Durie, A., Yeoman, I.S. and McMahon-Beattie, U. (2006) How the history of Scotland creates a sense of place. *Place Branding* 2 (1), 43–52.

Groves, A.M. (2001) Authentic British food products: A review of consumer perceptions. *International Journal of Consumer Studies* 25 (3), 246–254.

Hay, R. (1998) Sense of place in developmental context. *Journal of Environmental Psychology* 18, 5–29.

Holloway, J.C. (1994) *The Business of Tourism* (4th edn). Essex: Addison Wesley Longman.

Howell, R. (1985) *Fedw Villages - a Lower Wye Valley History.* Old Cwmbran: Village Publishing.

Jamal, T. and Hill, S. (2004) Developing a framework for indicators of authenticity: The place and space of cultural and heritage tourism. *Asia Pacific Journal of Tourism Research* 9 (4), 353–371.

Jones, E. and Haven-Tang, C. (2005) Tourism SMEs, service quality and destination competitiveness. In E. Jones and C. Haven-Tang (eds) *Tourism SMEs, Service Quality and Destination Competitiveness* (pp. 1–24). Wallingford: CABI.

Klingmann, A. (2007) *Brandscapes: Architecture in the Experience Economy.* Cambridge, MA: Massachusetts Institute of Technology.

Kneafsey, M. (1998) Tourism and place identity: A case-study in rural Ireland. *Irish Geography* 31 (2), 111–123.

LaSalle, D. and Britton, T. (2003) *Priceless: Turning Ordinary Products into Extraordinary Experiences.* Boston, MA: Harvard Business Press.

Lynch, P.A. (2000) Networking in the homestay sector. *Service Industries Journal* 20 (3), 95–116.

McKercher, B. and du Cros, H. (2002) *Cultural Tourism: The Partnership Between Tourism and Cultural Heritage Management.* New York: The Haworth Hospitality Press.

McLean, F. and Cooke, S. (2003) Constructing the identity of a nation: The tourist gaze at the Museum of Scotland. *Tourism, Culture and Communication* 4 (3), 153–162.

Michael, D.P.M. (1985) *The Mapping of Monmouthshire.* Bristol: Regional Publications (Bristol).

Monmouthshire County Council (2006) *STEAM Report 2005.* Cwmbran: Monmouthshire County Council.

Nickerson, N.P. (2006) Some reflections on quality tourism experiences. In G. Jennings and N.P. Nickerson (eds) *Quality Tourism Experiences* (pp. 227–235). Burlington: Elsevier.

Office for National Statistics (2003) *Social Capital – Measuring Networks and Shared Values.* Online document. On WWW at http://www.statistics.gov.uk/CCI/nugget.asp?ID=314. Accessed 03.06.10.

Ooi, C.C. (2004) Poetics and politics of destination branding: Denmark. *Scandinavian Journal of Hospitality and Tourism* 4 (2), 107–128.

Pine, B. and Gilmore, J. (1998) Welcome to the experience economy. *Harvard Business Review* 76 (4), 97–105.

Pine, J.B. and Gilmore, J.H. (1999) *The Experience Economy.* Boston, MA: Harvard Business School Press.

Placebook Scotland (2008) *Sense of Place: The Power of Scotland's Places.* Online document. On WWW at http://www.placebookscotland.com/page/page/show?id=2324419%3APage%3A576. Accessed 03.06.10.

Relph, E.C. (1976) *Place and Placelessness.* London: Pion.

Richards, G. and Wilson, J. (2006) Developing creativity in tourist experiences: A solution to the serial reproduction of culture? *Tourism Management* 27 (6), 1209–1223.

Ritchie, B.R. and Crouch, G. (2003) *The Competitive Destination: A Sustainable Tourism Perspective.* Wallingford: CABI.

Ritzer, G. (1998) *The McDonalization Thesis.* London: Sage.

Schouten, F. (2007) Cultural tourism: Between authenticity and globalization. In G. Richards (ed.) *Cultural Tourism: Global and Local Perspectives* (pp. 25–38). New York: The Haworth Hospitality Press.

Sharpley, R. (2007) Flagship attractions and sustainable rural tourism development: The case of the Alnwick Garden, England. *Journal of Sustainable Tourism* 15 (2), 125–143.

Stenger (1992) The sense of place. Online document. On WWW at http://www.mtbaker.wednet.edu/tlcf/The%20Sense%20of%20Place.htm. Accessed 03.06.10.

Stewart, E.J., Hayward, B.M., Devlin, P.J. and Kirby, V.G. (1998) The 'place' of interpretation: A new approach to the evaluation of interpretation. *Tourism Management* 19 (3), 257–266.

Stokowski, P.A. (2002) Languages of place and discourses of power: Constructing new senses of place. *Journal of Leisure Research* 34 (4), 368–382.

Vanclay, F. (2008) Place matters. In F. Vanclay, M. Higgins and A. Blackshaw (eds) *Making Sense of Place: Exploring Concepts and Expressions of Place Through Different Senses and Lenses* (pp. 3–11). Canberra: National Museum of Australia Press.

Wales Tourist Board (2000) *Achieving Our Potential: A Tourism Strategy for Wales*. Cardiff: Wales Tourist Board.

Wales Tourist Board (2003) *Cultural Tourism Strategy for Wales*. Cardiff: Wales Tourist Board.

Wales Tourist Board (nd) *Sense of Place Toolkit*. Cardiff: Wales Tourist Board.

Welsh Assembly Government (2008) *Croeso Cynnes Cymreig – A Warm Welsh Welcome*. Cardiff: Welsh Assembly Government.

Williams, C. and Ferguson, M. (2005) Recovering from crisis: Strategic alternatives for leisure and tourism providers based within a rural economy. *International Journal of Public Sector Management* 18 (4), 350–366.

Williams, D.R., McDonald, C.D., Riden, C.M. and Uysal, M. (1995) *Community attachment, regional identity and resident attitudes toward tourism*. Online document. On WWW at http://www.fs.fed.us/rm/value/docs/ttra95.pdf. Accessed 03.06.10

Wilson, S., Fesenmaier, D.R., Fesenmaier, J. and van Es, J.C. (2001) Factors for success in rural tourism development. *Journal of Travel Research* 40 (2), 132–138.

Chapter 10

Theatre in Restaurants: Constructing the Experience

DARRYL GIBBS AND CAROLINE RITCHIE

Introduction

As William Shakespeare (1599) once said:

All the world's a stage,
And all the men and women merely players;
They have their exits and their entrances,
And one man in his time plays many parts.

(*As You Like It* Act 2, scene 7: 139–143)

This quote, written some 400 years ago, can be appropriately applied to dining out in the 21st century. In a restaurant the players, management, staff and customers all have allocated roles and allocated areas of the space in which to perform those roles. However, there are many variations and role changes within this enduring cycle. For example, when a waiter leaves 'their' restaurant and joins friends for dinner in another, they take on the customer's role. Understanding the role being performed by each participant in each meal event can enable the 'stage' management to meet expectations and provide memorable experiences.

As Meiselman (2006) discusses, although now part of the classical school of management theory, scientific rationalism still dominates and underpins much current management research and praxis in the hospitality industry. As Crang (1994) also discusses, overtly or covertly referencing the motivational theories of the great pioneers such as Taylor, Maslow, Alderfer and Herzberg, an assumption is often made that academics should work to identify the individual component parts of a memorable experience; see for example, the Five Aspects Meal Model (FAMM), (Edwards & Gustafsson, 2008; Gustafsson *et al.*, 2006). Management theory is then developed, enabling staff to be trained to deliver those components of each meal event identified as significant, in the most efficient way so that each occasion can be made memorable.

This chapter argues that while there can be great comfort and safety in participating in any event where the rituals and culture are well known, in other circumstances many consumers will actively seek out the risk of the unknown (Beardsworth & Keil, 2000; Bourdieu, 1977;

Christy & Norris, 1999; Ritchie, 2007; Rozin, 2006; Telfer, 1996). The authors argue that management cannot and should not attempt to script for the memorable experience since it would then immediately become just another act in the waiters' repertoire.

We go to the theatre to watch a new play or new production of a favourite and much loved one in the anticipation that we will be pleasurably surprised and perhaps challenged by the new production. We go with friends to watch a stand up comedian and thoroughly enjoy the heckling and banter that takes place, whether or not we are directly involved. We use food and drink both to share pleasure with our friends, and to challenge them in the form of new and different foods. We socialise in local familiar places or try out new cutting edge establishments. We understand that professional skills are used in order to produce each of the above experiences – the play, the comedy and the food. We also understand that when seeking out the unknown, the frisson of risk-taking is part of the joy of the occasion. Therefore, the authors argue that, in contrast to seeking to script for every need, memorable hospitable experiences are only truly experienced if the moment is spontaneous.

This chapter discusses the importance of developing an understanding of the skills required to 'put on a good show' in order to meet customer expectations, enhance the hospitality experience and ensure continued custom. This chapter also shows that, just as the play differs from the stand-up comedy, so different performances are required from staff within bar and food service environments to support appropriate experiences. Furthermore the authors argue that, in order to ensure that the risky off-script experience is positive, there is a need for staff to be sufficiently skilled and empowered so as to be able to support the experience effectively as it, and however it, develops.

The analogy of the theatrical experience of a meal event is not a new phenomenon; in medieval times those of less social status would go to watch the intricate rituals of those with greater status dining. During a Renaissance feast, the 'gastronomic theatre' had to be large and loud enough to be visible to all, 'including spectators' (Jones, 2007: 284). Enormous prestige could be attached to roles such as those of ewerer or cup-bearer (Black, 1993: 116) which today could be considered low-status waiting type roles. Those with appropriate skills and ability (and birth) to perform the elaborate rituals would be regarded as celebrities perhaps in a similar way to some celebrity chefs or mixologists today.

In more recent times, others have also made explicit reference to the innate theatricality of the dining out experience. Ingemar Lindh, 20th century improvisationist and founder of the Institute for Scenkonst (Institute for Scenic Art) discussed in his House Project, (the provision of living space for actors and guests), the collaborative context of the provision of hospitality. In particular, he identified with:

the mechanics of encounter and the sensitivity to the other that permeate hospitality... the performers work upon oneself; the relationship with space and text; the role of the spectator; and the discipline of the work. (Camilleri, 2008: 249)

The architect Frank Lloyd-Wright simply said, 'Dining is and always was a great artistic opportunity' (Lloyd-Wright quoted in Secrest, 1992: 202).

From a more philosophical perspective, Immanuel Kant considered it significant that, in modern language usage, the word 'taste' is a recognised term both for the basic in-your-mouth gustatory experience as well as aesthetic knowledge and reflection. He suggested that:

there is no situation in which sensibility and understanding, united in enjoyment, can be as long continued and as often repeated with satisfaction as a good meal in good company. (Kant, 2005: 214)

Telfer (1996) suggests that the concept of enjoyment is significant in the provision of hospitality. Thus, since currently much research into private sector catering is predicated upon the notion that we rarely feed someone just to sate hunger, she suggests that the terms 'entertainment' and 'hospitality' can be used synonymously particularly at meal events (social occasions) rather than feeding events (to satisfy hunger). The authors suggest, however, that many eating out occasions are literally that, eating to satisfy hunger (the lunchtime snack, the motorway café meal). They are functional meals taken simply to refuel and refresh the body; no entertainment is required before moving on to the next activity of the day. In contrast, many other meals are taken in company with others as part of friendship or political cultural exchanges where the meal is an integral part of the enjoyment of the whole occasion. The authors suggest that it is upon these occasions that the memorable experience is more often sought and welcomed.

Reflecting this difference, Black (1993), Jones (2007), Kant (2005), Secrest (1992) and Telfer (1996) all suggest that when a meal is the mechanism for creating a social occasion, tacit acknowledgement of the theatrical conviviality of the meal event has always been made with particular potential for memorable experiences to be welcomed. In conjunction with this, statistical reports such as Mintel (2007, 2008) show that customer interaction with staff is one of the most significant reasons for dining out in a particular place.

However, it is only recently that academics and hospitality practitioners have begun to reflect in depth upon both the significance and construction of what Lugosi (2008) describes as 'communitesque' hospitable moments. These are the unscripted moments when some or all staff and customers come together in an intense, perhaps surreal, unforgettable experience. Spontaneous singing or dancing; sitting on a bar terrace when the sun really does set in spectacular fashion; the draw of an open fire in a pub on a cold winters' evening; being met by elephants instead of mini-buses as transport to the Chitwan National Park in Nepal after a freak flash flood. In all these instances, strangers who would probably never talk together interact as friends and equals until the experience ends and then they part.

Direct Application of the 'Theatre Experience' to the 'Restaurant Experience'

Theatrical and dramaturgical (Erikson, 2004a) metaphors for the service encounter have been applied by various authors (Morgan *et al.*, 2008) across a number of service industries and disciplines, as they seek to explore the insights that theatricality provides for the relationship between the consumer and the foodservice provider. Berry's (1981) case study of the Disney Corporation provides an early example of academic application of theatrical metaphor and language. In the management of Disney's theme parks, staff became the 'cast' and as the 'cast' they are either performing 'onstage' or they are 'backstage' (Morgan *et al.*, 2008). Grove and Fisk (1989) built on the work of Booms and Bitner (1981) developing a coherent framework of theatricality and performance for analysing the service encounter and experience. In this drama metaphor framework the consumers become both actors and audience, the restaurant servicescape becomes the theatre and the whole process becomes a live performance. This approach derives from symbolic interaction (Goffman, 1959), which recognises that humans use symbols (i.e. colour or memorabilia) to enable interaction with each other based on interpretations made of the context in which they interact (Gardner & Woods, 1991; Lundberg & Mossberg, 2008).

Bitner (1992) identified the concept of 'servicescape' as a metaphor for the physical environment that inevitably influences and shapes the participants' perceptions of the performance experience. This servicescape becomes the stage on which the performance is set (Morgan *et al.*, 2008). A number of authors have since merged the concepts and language of servicescape and stage management to explore how both the stage and the performance influence and shape the whole of the restaurant experience (Andersson & Mossberg, 2004; Gustafsson *et al.*, 2006; Hansen *et al.*, 2005; Warde & Martens, 2000).

The restaurant has been described as a 'stage for service' (Erikson, 2004a: 77), whereby the workers are hosts to the guests, and as such, function like tour guides to the social rules that govern the restaurant space. She further suggests that, particularly in the highly pressurised environment of fast food provision, the service exchange can better be viewed as a dance which may include the physical/sexual nuances of carnival. When the service exchange is viewed as a dance and the restaurant imagined as a stage on which the dance is performed, the line between front of house and back of house is demarcated, as Orwell (1933) suggested, not by a curtain but on the line where the kitchen tile turns into dining room carpet. In a similar way to Orwell, Erikson (2004a) suggests that the space for the customers, the audience of the staged service, is 'subtly demarcated from workspace where workers put the show together' (Erikson, 2004a: 79). The back of house is a constructed place/ space in which evidence of workers' labour is subtly hidden. Foodservice personnel use the back of house space not only to assemble food and beverages, but also to drop their character before returning to the front of house stage.

Williams and Anderson (2005) also applied a theatre/drama perspective in their research in which they sought to gain insights into the participatory nature of service creation. They argued that drama production principles can be applied to situations where customers 'co-create the service offering' (Williams & Anderson, 2005: 13). They suggested that elements in any service encounter can be delineated into director, lead actor, set designer, scriptwriter, supporting cast member and/or traditional audience roles. Furthermore, they proposed that by merging theories from theatre and services literature, a means of assessing the relative importance of each service component across service encounters and service scenarios could be more fully illustrated.

Morgan *et al.* (2008) argue that many of these approaches take an operational (scientifically rational) perspective, which seeks to describe and view the whole of the meal experience as something functional which is designed for the consumer by the professionals. This approach views the meal experience as something to be used mainly in the training of staff and the management of the service experience, rather than an approach which is customer-centred and orientated (Gustafsson, 2004; Gustafsson *et al.*, 2006).

In contrast, researchers in the field of experience management have applied the use of theatricality and performance to develop a more strategic use of the theatrical metaphor in the construction and management of experiences (Pine & Gilmore, 1999; Schmitt, 1999, 2003; Shaw, 2005; Smith & Wheeler, 2002) and of the components that make up that experience (Stuart, 2006). This work focuses on dramatising the service performance thus creating uniquely memorable experiences in the emerging 'experience economy' (Pine & Gilmore, 1999). They develop and extend Schechner's (1977) earlier performance theory in which drama is any activity where one group performs in front of another, to analyse encounters between service staff and consumers.

Pine and Gilmore (1999) further suggested that this drama then becomes the strategy of the company, which then becomes the processes that the staff must enact in order to achieve the goals and strategy of the company. In this scenario, the theatre is the workplace where the performance, the service to the consumer, takes place. Pine and Gilmore's (1999) concept sees the consumers as an audience to be entertained, involved and drawn in as they too becomes participants in the whole of the drama. They argued that the work of theatre is not so much a metaphor, but rather, a model of reality. Their overall aim was to create an impression and an emotional response from the consumer, the participant of the drama. Gardner and Woods' (1991) work suggests that this is often in the hope of increasing sales and tips.

Again, the work of researchers in the discipline of experience management has been criticised by some (Morgan *et al.*, 2008), this time for being too production-centric. The emphasis on the design, direction and stage management of the consumer experience has been criticised as superficial. It does not allow customers to create experiences that suit their own needs and level of involvement and performance (Holbrook, 2001; Prahalad & Ramaswamy, 2004). Instead it is suggested that consumers come to the restaurant stage to create their own experience through social interaction with others, particularly others participating in the meal occasion.

This view of the restaurant experience recognises and values the experience as having the potential for emotional, symbolic and transformational significance for the consumer (Caru & Cova, 2003; Gillespie, 2001). It argues that in a restaurant experience, customers actively interact with the physical setting and with other people in order to create their own personal event through that interaction (Gupta & Vajic, 2000). Whilst this may or may not involve overt interaction with others, it certainly includes the awareness of, and sensitivity towards 'others' that Lindh (cited in Camilleri, 2008) alluded to. This concept of 'co-creation' (Camilleri, 2008; Gillespie, 2001; Morgan *et al.*, 2008; Prahalad & Ramaswamy, 2004) seems to confirm the significance of all of the roles (the consumer, the food, the staff and the setting) in the drama of the restaurant experience.

In this paradigm, which views the service performance as a theatrical event, the service staff do not play the leading role even though their supporting role may appear to be the leading one. It could, for example, involve acting as a gastronomic or wine consultant by describing the menu in an effective, engaging way (Hall *et al.*, 2001; Kivela *et al.*, 2000) or serving the dishes with style including preparation of elements of the dish at the table (Hemmington, 2007). Acute awareness of the needs of others, the customer, enables skilled staff to apparently take the lead, but only with the active collusion of the real central characters. When that act is complete, control, apparently and reassuringly (Noone, 2008), passes back to the consumer. As in the case of the theatre itself, good supporting actors always avoid upstaging the leading character/s. From this perspective, the managerial role becomes one of provisioning/staging the space in which the experience may occur (Morgan *et al.*, 2008).

The Nature of Hospitableness/Natural Hospitality

The previous discussion suggests that deeper insights can be garnered by regarding the customers not as the audience but as skilled performers in their own right. Many social scientists have shown both how the public consumption of food is used to demonstrate cultural capital and how important the concept of hospitality is within society, for example, Beardsworth and Keil (2000), Bourdieu (1977) and Rozin (2006). Customers come to a restaurant to act out particular social roles in the context of that occasion; staff must react appropriately if the performance is to be successful. Lashley *et al.* (2004) suggest that many customers use comparison with home meal experiences to judge authenticity. The art of the theatre of the restaurant is to naturalise the hospitality offered so that it conforms with the cultural expectations of the customer. However, as O'Connor (2005) argues, customers are quick to know when true, authentic, natural hospitality is being offered and when it is a superficial act.

The observation of philosopher Max Beerbohm proves useful in understanding the pragmatic realities of measuring levels of natural hospitableness:

> In every human being, one or the other of these two instincts is prominent: the active or positive instinct to offer hospitality and the negative or passive instinct to accept it. And either of these instincts is so significant of character that one might well say that mankind is divisible into two classes: hosts and guests. (Beerbohm, quoted in Pritchard, 1981)

Lovell (2009) suggests that many who work in the service industries do so because they are Beerbohm's 'natural hosts'. Since food service staff, along with most other employees, seek job satisfaction they will instinctively react to the needs of others in their area of care, thus providing an authentic experience. Telfer's (2000) work concurs with this view, reinforcing the suggestion that many workers employed in service industries such as hospitality and tourism have chosen hospitableness as their way to show both generosity and kindness. They like to make people happy and choose to do this in the commercial setting of a food service environment. Thus, it can be argued that hospitableness is a natural and authentic part of the lives of good service staff (Walter, 2008).

Baum (2006) suggests that where staff and customers have the same cultural understanding and use the same cultural symbols, then again the offer of hospitality may be perceived as more natural (i.e. given in friendship not just offered for payment) and authentic. O'Connor (2005) points out that if hospitality is indeed a personality characteristic and a virtue belonging to and inherent within human nature, then for a hospitality employee to be perceived as being genuinely hospitable, they must 'perform' their hospitable actions naturally. Agreeing with War-hurst and Nickson (2001) he suggests that the hard, technical skills needed to perform the job of foodservice personnel could be developed through training and experience. However, the more important skill which needs to be taken into account when employing staff is their level of natural hospitableness.

Skills Needed to Support the 'Experience'

Much hospitality work is widely characterised in both the popular press and in research-based academic literature and sources as dominated by a low-skills profile (Baum, 2006; Shaw & Williams, 1994; Westwood, 2002). Burns (1997) questions the very basis for categorising employment per se into 'skilled' and 'unskilled' categories. Burns' argument rests with the postmodernist viewpoint that this separation is something of a social construct. Burns suggests that skills within 'organised' sectors of the hospitality industry (such as airlines and large hotel chains) are recognised and valued, whereas skills within catering and fast food (where labour is seen in terms of costs which must be kept at the lowest possible level) (Lashley *et al.*, 2002) are not valued or developed. Burns' definition of hospitality skills, therefore, seeks to go beyond the purely technical capabilities that those using either 'skilled' or 'unskilled' descriptors traditionally assume.

In recent years, several studies have been published which review employee skills central for the creation of successful service encounters (Lundberg & Mossberg, 2008). Some studies concentrate on the so-called 'hard' skills which relate to the technical performance of hospitality work such as wine knowledge and silver service skills (Burns, 1997; Pratten, 2003). Others have focused on the so-called 'soft' skills which are often composed of attitudinal aspects of work (Guerrier & Adib, 2003; Hallier & Butts, 1999; Hochschild, 1983). As previously discussed these skills are also alluded to by Lovell (2009), Telfer (2000) and Walter (2008).

Much recent research has found that employers within both the hospitality and tourism industries increasingly desire employees that possess and display the right attitude and appearance (Chan & Coleman, 2004; Nickson *et al.*, 2005). Nickson (2007) subsequently developed this argument to suggest that this encompasses aspects such as social and interpersonal skills, which are largely concerned with ensuring employ-ees in the hospitality industry are responsive, courteous and under-standing with customers. In taking the argument to its next logical step, Nickson (2007) developed the term 'aesthetic labour' – which he describes as the ability to either 'look good or sound right' (Nickson, 2007: 93). Although aesthetic labour is primarily about appearance, it can also, as previously discussed, be underpinned by 'cultural cache' (Baum, 2006: 135) – the ability of frontline staff to understand and engage culturally with their customers on terms dictated by the customer.

Lashley *et al.*'s (2004) research highlights that, from the customer perspective, the concepts of satisfaction and nurturing are more valued than other technical aspects of service such as silver service skills and detailed menu knowledge. Time and time again throughout Lashley *et al.*'s (2004) research it is, as Burns (1997) argued, the 'soft-skills' described by the respondents as 'attentiveness', 'attention to detail', 'flexibility', 'tolerance', 'amiability' and 'desire to serve' (Lashley *et al.*, 2004: 178–179) that dominate and are of tremendous importance for the whole meal experience. The authors observed a common thread through the narratives of almost all the respondents involved in the research – namely recognition that the service encounter inevitably involves the management of emotions. Insightfully, there is specific reference made by one respondent to 'the staff's successful emotional management of the customers' (Lashley *et al.*, 2004: 179). This service attribute has been described as 'emotional comfort' (Johns & Howard, 1998: 251) – i.e. the need to make the guests feel at ease or 'at home' whilst still respecting their social space.

It has long been recognised that providing emotional labour is an important element of interactive service work. The role of the waiter performing this 'emotional labour' is probably best summed up in this much loved and much quoted extract from Orwell's description of his life working in hotels in Paris in the 1930s:

> It is an instructive sight to see a waiter going into a hotel dining room. As he passes the door a sudden change comes over him. The set of his shoulders alters; all the dirt and hurry and irritation have dropped off in an instant. He glides over the carpet with a solemn priest-like air...And you (cannot) help thinking, as you (see) him bow and smile, with the benign smile of the trained waiter, that the customer (is) put to shame by having such an aristocrat serve him. (Orwell, 1933: 74)

However, when discussing the notion of emotion, it is interesting to compare Orwell's description of a waiter with the actress Sarah Bernhardt's contemporaneous description of an actor:

The artist's personality must be left in his dressing-room; his soul must be denuded of its own sensations and clothed with the base or noble qualities he is called upon to exhibit.... [he] must leave behind him the cares and vexations of life, throw aside his personality for several hours, and move in the dream of another life, forgetting everything. (Bernhardt, 1920: 76)

As can be seen in the description of the mental state of the service provider, whether actor or waiter, is very similar. However, whilst the actor has always been expected to slip into an alter ego, it has often been irrationally assumed that a good waiters' persona is real reflecting natural hospitableness, warmth and cultural compatibility. Hochschild's (1983) seminal work introduced the concept of emotional labour within the services economy. She pointed out that service employees are required to manage their emotions for the benefits of customers and are, in part, paid to do this; as in fact are actors. Academics have since studied the demand to fabricate emotions in the workplace for the benefit of co-workers, managers and customers (Erikson, 2004b).

Baum (2006) argues that the expectations of emotional labour add significantly to the skills demands of work in the hospitality industry. Lashley *et al.* (2004) also suggested that this concern for the emotional dimension of the service encounter may represent a key critical factor contributing to the success of any meal occasion. Their findings highlight the role of guest contact with employees during the service encounter as an integral and pivotal part of the commercial product. Therefore, the 'emotional intelligence' (Stein & Brooks, 2000) and awareness of Others required of frontline service staff is of paramount importance.

The work of Erikson (2004b) adds a further dimension to the study of the emotional content of interactions between customers and workers in constructing the restaurant experience. She argues that since the work of foodservice personnel hinges on their ability to perform and endure emotional labour, two primary strategies have evolved. These are described as 'detachment' and 'investment' (Erikson, 2004b: 550). She argues that workers who use detachment strategies seek to protect themselves from the emotional demands of the job by psychologically distancing themselves from the service exchange. In contrast, workers who 'invest' view the service exchange as pleasant social interactions. Consistent with the views of Lovell (2009), Erikson (2004b) argues that much previous research has focused on the cost of emotional labour to workers. However, other more recent research suggests that those service workers who invest in the emotional demands and emotional caring they are expected to perform, take pleasure in the emotional requirements of their job. Supporting the views of Telfer (2000) and Walter (2008), this seems to confirm that there are significant potential benefits within emotional labour exchange for particular hospitality staff.

These arguments may seem to have emphasised the need for soft-skills as being the most significant determinant of the empathy required to support a memorable customer experience. However, there is research contradicting the importance of the soft-skills argument (Johanson & Woods, 2008; Lundberg & Mossberg, 2008; Noone, 2008; Raub, 2008). Their work suggests that it is only those staff who feel technically skilled and confidently empowered who are actually able to support and authenticate the improvised nature of the theatrical meal event experience. That whilst the customer is apparently in charge of the performance, it is only skilled, confident frontline staff are able to stray from the official script, and support an improvised experience whilst ensuring that the physical comfort of the customer is maintained throughout.

Gillespie's (2001: 23) experience at the Bocuse Restaurant in Lyon, or customers seeking the Heston Blumenthal experience at the 'Fat Duck' in Bray confirm that professional staff can create highly memorable meal events which may not need to stray from the script, in the same way that actors in a play deliver their scripted lines. However, Lugosi's (2008) work suggests that in other situations memorable experiences are, or appear to the customer to be, spontaneous; more reminiscent of the stand-up comedian than the formal play. Lugosi discusses how after the formal floor show (comprising of pianist and singer) had finished, a customer asked the pianist to play a particular song to which she sang. Others not in her party were drawn to join in until the whole 'audience', customers of the bar, were either singing or listening to this impromptu performance.

Whilst to the external observer the memorable moment appears to have been caused by customers spontaneously singing/creating a musical event (Lugosi, 2008) this would not have been possible if the bar had not employed a good piano player to 'co-create' the experience. Each customer may indeed have considered their experience 'unique' but, as is demonstrated, each 'unique' musical event occurring in that bar was in fact supported by management, bar staff, entertainment staff and the customers themselves (Lugosi, 2008). One of the authors of this chapter was enchanted, upon moving to a new area, to discover a local pub wherein, apparently, the locals spontaneously broke into extraordinarily harmonious song on a regular basis. Later it was discovered that the landlord paid a pint per person for the singing and that the singers were gifted locals using the pub as a practice venue. Either way the atmosphere was excellent and the pub always full.

These experiences reinforce the idea that memorable experiences are co-created by staff, management and customers themselves, and that all have significant parts to play. However, it also introduces a paradox referred to at the start of the chapter. If restaurant and bar staff jobs are generally considered to be low skilled and subject to frequent turnover, how can the hospitality industry develop the confident and skilled staff needed to support a memorable experience?

Constructing the Bar and Restaurant 'Experience'

As Lashley *et al.* (2002) show there are employers for whom staff are simply a low-skilled constantly changing part of the service equation. Perhaps, as previously mentioned, for those consumers participating in a feeding event rather than a meal occasion, staff interaction is not particularly relevant. Indeed, if in a hurry, for example, the development of an off-scripted potentially delaying experience may be extremely unwelcome. In food service outlets catering primarily to these types of need, the highly scripted functional behaviour required by large companies to attain a uniform standard of service amongst inexperienced staff may be the most appropriate. However, in those outlets purporting to offer the enjoyment, entertainment (Telfer, 1996) and hospitality required for social dining out occasions, as Harris *et al.* (2003), Johanson and Woods (2008) and Lynch (2005) argue, detailed scripting of the service encounter may lead to 'mindless' and 'habitual' behaviour. This in turn leads to an inauthentic and unconvincing hospitality experience.

Following the analogy of applying theatrical metaphors for the restaurant experience, there is a considerable difference between an actor simply reciting a given script and that actor acting authentically in role and/or character. The implication here for the delivery of a truly authentic and genuine restaurant experience lies in the ability of management to empower their technically skilled staff to go 'off-script'. In fact, Lundberg and Mossberg (2008) suggest that many of the soft-skills required to do this are learnt by IWOL (informal word-of-mouth). Whist Lugosi and Bray (2008) suggest that IWOL has the benefit of developing experiential knowledge and thus self confidence; it is also, by definition, often beyond the control of management.

Hochschild (1983) was one of the first to discuss the concept of deep and shallow acting to describe how staff cope with the demands of emotional labour, that is to say the role and behaviour which management expect from staff in the inevitable staff customer interaction of a hospitable experience. Deep acting is where the employee genuinely takes on the role that they are playing, shallow acting is when, as Erickson (2004a) confirms, the employee detaches themselves emotionally from the activity of providing service, the Orwellian approach. Crang further notes a third acting approach whereby a busy member of waiting staff, using urgent posture and movement, can deliberately temper 'any frustration felt by customers with a notable performance of [a] dutiful work rate' (Crang, 1994: 689).

Kim (2008) and Lovell (2009) both suggest that those service staff who choose to engage in deep acting, the development of trust and natural hospitality during the service encounter, find the experience emotionally rewarding. They enjoy the activity of serving customers, enjoy hosting the event and enjoy developing a long term relationship with regular customers. Luria and Yagil (2008) suggest that in a restaurant business which has a culture of ethical and fair behaviour towards their employees, the employees will naturally behave in a fair and ethical way towards the customers. This is because they feel empowered and, as Raub (2008) confirms, empowered employees are more likely to be able to be spontaneous, thus enabling a natural experience to occur. This, along with previous discussion (Baum, 2006; O'Connor, 2005; Walter, 2008; Warhurst & Nickson, 2001), suggests that the best service staff are those who are naturally hospitable and work in an environment which empowers them to utilise their hard and soft-skills whenever the moment requires it.

However, there is evidence that the type of interaction/performance required varies between servicescapes, particularly between the restaurant and bar. Erickson (2004a, 2004b), Lundberg and Mossberg (2008), Raub (2008), Seymour and Sandiford (2005) all show that bar staff and restaurant staff view their participation differently. They also suggest that the nature of the occasion itself, feeding or meal, restaurant or pub (drink led), will influence how the same member of staff will act within each servicescape.

Seymour and Sandiford (2005) carried out an ethnographic study of individual units of a medium-sized chain of English public houses that manage approximately 160 properties. The interviewees in their research were partly made up of bar staff who worked in both the bar area as well as the pubs' restaurants. Many explained that they preferred to work in the bar rather than the restaurant. Supporting Erickson's (2004a) findings in a small family-style Tex-Mex restaurant in Minneapolis, Minnesota, USA, Seymour and Sandiford showed that there seemed to be a general feeling that restaurant service required a different approach to service from that found in the bar area.

In Seymour and Sandiford's (2005) work, a number of the staff highlighted the level of formality and personal authenticity required by customers in the bar and restaurant areas as being important differences between working in a bar or restaurant servicescape. The staff who expressed a preference for working behind the bar explained that they felt it was acceptable to show their own personality in the bar area, rather than feeling limited by a stuffy restaurant setting where they would feel obliged to take on a more prescribed and formal role. The implication here is that working in a public-house bar empowers service personnel to use their own judgement and construct their own 'script' much more than in the formal prescribed service encounter of a restaurant servicescape. However, since wages in a pub/bar in the UK are not usually dependant upon tips unlike most restaurants, Crang's (1994) and Gardner and Woods' (1991) findings may suggest that there is a greater need to 'work' the customers in a restaurant setting. This may impact consciously or unconsciously upon perceptions of behaviours required in the different servicescapes.

Seymour and Sandiford's (2005) findings were replicated in more recent research conducted by Gibbs (2008) who conducted research with employees who worked in the bar and bistro servicescapes of one case study hotel in South Wales, UK. Some staff worked in both areas, some in only one. One interviewee specifically commented on how the bar staff and bistro staff seem suited to different personality types and personality predispositions. She remarked that:

> You've got different personalities on the bar and the bistro...I think there are certain members of staff that work on the bar that are suited to the bar and wouldn't be suited to the bistro and vice versa...It's more jokey and casual and fun in the bar and that tends to suit the personalities who work there...I think that the staff who work in the bistro also tend to be more serious than those who work in the bar. (Gibbs, 2008: 59)

Another interviewee, commenting upon personality types and place of service, explained that although she felt she was the same person and retained her integrity and authenticity in both the bar and the bistro, she was aware that others behaved differently:

> I know that I'm the same person whether I'm doing a shift in the bar or the bistro, but there are other members of staff here who do put on an act and change a lot when they're working in the bistro. I think they might think they have to be a different person when they're in the bistro because there's a different environment down there. (Gibbs, 2008: 60)

There was a perception that those who worked behind the bar were allowed/encouraged to express their own personalities. More significantly, there was a commonly held perception that the same customers were more likely to treat the bar staff as social equals than staff encountered in the bistro/restaurant. Again this may have a relationship to tipping cultures since you don't tip peers, friends or equals.

Erickson's (2004a) work suggested that there is a further subculture at work even when the bar and restaurant are part of the same physical building or space. It suggests that the bar is viewed by staff and customers as a more sexual, freer space than the restaurant. Supporting this view, Jonsson *et al.* (2008) and Lin *et al.* (2008) both also suggest that suitability for the service role in a particular servicescape may be gender dependant. All of this discussion suggests that perhaps the bar is analogous to the stand-up comedians' act which depends upon interaction with the audience, whilst the restaurant is more referent to the staged play; we watch, our emotions are engaged but we don't have to participate actively.

Managing Rationally or Enabling Memorable Moments?

The creation of theatre in restaurant certainly seems to be dependant upon skilled and empowered staff choosing voluntarily to collaborate with customers to create memorable experiences as they occur. Since this inevitably means varying from the basic routine it may well incur time costs (Noone, 2008). Good musicians and actors are all highly trained and their skills highly regarded; they are also paid to reflect and perform these skills. The employment of technically skilled, professional, empowered front of house staff would increase labour costs as well as time costs. However, it is also likely to have the benefit of being able to support positive experiences and memories which will be shared with others who may then be encouraged to actively seek a similar experience at the same establishment for themselves.

Conversely, the authors agree with Lugosi (2007) in suggesting that some memorable experiences happen spontaneously. Therefore, the question has to be asked as to whether memorable experiences should be managed at all since this has the potential to turn the experience into a Disneyesque replica of an authentic experience? However, the staged performance, gustatory experience, that Gillespie (2001) describes certainly suggests that some memorable experiences can, may even need to, be managed and yet they will still retain their authenticity. Paradoxically, as this chapter has pointed out, not all consumers are looking for memorable experiences each time they eat outside the home. In many situations a functional, pragmatic familiar service may well meet their needs providing the experience they want at that time. Therefore, the authors also question whether or not the hospitality industry really needs to seek to provide memorable experiences in all food and drink servicescapes. Is it really cost effective to do so?

Lugosi's (2007) examination of the role of customers' participation in the production of commercial hospitality argued that existing academic approaches are inadequate in so far that they have tended to focus narrowly on the managerial aspects of both participation and performance in the service encounter. The authors of this chapter concur but also argue that whilst it is very important to provide customers with the experience they want each time they eat out, we are only at the beginning of understanding what constitutes a memorable experience for differing customers at different moments in time. Was it the unexpected offer of a baby's high chair to a harassed parent; that moment when Gordon Ramsey came into the restaurant and stopped at the table to chat; when the barman created a cocktail to celebrate your engagement; when the person at the table next door turned out to be a long-lost old friend?

This chapter suggests that just as sometimes we want to go to a play, sometimes to a comedy show and sometimes are happy to be entertained by street performances, so we require differing experiences and differing levels of staff support and interaction across a range of situations. What we don't fully understand as yet is how to meet a range of customer needs which create a range of memorable moments. Further research is therefore needed in order to establish consumer perceptions of what constitutes a feeding event and what constitutes a meal experience. It will then be possible to more fully understand how to construct appropriate meal experiences.

References

Andersson, T.D. and Mossberg, L. (2004) The dining experience: Do restaurants satisfy customer needs? *Food Service Technology* 4, 171–177.

Baum, T. (2006) *Human Resource Management for Tourism, Hospitality and Leisure: An International Perspective*. London: Thompson.

Beardsworth, A. and Keil, T. (2000) *Sociology on the Menu*. London: Routledge.

Bernhardt, S. (1920) *The Art of the Theatre*. London: Geoffrey Bles.

Berry, L. (1981) The employee as customer. *Journal of Retail Banking* 3, 33–40.

Bitner, M. (1992) Servicescapes: The impact of physical surroundings on customers and employees. *Journal of Marketing* 56, 57–71.

Black, M. (1993) Medieval Britain. In M. Black (ed.) *A Taste of History: 10,000 Years of Food in Britain* (pp. 95–136). London: English Heritage in association with British Museum Press.

Booms, B. and Bitner, M. (1981) Marketing strategies and organisational structures. In J. Donnelly and W. George (eds) *Marketing of Services* (pp. 47–51). Chicago, IL: American Marketing Association.

Bourdieu, P. (1977) *Outlines of a Theory of Practice* (R. Nice, trans.). Cambridge: Cambridge University Press.

Burns, P. (1997) Hard-skills and soft-skills: Undervaluing hospitality service with a smile. *Progress in Tourism and Hospitality Research* 3, 239–248.

Camilleri, F. (2008) Hospitality and the ethics of improvisation in the work of Ingemar Lindh. *New Theatre Quarterly* 24 (3 No.95), 246–259.

Caru, A. and Cova, B. (2003) Revisiting consumption experience: A more humble but complete view of the concept. *Marketing Theory* 3, 267–286.

Chan, B. and Coleman, M. (2004) Skills and competencies needed for the Hong Kong hotel industry: The perspective of the hotel human resources manager. *Journal of Human Resources in Hospitality and Tourism* 3 (1), 3–18.

Christy, R. and Norris, G. (1999) Discovery markets: Communicating product identities in specialised sectors. *British Food Journal* 101 (10), 797–808.

Crang, P. (1994) It's showtime: On the workplace geographies of display in a restaurant in southeast England. *Environment and Planning: Society and Space* 12, 675–704.

Edwards, J.S.A. and Gustafsson, I-B. (2008) The five aspects meal model. *Journal of Foodservice* 19 (1), 4–12.

Erikson, K. (2004a) Bodies at work: Performing service in American restaurants. *Space and Culture* 7 (1), 76–89.

Erikson, K. (2004b) To invest or detach? Coping strategies and workplace culture in service work. *Symbolic Interaction* 27 (4), 549–572.

Gardner, K. and Woods, R.C. (1991) Theatricality in food service. *International Journal of Hospitality Management* 10 (3), 267–278.

Gibbs, D. (2008) Service with a smile? A case study exploring the relationship between the service encounter and the meal experience. MA Thesis, University of Wales Institute.

Gillespie, C. (2001) *European Gastronomy into the 21st Century.* Oxford: Elsevier Butterworth Heinemann.

Goffman, E. (1959) *The Presentation of Self in Everyday Life.* New York: Doubleday.

Grove, S.J. and Fisk, R.P. (1989) Impression management in services marketing: A dramaturgical perspective. In R. Giacalone and P. Rosenfield (eds) *Impression Management in the Organisation* (pp. 427–438). Hillsdale, NJ: Lawrence Erlbaum.

Guerrier, Y. and Adib, A. (2003) Work at leisure and leisure at work: A study of the emotional labour of tour reps. *Human Relations* 56 (11), 1399–1417.

Gupta, S. and Vajic, M. (2000) The contextual and dialectical nature of experiences. In J.A. Fitzsimmons and M.A. Fitzsimmons (eds) *New Services Development: Creating Memorable Experiences* (pp. 33–51). Thousand Oaks, CA: Sage.

Gustafsson, I.B. (2004) Culinary arts and meal service – a new scientific research discipline. *Food Service Technology* 4, 9–20.

Gustafsson, I.B., Ostrom, A., Johnson, J. and Mossberg, L. (2006) The five aspects meal model: A tool for developing meal services. *Journal of Foodservice* 17, 84–93.

Hall, J., Lockshin, L. and O'Mahoney, B. (2001) Exploring the links between wine choice and dining occasions: Factors of influence. *International Journal of Wine Marketing* 13 (1), 36–53.

Hallier, J. and Butts, S. (1999) Employers' discovery of training: Self-development, employability and the rhetoric of partnership. *Employee Relations* 21, 80–95.

Hansen, K.V., Jensen, O. and Gustaffson, I.B. (2005) The meal experiences of a la carte restaurant customers. *Scandinavian Journal of Hospitality and Tourism* 5, 135–151.

Harris, R., Harris, K. and Baron, S. (2003) Theatrical service experience. *International Journal of Service Industry Management* 14, 184–199.

Hemmington, N. (2007) From service to experience: Understanding and defining the hospitality business. *Service Industries Journal* 27 (6), 747–755.

Hochschild, A. (1983) *The Managed Heart.* Berkeley: University of California Press.

Holbrook, M.B. (2001) Times Square, Disneyphobia, HegeMickey, the Ricky principle, and the downside of the entertainment economy. *Marketing Theory* 1, 139–163.

Johanson, M.M. and Woods, R.H. (2008) Recognising the emotional element in service excellence. *Cornell Hospitality Quarterly* 49 (3), 310–316.

Johns, N. and Howard, A. (1998) Customer expectations versus perceptions of service performance in the foodservice industry. *International Journal of Service Industry Management* 9 (3), 248–265.

Jones, M. (2007) *Feast: Why Humans Share Food*. Oxford: Oxford University Press.

Jonsson, I.M., Ekstrom, M.P. and Nygren, T. (2008) Key concepts towards a stance on gender in the restaurant. *Journal of Foodservice* 19, 53–62.

Kant I. (2005) Objective and subjective senses: The sense of taste. In C. Korsmeyer (ed.) *The Taste Culture Reader: Experiencing Food and Drink* (pp. 209–214). New York: Berg.

Kim, H.J. (2008) Hotel service providers' emotional labour: The antecedents and effects on burnout. *International Journal of Hospitality Management* 27, 151–161.

Kivela, J., Inbrakaran, R. and Reece, J. (2000) Consumer research in the restaurant environment – Part 3: Analysing, findings and conclusions. *International Journal of Contemporary Hospitality Management* 12, 13–30.

Lashley, C., Morrison, A. and Randall, S. (2004) My most memorable meal ever! Hospitality as an emotional experience. In D. Sloan (ed.) *Culinary Taste: Consumer Behaviour in the International Restaurant Sector* (pp. 165–184). Oxford: Elsevier Butterworth Heinemann.

Lashley, C., Rowson, W. and Thomas, R. (2002) *Employment Practices and Skill Shortages in Greater Manchester's Tourism Sector*. Leeds: Leeds Metropolitan University.

Lin, M-Q., Huang, L-S. and Chiang, Y-F. (2008) The moderating effects of gender roles on service emotional contagion. *The Service Industries Journal* 28 (6), 753–767.

Lovell, G. (2009) Can I trust you? Meaning, definition and application of trust in hospitality service settings. *Tourism and Hospitality: Planning and Development* 6 (2), 145–157.

Lugosi, P. (2007) Consumer participation in commercial hospitality. *International Journal of Culture, Tourism and Hospitality Research* 1 (3), 227–236.

Lugosi, P. (2008) Hospitality spaces, hospitable moments: Consumer encounters and affective experiences in commercial settings. *Journal of Foodservice* 19, 139–149.

Lugosi, P. and Bray, J. (2008) Tour guiding, organisational culture and learning: Lessons from an entrepreneurial company. *International Journal of Tourism Research* 10, 467–479.

Lundberg, C. and Mossberg, L. (2008) Learning by sharing: Waiters' and bartenders' experience of service encounters. *Journal of Foodservice* 19, 44–52.

Luria, G. and Yagil, D. (2008) Procedural justice, ethical climate and service outcomes in restaurants. *International Journal of Hospitality Management* 27, 276–283.

Lynch, P. (2005) Sociological impressionism in a hospitality context. *Annals of Tourism Research* 32, 527–548.

Meiselman, H.L. (2006) The role of context in food choice, food acceptance and food consumption. In R. Shepherd and M. Raats (ed.) *The Psychology of Food Choice* (pp. 179–200). Wllington: CABI.

Mintel International Group Ltd. (2007) *Eating Out Review*. London: Mintel Publications.

Mintel International Group Ltd. (2008) *Consumer Attitudes Towards Customer Service in Eating Out*. London: Mintel Publications.

Morgan, M., Watson, P. and Hemmington, N. (2008) Drama in the dining room: Theatrical perspectives on the foodservice encounter. *Journal of Foodservice* 19, 111–118.

Nickson, D. (2007) *Human Resource Management for the Hospitality and Tourism Industries.* Oxford: Elsevier Butterworth Heinemann.

Nickson, D., Warhurst, C. and Dutton, E. (2005) The importance of attitude and appearance in the service encounter in retail and hospitality. *Managing Service Quality* 15 (2), 195–208.

Noone, B.B. (2008) Customer perceived control and the moderating effect of restaurant type on evaluations of restaurant employee performance. *International Journal of Hospitality Management* 27, 23–29.

O'Connor, D. (2005) Towards a new interpretation of "hospitality". *International Journal of Contemporary Hospitality Management* 17 (3), 267–271.

Orwell, G. (1933) *Down and Out in Paris and London.* London: Penguin.

Pine, B.J. and Gilmore, J.H. (1999) *The Experience Economy: Work is Theatre and Every Business is a Stage.* Boston, MA: HBS Press.

Prahalad, C.K. and Ramaswamy, V. (2004) *The Future of Competition: Co-Creating Unique Vale with Customers.* Boston, MA: Harvard Business School Press.

Pratten, J.D. (2003) Customer satisfaction and waiting staff. *International Journal of Contemporary Hospitality Management* 16 (6), 385–388.

Pritchard, M. (1981) *Guests and Hosts.* Oxford: Oxford University Press.

Raub, S. (2008) Does bureaucracy kill individual initiative? The impact of structure on organisational citizenship behaviour in the hospitality industry. *International Journal of Hospitality Management* 27, 179–186.

Ritchie, C. (2007) Beyond drinking: The role of wine in the life of the UK consumer. *International Journal of Consumer Studies* 31, 534–540.

Rozin, P. (2006) The integration of biological, social, cultural and psychological influences on food choice. In R. Shepherd and M. Raats (eds) *The Psychology of Food Choice* (pp. 19–40). Wallingford: CABI.

Schechner, R. (1977) *Performance Theory.* London: Routledge.

Schmitt, B.H. (1999) *Experiential Marketing: How to Get Companies to Sense, Feel, Think, Act and Relate to Your Company and Brands.* New York: Free Press.

Schmitt, B.H. (2003) *Customer Experience Management: A Revolutionary Approach to Connecting with Your Customers.* Hoboken, NJ: John Wiley.

Secrest, M. (1992) *Frank Lloyd Wright: A Biography.* Chicago, IL: University of Chicago Press.

Seymour, D. and Sandiford, P. (2005) Learning emotion rules in service organisations: Socialisation and training in the UK public-house sector. *Work, Employment and Society* 19, 547–563.

Shakespeare, W. (1599) *As You Like It.* London: Penguin.

Shaw, C. (2005) *Revolutionise Your Customer Experience.* Basingstoke: Palgrave Macmillan.

Smith, S. and Wheeler, J. (2002) *Managing the Customer Experience: Turning Customers into Advocates.* Harlow, Essex: FT Prentice Hall.

Shaw, G. and Williams, A. (1994) The effects of diversity on small group work processes and performance. *Human Relations* 51 (10), 1307–1325.

Stein, S. and Brooks, H. (2000) *The EQ Edge: Emotional Intelligence and Your Success.* London: Kogan Page.

Stuart, I.F. (2006) Designing and executing memorable service experiences: Lights, camera, experiment, integrate, action! *Business Horizons* 49, 149–159.

Telfer, E. (1996) *Food for Thought; Philosophy and Food.* London: Routledge.

Telfer, E. (2000) The philosophy of hospitableness. In C. Lashley and A. Morrison (eds) *In Search of Hospitality: Theoretical Perspectives and Debates* (pp. 38–55). Oxford: Elsevier Butterworth Heinemann.

Walter, U. (2008) The meeting aspect and the physical setting: Are they important for the guest experience? *Journal of Foodservice* 19, 87–95.

Warde, A. and Martens, L. (2000) *Eating Out: Social Differentiation, Consumption and Pleasure*. New York: Cambridge Press.

Warhurst, C. and Nickson, D. (2001) *Looking Good and Sounding Right*. London: Industrial Society.

Westwood, A. (2002) *Is New Work Good Work?* London: The Work Foundation Press.

Williams, J.A. and Anderson, H.H. (2005) Engaging customers in service creation: A theatre perspective. *Journal of Services Marketing* 19 (1), 13–23.

Chapter 11

Tourism Memorabilia and the Tourism Experience

NICOLE FERDINAND and NIGEL L. WILLIAMS

Introduction

This chapter seeks to provide an understanding of the significant role that production and sale of tourism memorabilia has for the tourism industry and the tourism experience that organisations provide. It begins by outlining the range of items that constitute tourism memorabilia and the multiple meanings and functions these items have for both their consumers and producers. It then explores the significant benefits that tourism memorabilia provides for tourists, businesses in tourism and related industries, governments and destinations. The central focus of the chapter is how different concepts of the tourism experience can uncover a range of opportunities for organisations to utilise tourism memorabilia to enhance their offerings to tourists. Examples are drawn from North America and Europe to show how organisations ranging from cultural preservation societies and museums to airlines and hotels can use tourism memorabilia to enhance the tourism experience they provide. Also discussed is the potential for tourism memorabilia to provide authenticity and to commoditise the tourism experience. The chapter closes with a case study of a local souvenir provider from the Caribbean which illustrates previously highlighted issues.

What is Tourism Memorabilia?

Tourism memorabilia or souvenirs cover a wide range of merchandise purchased by tourists within destinations. They can be described as commercially produced and purchased objects used to remind the purchaser of the tourism experience (Swanson & Horridge, 2006). These objects can range from jewellery trinkets and T-shirts to expensive, highly ornate crafts, artworks and clothing (Weaver & Lawton, 2006). However, memorabilia can also include items that are not commercially produced or purchased such as ticket stubs, rocks, drift wood or sea shells.

The buying and selling of memorabilia has always been part of the tourism experience and contributes to the viability of the retail trade in many tourism destination areas (Jansen-Verbeke, 1998). From the time of the earliest tourists, there has been a human impulse to acquire memorabilia or souvenirs to commemorate the tourism experience. Inscriptions, dating back to 1244 BC, were found in ancient Egyptian pyramids and monuments, which describe the acquisition of souvenirs by ancient tourists. The acquisition of souvenirs was also prevalent among the young men of the aristocratic classes embarking on Grand Tours during the mid-16th to 19th centuries. These travellers, mainly young men from the United Kingdom and other parts of northern Europe, brought back goods which significantly influenced social and cultural trends at the time. Their demand for souvenirs also had economic impacts for the destinations they visited, through the establishment of souvenir trade by locals (Weaver & Lawton, 2006).

For the tourist, the acquisition of tourism memorabilia can vary significantly in terms of function and meaning. Gordon's (1986) typology of souvenirs illustrates the various functions and meanings that tourism memorabilia have for tourists. The typology identifies five categories of souvenirs-pictorial image, piece-of-the-rock, symbolic shorthand, markers and local products. Each of the categories reveals a particular function or meaning for tourism memorabilia. Pictorial images (for e.g. post cards or photographs) are either sent to someone else or kept by the tourist. In both instances, the pictorial image is meant to serve as a snapshot of the location visited. Pieces of rock souvenirs are gathered from nature to represent non-urban environments. Examples of piece of rock souvenirs can include pinecones, seashells, rocks and pebbles. A symbolic shorthand souvenir is a manufactured object that evokes a short hand code or message about the place it came from. Typical symbolic shorthand souvenirs are miniature replicas of iconic buildings and other landmarks. They often serve functional purposes such as key chains, coffee mugs or letter openers, allowing the symbol of the extraordinary tourism experience to be used in everyday life. Markers are items inscribed with words that locate them in a certain place and time. Perhaps the most readily recognisable markers are printed T-shirts. Local product souvenirs such as food and clothing are made from indigenous materials and serve as cultural artefacts of the country or region from which they originated.

It is also possible to view tourism memorabilia from the perspective of the producers rather than the buyers of these items. In this case, they will be defined by the purpose for which they were produced. When these items are produced for the branding or promotion of a company or destination, they will be viewed as part of the promotional mix used by a company or country to publicise its tourism product (Pine & Gilmore, 1999).

If these items are produced as cultural artefacts of a particular country, city or village, they can be viewed as signifiers of ideological meanings and reflections of social and political relations (Shenhav-Keller, 1993).

Conversely, the cultural artefacts that are offered for sale as memorabilia, in a particular destination, can also reveal the extent to which tourism has eroded the meaning and authenticity of the items sold. They can powerfully demonstrate how tourism has commoditised a destination's culture by the extent to which they have been altered in response to the perceived or actual demands of the tourist market (Greenwood, 1989; King & Stewart, 1996).

The Importance of Tourism Memorabilia for Tourism and Related Industries

Just as tourism experiences are viewed as part of a wider experience economy as defined by Pine and Gilmore (1999), tourism memorabilia can be seen as part of the wider memorabilia industry which is worth billions of dollars (US) worldwide. This is an extremely profitable business as these items 'generally sell at price points far above those commanded by similar items that don't commemorate an experienced locale or event' because 'the price point functions as less of an indicator of the costs of the goods than of the value the buyer attaches to remembering the experience' (Pine & Gilmore, 1999: 57). Thus the sale of memorabilia provides attractive financial opportunities to the providers of tourism experiences to substantially increase their revenues by capitalising on their customers' desires for nostalgia.

Tourism memorabilia can also be viewed as part of tourist shopping, which has been acknowledged as one of the most important aspects of tourism (Law & Au, 2000). Tourists often spend more on shopping than they do on food, lodging, or other activities (Jansen-Verbeke, 1991; Timothy & Butler, 1995). For some tourists shopping can be important motivational factor for making a trip (Timothy, 2005) or a pull-factor of a particular destination (Oh *et al.*, 1995). Researchers have also found that without shopping activity, a tour cannot be a complete travelling experience (Hudman & Hawkins, 1989; Keowin, 1989).

Additionally, due the vast range of products that constitute tourism memorabilia, the tourism memorabilia business can be seen as one that cuts across sectors (e.g. clothing, food, arts and crafts) providing opportunities for a range of producers from large operators of visitor attractions, hotel chains and packaged tours to cottage industries producing local handicraft items. The variety of tourism memorabilia items also presents opportunities for producers to target a range of customer segments. Littrell *et al.* (1994) developed four tourist profiles based on their purchase of tourism memorabilia. These were ethnic, arts, and people; history and parks; urban entertainment; and active outdoor. Ethnic, arts, and people-oriented tourists were described as those that purchased jewellery, local foods, antiques and books. History and parks-oriented tourists bought crafts, postcards, books about the area, local foods and items chosen as part of a collection. Urban entertainment-oriented tourists were likely to buy markers such as T-shirts or other mementos that symbolised the destination visited. The final tourism style, active outdoor-oriented did not view souvenir purchasing as particularly important but when they did buy souvenirs, they chose to purchase T-shirts, sweatshirts and items that originated in nature.

Each of these perspectives serves to highlight the significant economic benefits the sale of tourism memorabilia can generate in terms of revenue and also employment for tourism and related industries. Furthermore, the sale of tourism memorabilia can also have positive spill-over effects for a destination. A well managed tourist shopping experience has the potential to contribute to a more favourable image of a tourist destination (Tosun *et al.*, 2007), and the sale of cultural products that are specific to a country or region can provide a competitive advantage for a destination (Pugh & Wood, 2004). The production of tourism memorabilia, especially handcrafted items, has also been used by governments as a means of cultural regeneration. A strategy which involves the targeting of tourist markets for locally made, handcrafted items can potentially revitalise dying art forms, maintain traditional ways of life and build community pride whilst at the same time generating revenue and creating jobs which can substantially improve the economic outlook for a destination. However, as highlighted previously, if care is not taken in pursuing these benefits such initiatives can become simply 'a gimmick to attract more tourists' and render the items produced 'commodities to be traded in the global cause of tourism development' (Clarke, 2000: 33).

Models of Tourism Experience and their Implications for the Role of Tourism Memorabilia

The tourism experience is a widely researched topic within the social sciences as well marketing and management. Academics have put forward a plethora of models of the tourism experience (see Chapter 1). However, none of them concretely define the components of tourism or explain what exactly constitutes a tourism experience. This makes understanding the role of tourism memorabilia in the tourism experience problematic, as its role(s) can be understood in a range of contexts, according to the paradigm by which the tourism experience is conceived. The models that are described below are illustrative of this point. Each provides a set of opportunities for tourism memorabilia to be used to enhance the tourism experience.

Tourism as a temporal experience

Killion (1992) using the Clawson (1963) recreation experience model defined the 'travel' experience in terms of five phases. These consisted of a planning phase, a travel to phase, an on-site activities phase, a return travel phase and a re-collection phase. The key difference between Killion's and Clawson's model, is Killion's presentation of the experience as circular. Clawson in contrast, represents the experience as a linear model with specific beginning and end points. A simpler model proposed by Craig-Smith and French (1994), views the 'vacation' experience as three linear phases with previous experiences informing future ones. These are an anticipatory phase, an experiential phase and a reflective phase. Both these models define the tourism experience in terms of the passage of the time and seek to chronologically map the experience. They therefore suggest opportunities for tourism memorabilia to enhance the tourism experience during specific time periods.

Pre-experience ('planning' or 'anticipation' phase)

Tourism memorabilia items are typically purchased during or after the completion of the tourism experience. Thus, there may be a tendency to overlook opportunities to enhance the tourism experience, prior to the tourist's visit to a destination. However, tourism memorabilia when sold as promotional items, in addition to promoting tourism experiences, as part of a company or a destination's promotional mix, can potentially serve to shape a customer or a visitor's prior expectations of the tourism experience. Memorabilia items are usually bought to be displayed in the owner's country of origin as status symbols. They may also be frequently worn pieces of clothing and accessories, such as hats, T-shirts, bags and necklaces (Weaver & Lawton, 2006). Returning tourists, as a result, become walking advertisements for the company's services they have used or the destination they have visited. Additionally, as observed by Pine and Gilmore (1999), one of the key functions of memorabilia is the transmission experiences to others by the generation of conversation. Thus, items that commemorate particularly memorable experiences of a trip can generate valuable word-of-mouth advertising for companies or destinations which creates anticipation and excitement and which can shape the travel plans of potential customers.

During the experience ('on-site activities' or 'experiential' phase)

The importance of shopping as a part of the tourism experience has already been highlighted as the absence of it could render a tour incomplete. Shopping is also highlighted as a common preferred tourism activity for many destinations (Cook, 1995; Jansen-Verbeke, 1991; Timothy & Butler, 1995). Onderwater *et al.* (2000) also argue that the purchase of tourism memorabilia influences visitors' overall tourism experiences while visiting a destination. The importance of shopping and the purchase of tourism memorabilia during the 'on-site activities' or 'experiential' phases of the tourism experience, demonstrate the potential for the purchase of tourism memorabilia to be used both as an enhancement and as integral part of the tourism experience.

Real (2000) outlines how HandMade in America, a non-profit organisation, dedicated to preserving the quality of life in the western region of North Carolina, took advantage of the link between shopping and cultural tourism. The organisation devised a unique shopping experience for tourists interested in purchasing handcrafted items from the region. Working with representatives from over 20 countries, it designed a series of craft heritage trails through towns and villages where a visitor could discover the heritage of the area, as represented by its handcrafted traditions. The organisation also published these trails in a book entitled *The Craft Heritage Trails of West North Carolina*, giving each tour in the book a theme, with each tour including not only shops where authentic American and North Carolinian items are sold, but also restaurants, accommodations and other attractions that focus on providing an authentic experience.

The craft heritage trails of West North Carolina illustrate how shopping for tourism memorabilia can become an integral part of the tourism experience that can be combined with other activities such as visits to restaurants and historical sites for a truly unique, packaged tour. The book, also a piece of tourism memorabilia, enhances the tourism experience, by providing a comprehensive guide of recommended, authentic shops, accommodation and heritage sites. It gives tourists a range of vetted options on which they can design their own itineraries, which saves time and eliminates risk, allowing them to concentrate on enjoyable activities.

Post-experience ('re-collection' or 'reflexive' phase)

Gordon's (1986) typology of souvenirs mentioned previously, illustrates the range of meanings and functions tourism memorabilia can have for the tourist. After their return from a destination souvenirs may serve as pictorial or symbolic reminders of a destination, markers which commemorate a moment in time, representations of the local environment or cultural artefacts from a particular place or culture. The purchase of tourism memorabilia also satisfies tourists' desires for novelty (Lee *et al.*, 2009), 'authenticity' (Littrel *et al.*, 1993), collecting (Squire, 1994) social status and even the envy of others (Pine & Gilmore, 1999). By understanding the range of desires that tourism memorabilia satisfies for tourists and the specific needs of individual customer segments, the producers of these items can significantly enhance buyers' post-tourism experiences.

Research undertaken by Squire (1994) highlights how Hill Top Farm fulfils the needs and desires of its female buyers of tourism memorabilia, thereby facilitating their enhanced post-tourism experiences. Hill Top Farm is a commemorative museum dedicated to the memory of Beatrix Potter, deceased author of the popular children's book *The Tale of Peter Rabbit*. Recognising the role of women as mothers and custodians of family tradition and their potential to forge associations between Potter, childhood and family life, Hill Top Farm targets its marketing and merchandising activities primarily towards women and children. Interviews of female visitors undertaken by Squire revealed that women visiting the Hill Top shop bought souvenirs as gifts, functional items to be used in nurseries, collectables and in the case of the female Japanese visitors, status symbols. Some also bought souvenirs simply to engage in childhood nostalgia. The Hill Top shop offers a range of items to satisfy these needs and desires including, books, nursery furnishings, china, figurines, toys and handkerchiefs.

In-between experiences ('travel to' and 'return travel' phases)

Transportation operators play an important role in the tourism experience. However, as observed by Jennings and Weller (2006: 63) transportation providers as 'informal brokers' of the tourism experience are largely invisible and thus they go unnoticed and unrewarded. This suggests that the travel time to and from destinations will not be occasions that tourists want to remember or commemorate with memorabilia. Pine and Gilmore (1999), in contrast, propose any business, given the proper stage setting, can mix memorabilia into its offering. They assert that if airlines staged well managed experiences more passengers would want to shop in the seat-pocket catalogues for mementos.

KLM Royal Dutch Airlines, through its use innovative of souvenirs, have turned the routine task of air travel into something that their customers look forward to. Michaels (2008) relates how even in times when airlines are faced with increasing pressures to cut costs, KLM have not stopped producing their Dutch house-shaped liquor bottles. He explains that today, they remain a rare symbol of frivolity of times past. The bottles were launched in 1952 and became an instant hit. They were initially only given to first-class passengers and became a symbol of success and of an international jet-setting life-style, prominently displayed in homes as trophies. Even though KLM no longer offers first-class, the 'houses' as they are called, are still highly sought after by business-class passengers, who often jockey for first pick of the items to assemble complete collections. The airline only carries thirty houses on each flight, which are given to business-class passengers only, so assembling the complete collection of 88 houses is quite a feat. Passengers pay as much as $US40 to buy the houses from other sources, with the special edition houses trading for $US1000 or more. Once when a KLM airliner accidentally took off without its cargo of houses, the pilot radioed ahead to arrange for houses to be available at the landing gate in Amsterdam. Upon arriving at their destination, instead of exiting the plane, business-class passengers waited patiently to collect them.

In an industry faced with soaring fuel prices and cutbacks, KLM airlines still offers its customers seemingly frivolous items of memorabilia. The airline does not sell the items and limits their supply to 30 each flight, ensuring the tiny trophies retain their status. The competition amongst business-class passengers for first pick of the houses and the sheer joy and pride of those with complete collections, clearly illustrate how memorabilia can be used to transform the mundane experience of air travel into something special which adds to the overall tourism experience, instead of being viewed as an interruption or annoyance.

The tourism experience as a staged show

Pine and Gilmore (1999) proposed that businesses were entering an experience economy and that the orchestration of experience will become as much a part of doing business as product and process design, with real life becoming more like show business every day. From their observations of pioneering enterprises, such as popular tourist destinations Disney World and the Hard Rock Café, they provide the following steps for businesses wishing to stage memorable experiences:

Step 1 - Theme the experience.
Step 2 - Harmonise impressions with positive cues.
Step 3 - Eliminate negative cues.
Step 4 - Mix in memorabilia.
Step 5 - Engage the five senses.

They assert that companies should stage unified experiences in which all elements are focused on a well-defined theme. Thus, tourism experience providers following these guidelines should view the theme of their experiences as the central focus and use tourism memorabilia as an element to be added to a mix of impressions and cues, which engage the senses. The authors suggest four ways of by which this can be achieved:

(1) Selling memorabilia associated with the experience.
(2) Turning items inherently associated with the experience into personalised memorabilia.
(3) Giving away limited edition memorabilia items as keepsakes.
(4) Developing new and innovative memorabilia items which customers can personalise for themselves.

In each case, they emphasise the need for memorabilia to be reflective of the theme of the experience provided and to be engaging to the customer. In their book *The Experience Economy: Work is Theatre and Every Business a Stage*, the example of the Ritz, Carlton in Naples Florida, is used as an illustration of how a piece of memorabilia can perfectly reflect the theme of an establishment and capture the imagination of its customers. The hotel, instead of throwing away its old doorknobs, turned them into 463 limited edition paperweights. These were then given to guests who submitted stories of memorable stays at the Ritz, Carlton and with more that 6000 guests sending in stories, the items became a treasured physical reminder of a special experience.

Tourism as a combination of 'peak', consumer and routine experiences

Quan and Wang (2004) have proposed a structural model of the tourist experience which strives to integrate the different dimensions of the tourism experience into a structured whole. They contend for too long the tourism experience has been one-sidedly understood as either a 'peak' experience or a consumer experience.

On reviewing the literature of tourism social science, Quan and Wang concluded that the tourism experience is artificially 'purified' as an experience that is 'in sharp contrast or opposing to the daily experience' (2004: 298), hence the term 'peak' experience. They also highlight the limitations of the treatment of the tourism experience in marketing/ management literature. Too much focus is given to the operational aspects of consumer experiences or behaviours, without fully considering the relationship between supporting consumer experiences and peak experiences. Thus, a conceptual model is proposed, which shows the tourist experience as a combination of peak, consumer and routine experiences.

Using food consumption as illustrative example, Quan and Wang show how different elements of the tourist experience can be either peak experiences or supporting consumer experiences, depending on specific situations. They also assert their structural model is not only applicable to the analysis of the role of food experiences in tourism but a wider range of experiential factors in the tourism experience.

If this model is applied to tourism memorabilia, the ways in which souvenirs have been used by the organisations discussed earlier on in the chapter can be seen as examples in which the purchase of tourism memorabilia have been used as both peak and supporting consumer experiences. The houses given to business-class passengers on KLM airlines also demonstrate how tourism memorabilia can transform a supporting consumer experience like air travel, into a peak experience.

Tourism Memorabilia, the 'Authentic' and the Commodification of Culture

The role of tourism memorabilia in the 'authentic' tourism experience

The use of tourism memorabilia by tourists as a means of satisfying their desires for the 'authentic' has already been identified. One of the key themes in tourism research is tourists' search for the 'authentic'. MacCannell (1976) suggests tourism provides an opportunity for tourists to experience the pristine, primitive and natural, by undertaking a pilgrimage to that which is untouched by modernity. It is assumed that these conditions exist in earlier eras and other places. He asserts that tourists therefore seek out such places to escape from the alienation and meaninglessness of modern life and connect with what is described as the 'authentic'. Cohen's (1989) analysis of Thai hilltribe tourism posters confirms this view of the authentic as the images of timelessness, primitiveness, naturalness and the exotic were found to create the expectation of a tourist adventure among people frozen in time. In other research Cohen asserts '"authenticity" is a socially constructed concept and its social connotation is, therefore, not given, but "negotiable"' (1988: 374). Authenticity is therefore a personally constructed, contextual and changing concept which makes tourists active creators of meaning in the tourism experience rather than passive receivers.

Research on the purchase of memorabilia by tourists, suggests that these items provide opportunities for tourists to preserve their memories of finding the authentic. Gordon (1986) suggested that souvenirs serve as reminders of experiences with people, places and events apart from their daily routine. Littrell (1990) proposed souvenirs inspired tourists to contrast trips with their everyday experiences, to expand their world-view, to differentiate themselves from others, and to experience a more authentic cultural life. Littrel et al. (1993) highlight that the search for authentic souvenirs may become a frantic activity for some tourists, leading them to engage in uncharacteristically extravagant spending. Old and well-used tribal crafts may also appeal to the tourist who buys only new and pristine products when at home (Graburn, 1982). Littrel et al. (1993) found that for tourists authentic souvenirs were those that were unique or original, exhibited a handmade appearance and high-quality workmanship, met aesthetic criteria for colour and design, were functional and useful, illustrate cultural and historical ties, were made with local materials by local artisans and/or sold with information about the maker or written evidence of genuineness. However, some research-ers argue that not all tourists are alienated from their worlds and not all of them are seeking authenticity from the tourism experience (Bruner,

1991). For these tourists what Bruner describes as 'authentic reproductions' (1991: 240–241) may suffice as authentic souvenirs.

Tourism memorabilia and the 'commodification' of culture

The 'commodification' of culture is a concept that has been discussed alongside notions of authenticity in tourism research. Tourism memorabilia has been observed to enhance the authentic tourism experiences of tourists (Gordon, 1986; Littrell, 1990) and also the 'commodification' of those experiences (Graburn, 1982). The 'commodification' of a destination's culture or its transformation into a commodity to satisfy the perceived or actual demands of tourists is highlighted as one of the primary negative socio-cultural impacts of tourism (Greenwood, 1989; King & Stewart, 1996). Weaver and Lawton (2006) note, that the commodification of culture may not necessarily be harmful. It is when the inherent quality and meanings of cultural artefacts and performances become less important than the goal of earning revenue from their reproduction or sale that it becomes something that 'robs people of the very meanings by which they organise their lives' (Greenwood, 1989: 179). MacCannell (1976) suggests that if local people recognise what he describes as the distinction between the 'frontstage' and 'backstage' activities of a destination, they can prevent the negative aspects of commodification from occurring. Locals can select specific performances and displays to be modified for frontstage tourist consumption and set aside others for personal or local use backstage. Cole (2007) also asserts that despite the view of cultural commodification as cultural objectification of the 'West' of a cultural other, it also has the potential to instil a sense of empowerment and pride in local people.

Parananond (2000) provides an example in which the production of tourism memorabilia has been particularly damaging to local culture. Parananond asserts that the way in which the local craftspeople of the Thai city of Chiang Mai have adapted their trade for the tourist market, has led to 'the loss of local knowledge of traditional craft design and production techniques; and the loss of value and meaning of the crafts for the local community' (2000: 215). However, it could be argued that the local craftspeople, much like the native Indian communities in North America, are cultivating a traditional frontstage life for tourists, whilst living a modern life backstage (Weaver & Lawton, 2006). As Parananond (2000) observes, the availability of modern inventions such as refrigerators, enamelware, aluminium ware and plastic have rendered traditionally produced items such as pottery and Lacquer ware obsolete. Thus, the sight of the remaining traditional wooden utensils in huge scrap piles waiting to be turned into tourist souvenirs can be viewed in two ways. On the one hand, it can be viewed as a powerful signifier of the damage that the production and sale of tourism memorabilia has done to the local culture; and on the other, it can simply be viewed as proof of the modern lives that local craftspeople actually lead.

Case Study – PanLand Limited, Trinidad and Tobago – Pan Makers to the World

Trinidad and Tobago, the most southern of the Caribbean islands was discovered in 1498 by Christopher Columbus and remained in Spanish hands until its conquest by the British in 1798. African slaves were brought to the island to work in the sugar plantations and formed the largest segment of the local population. Drums and percussion instruments formed a key part (Barre, 1999) of local ceremonies for the former slaves. Carnival was the largest of these local ceremonies, an annual recreation of plantation fire drills in which the former slaves held parades. Conflict between the African population and the British colonial government resulted in the banning of ceremonial drumming in 1883. Drummers, seeking an alternative to drums, developed sticks made of the local grass bamboo, which could be tuned to provide a range of sounds. These instruments became known as 'Tamboo Bamboo'. Tamboo Bamboo was also declared illegal, and so the drummers developed instruments made from a range of discarded items, including tin cans (Maxime, 1997).

Local musicians soon realised that discarded biscuit and paint tins could be shaped to produce different notes when struck. Winston 'Spree' Simon, a local drummer, began playing melodies on the crude tin instruments in 1939, refining the instrument's shape into a convex (dome-shaped) steel pan (Barre, 1999). Music played on these pans became popular, with the biscuit and paint tins being replaced with oil drums discarded from the local oil industry. In 1946, Ellie Manette created the first steel drum in its concave form, made from a steel 55 gallon oil drum, which remains the dominant design today (Gay, 2005). Steel pan music has continued to develop and is seen as a symbol of Caribbean culture. Orchestras have been formed of various types of pans and they perform in Trinidad and Tobago for Carnival and other festivals. Steel Orchestras also tour internationally, performing to music enthusiasts in Europe, America and Asia. Pans are traditionally produced by hand, by craftsmen in small workshops for use during the Carnival season, which takes place during either the months of January and February or February and March each year.

PanLand Limited was started in 1993 by a local mechanical engineer to manufacture instruments for professional musicians. Its factory was set up in Laventille, a depressed area in Trinidad's capital, near to where innovators such as Winston 'Spree' Simon created the first steel pans. The factory, the largest of its kind, also incorporated customised processing equipment developed by a local research institute. From inception, PanLand Limited targeted export markets as local demand was not sufficient to absorb the factory's output.

While the company sells a range of full sized instruments targeted at professional steel pan musicians, it also produces a range of miniature playable souvenir pans. These souvenirs, which sometimes outsell the professional instruments, attract two main customer segments. The first are older pan players who purchase the items for their children in order to interest them in an aspect of the Trinidad and Tobago culture and the second are tourists who wish to have a unique souvenir item to demonstrate to their friends upon returning home. The souvenir pan's main appeal is its uniqueness. It is an attractive, playable instrument made of metal, in contrast to the typical tourist items of T-shirts and imported plastic products. Panland's original mission was to provide a reliable source of high-quality instruments for professional musicians. However, a significant portion of its revenues is derived from the tourist souvenir market. The souvenir pans are sold at the factory, in addition to a number of retail outlets throughout Trinidad and also at the local airport. The sale of these souvenirs, along with international exports, provides a valuable source of added revenue for the factory outside of the carnival season when most of the professional steel pan instruments are sold.

The souvenir steel pan produced by PanLand Limited is an example of how an item of souvenir memorabilia can serve a variety of needs for both the local community and tourists. The souvenir steel pan provides an opportunity for local professional musicians to introduce a cultural tradition to the next generation. It also provides year round revenues to the local pan factory, making it sustainable, even though the local demand for the instruments is not sufficient to utilise its production capacity. For tourists, the souvenir pan serves as an authentic reminder of Caribbean culture, which is also functional due to its playability, allowing for an authentic tourism experience to be carried over into every day life.

To some, the souvenir steel pan may be viewed as the commodification of a sacred instrument born out of the struggle of slavery. However, by producing a separate souvenir pan for tourists and steel pan instruments for musicians, PanLand Limited has kept the steel pan in its rightful place.

Conclusions

This chapter has highlighted the range of meanings, functions, needs and desires that items of tourism memorabilia have for tourists. Items can be practical and functional so that they go on to be used in every day life. They can also be highly symbolic, fulfilling personal needs and desires for social status, a more authentic way of life or simple nostalgia. Businesses and destination marketers that understand the range of needs and desires that tourism memorabilia meets for tourists can obtain several benefits from the production and sale of souvenirs. These include:

- Positive, promotion and branding through advertising and word-of-mouth recommendations.
- Increased customer satisfaction and loyalty.
- Additional revenue on top of that which is realised from the primary tourism experience offered.
- Increased employment opportunities and the instilling of a sense of pride and empowerment in local people.
- Cultural regeneration of communities.

Local organisations and governments seeking to exploit the financial opportunities of cultural tourism by selling local handcrafted items should be mindful of the potential damage the production and sale of tourism memorabilia can inflict on local cultures. Local communities can ensure that their cherished works of art and other precious objects do not become cheap souvenirs by keeping them backstage for personal and local use, instead of leaving them frontstage to be commoditised for tourist consumption. It is also important to understand that the Western concept of cultural commodification may not necessarily be the only way of viewing items of tourism memorabilia.

Acknowledgements

The authors would like to thank Mr Michael Cooper, owner and Chief Executive Officer of PanLand Limited, for his assistance in the documentation of the case study in this chapter. Further information on the steel pan and PanLand Limited can be found on the website http://www.panlandtt.com.

References

Barre, M. (1999) Steel pans: A brief history. Online document: On WWW at http://www.lafi.org/magazine/articles/steel.html. Accessed 12.08.09.
Bruner, E.M. (1991) Transformation of self in tourism. *Annals of Tourism Research* 18, 238–250.
Clarke, A. (2000) The power to define: Meanings and values in cultural tourism. In M. Robinson, P. Long, N. Evans, R. Sharpley and J. Swarbrooke (eds) *Expressions of Culture, Identity and Meaning in Tourism* (pp. 23–36). Sunderland: The Centre for Travel and Tourism in association with Business Education.
Clawson, M. (1963) *Land and Water for Recreation: Opportunities, Problems and Policies.* Chicago, IL: Rand Mc Nally.

Cohen, E. (1988) Authenticity and commoditization in tourism. *Annals of Tourism Research* 15, 371–386.

Cohen, E. (1989) "Primitive and remote": Hill tribe trekking in Thailand. *Annals of Tourism Research* 16, 30–61.

Cole, S. (2007) Beyond authenticity and commodification. *Annals of Tourism Research* 34 (4), 943–960.

Cook, S.D. (1995) 1996 outlook for travel and tourism basics for building strategies. In S.D. Cook and B. McClure (eds) *Proceedings of the Travel Industry Association of America's Twenty-first Annual Outlook Forum* (pp. 5–18). Washington, DC: Travel Industry Association of America.

Craig-Smith, S. and French, C. (1994) *Learning to Live with Tourism.* Melbourne: Pitman.

Gay, D. (2005) Steel drums to steel pans. Online document: On WWW at http://www.eng.uwi.tt/depts/elec/staff/ssutherland/dgay%20-%20steeldrums-steel pansII.pdf. Accessed 03.06.10.

Gordon, B. (1986) The souvenir: Messenger of the extraordinary. *Journal of Popular Culture* 20 (3), 135–146.

Graburn, N.H.H. (1982) The dynamics of change in tourist arts. *Cultural Survival Quarterly* 6 (4), 7–11.

Greenwood, D. (1989) Culture by the pound: An anthropological perspective on tourism as cultural commoditization. In V.L. Smith (ed.) *Hosts and Guests: The Anthropology of Tourism* (2nd edn) (pp. 171–185). Philadelphia, PA: University of Pennsylvania Press.

Hudman, L.E and Hawkins, D.E. (1989) *Tourism in Contemporary Society.* Englewood Cliffs: Prentice Hall.

Jennings, G. and Weller, B. (2006) Mediating meaning: Perspectives on brokering quality tourist experiences. In G. Jennings and N.P. Nickerson (eds) *Quality Tourism Experiences* (pp. 57–78). Oxford: Elsevier Butterworth-Heinemann.

Jansen-Verbeke, M. (1991) Leisure shopping: A magic concept for the tourism industry? *Tourism Management* 12, 9–14.

Jansen-Verbeke, M. (1998) The synergism between shopping and tourism. In W. Theobald (ed.) *Global tourism* (pp. 428–446). Oxford: Butterworth-Heinemann.

Keowin, C. (1989) A model of tourists' propensity to buy: Case of Japanese visitors to Hawaii. *Journal of Travel Research* 27 (3), 31–34.

Killion, G.L. (1992) *Understanding Tourism.* Study guide. Rockhampton: Central Queensland University.

King, D.A. and Stewart, W.P. (1996) Ecotourism and commodification: Protecting people and places. *Biodiversity and Conservation* 5, 293–305.

Law, R. and Au, N. (2000) Relationship modeling in tourism shopping: A decision rules induction approach, *Tourism Management* 21, 241–249.

Lee, Y., Kim, S., Seock, Y. and Cho, Y. (2009) Tourists' attitudes towards textiles and apparel-related cultural products: A cross-cultural marketing study. *Tourism Management* 30 (5), 724–732.

Littrell, M.A. (1990) Symbolic significance of textile crafts for tourists. *Annals of Tourism Research* 17, 228–245.

Littrel, M.A., Anderson, L.F. and Brown, P.J. (1993) What makes a souvenir craft authentic? *Annals of Tourism Research* 20, 197–215.

Littrell, M.A., Baizerman, S., Kean, R., Gahring, S., Niemeyer, S., Reilly, R. and Stout, J. (1994) Souvenirs and tourism styles. *Journal of Travel Research* 33 (1), 3–11.

MacCannell, D. (1976) *The Tourist: A New Theory of the Leisure Class*. New York: Schocken.

Maxime, G. (1997) The 52nd anniversary of steel bands on the streets. Online document: On WWW at http://www.tobago.org/trinidad/pan/ref/sbveaniv.htm. Accessed 24.08.09.

Michaels, D. (2008) The ultimate Dutch status symbol: House-shaped booze bottles. *The Wall Street Journal* (May 2008). On WWW at http://online.wsj.com/article_email/SB121217604543933443-lMyQjAxMDI4MTAyMjEwNzI2Wj.html. Accessed 18.12.08.

Oh, H., Uysal, M. and Weaver, P. (1995) Product bundles and market segments based on travel motivations: A canonical correlation approach. *International Journal of Hospitality Management* 14 (2), 123–137.

Onderwater, L., Richards, G. and Stam, S. (2000) Why tourists buy textile souvenirs: European evidence. *Tourism, Culture and Communication* 2, 39–48.

Parananond, P. (2000) Tourism and cultural changes: The crafts of the Chiang Mai. In M. Robinson, P. Long, N. Evans, R. Sharpley and J. Swarbrooke (eds) *Expressions of Culture, Identity and Meaning in Tourism* (pp. 215–229). Sunderland: The Centre for Travel and Tourism in association with Business Education.

Pine, B. and Gilmore, J. (1999) *The Experience Economy: Work is Theatre and Every Business a Stage*. Boston, MA: Harvard Business School Press.

Pugh, C. and Wood, E. (2004) The strategic use of events within local government: A study of London Borough councils. *Event Management* 9 (1–2), 61–71.

Quan, S. and Wang, N. (2004) Towards a structural model of the tourist experience: An illustration from food experiences in tourism. *Tourism Management* 25 (3), 297–305.

Real, T. (2000) Tourism, cultural heritage and shopping in the United States: Fruitful new linkages at the dawn of the 21st century. In M. Robinson, P. Long, N. Evans, R. Sharpley and J. Swarbrooke (eds) *Expressions of Culture, Identity and Meaning in Tourism* (pp. 291–320). Sunderland: The Centre for Travel and Tourism in association with Business Education.

Shenhav-Keller, S. (1993) The Israeli souvenir: Its text and context. *Annals of Tourism Research* 20, 182–196.

Squire, S.J. (1994) Gender and tourist experiences: Assessing women's shared meanings for Beatrix Potter' *Leisure Studies* 13 (3), 195–209.

Swanson, K.K. and Horridge, P.E. (2006) Travel motivations as souvenir purchase indicators. *Tourism Management* 27 (4), 671–683.

Timothy, D.J. (2005) *Shopping Tourism, Retailing and Leisure*. Clevedon: Channel View.

Timothy, D.J. and Butler, R.W. (1995) Cross-border shopping: A North American perspective. *Annals of Tourism Research* 22, 16–34.

Tosun, C., Temizkan, S.P., Timothy, D.J. and Fyall, A. (2007) Tourist shopping experiences and satisfaction. *International Journal of Tourism Research* 9, 87–102.

Weaver, D. and Lawton, L. (2006) *Tourism Management* (3rd edn). Milton: John Wiley.

Chapter 12
The Experience Economy 10 Years On: Where Next for Experience Management?

MICHAEL MORGAN

Introduction

In 1999, Pine and Gilmore declared that we were moving from a service to an Experience Economy in which the key to success would be to treat work as theatre and every business a stage. The book drew on a number of strands of academic and business thinking which had been developing over the previous decade and communicated them to a wide audience in a memorable phrase. This closing chapter will revisit the main elements of their analysis to see how they have been taken up by academics and professionals, particularly in leisure and tourism, and ask how robust their predictions and prescriptions have proved. In doing so we aim to examine the current state and future prospects for 'experience management'.

Background

As other chapters in this book reveal, interest in the experiential aspects of consumption can be traced back as far as Csikszentmihalyi (1975) and Holbrook and Hirschman (1982). That work, or at least service, has elements of theatrical performance had been recognised by service management writers since Booms and Bitner (1981). Grove and Fisk (1989) and Grove et al. (1992) drew together the drama-related dimensions of service performance from a number of authors (Berry et al., 1985; Gronroos, 1985; Lovelock, 1981) to create a drama-metaphor framework to be used in service management and marketing. An early example of academic use of the metaphor can be found in Berry's (1981) discussion of the Disney Corporation's show business terms in theme park management, where the staff are the 'cast' and they are either 'on-stage' or 'back-stage' (Morgan et al., 2008).

Pine and Gilmore claimed that they were going further. Theatre was not a metaphor for work, work was theatre. Their book's sub-title, 'work is theatre and every business a stage', sums up an approach that draws on Schechner's (1988) Performance Theory to analyse the customer–company interaction in terms of drama, scripts, sets, casting and performance rather than the conventional language of strategies, plans, plant, personnel and operations. The appeal of the book may have lain in the feeling that, while the military metaphors of strategic management and the classic models of Porter (1980) undoubtedly helped students and managers to analyse hospitality, tourism, leisure or retail businesses, they seemed to miss the essence of the consumer appeal of these service industries (Morgan, 2004). The advantage of the theatrical metaphor is that the consumers are no longer seen as a target to be hit or penetrated, but an audience to be entertained, involved and drawn into participating in the drama.

Tourism and the Experience Economy

Looking specifically at tourism, the old strategy-as-warfare models applied to UK tourism had seemed to produce strategies of price-driven competition, plans and processes based on mass movements of tourists, implemented in homogeneous, over-crowded resorts, staffed by seasonal workers with only basic training (Morgan, 1995, 2004). The theatre metaphor seemed more likely to create products and destinations attractive to what Poon (1993) called the new tourists, and Plog (2001) venturers – well educated, experienced foreign travellers, money-rich/time-poor professionals looking for more than sun, sand and sea in their precious limited time for holidays. What they were looking for were, indeed, experiences.

The heart of Pine and Gilmore's argument was that people would also pay more for these experiences than for undifferentiated products. Their assertion that the developed world was moving from a service– to an experience– economy was based partly on their analysis of the growth of US leisure and tourism attractions, such as theme parks, concerts, cinema and sports events, which they found to outperform other sectors in terms of price, employment and nominal Gross Domestic Product. This, they argued, was because experiences were a different type of offering to services or products. Experiences were events that engaged people in a personal way and because of this their value persisted long after the work of the event stager was done (Pine & Gilmore, 1999: 12–13).

Services, in contrast, were becoming commodities, in the sense that consumers regarded them as homogeneous and purchased them solely on price and availability. The widespread adoption of the internet encourages consumers to search for bargains and choose the cheapest offer regardless of which company provides it, since consumer protection measures and rising standards of service management have meant that quality and reliability can be taken for granted. Only by offering unique, un-missable events and experiences, it was argued, could an organisation stand out against the competition and command value-added prices.

Pine and Gilmore and their followers argue for the need to go beyond product and service orientations as a way of gaining competitive advantage, meeting the changing aspirations of affluent and well-informed consumers looking for authentic experiences, and so avoiding the trap of price-led commoditisation.

Key Elements of Experience Management

Morgan *et al.* (2009) identified a number of key recommendations for management which these authors derive from the 'work is theatre' metaphor:

- the importance of the setting, the design and ambience of the service environment or servicescape (Bitner, 1992; Pine & Gilmore, 1999);
- the importance of staff/customer interaction (Berry *et al.*, 1985; Gronroos, 1985; Grove *et al.*, 1992; Lovelock, 1981);
- the need for staff to put something of their own personality into their roles (Pine & Gilmore, 1999, after Schechner, 1988);
- an emphasis on charting and scripting each stage of the service encounter, often using metaphors from drama and storytelling (Grove *et al.*, 1992; Gyimóthy, 2000; Harris *et al.*, 2003; Pine & Gilmore, 1999; Schmitt, 2003; Shaw, 2005); and
- a view of service delivery as an integrated production in the cinematic rather than the factory sense of the word (i.e. a concern that each time the customer encounters the brand they should get the same high-quality experience) (Pine & Gilmore, 1999; Schmitt, 1999, 2003; Shaw, 2005; Smith & Wheeler, 2002).

Consumer satisfaction should, they say, be seen as something that emerges over the course of the whole experience, rather than as a response to individual attributes of the service. This requires a close analysis of the process, the dynamic interface (Schmitt, 2003), by which the customer interacts with the company, as well as analysis of the outcomes. For this, Pine and Gilmore use another metaphor, this time from film-making, and call it continuity management. This analysis involves considering all the five senses – sight, sound, touch, smell and taste – and understanding the emotional impacts of combustion points (Shaw, 2005) which require sensitive handling. New forms of research are put forward, such as experience mapping (Schmitt, 2003) or theatrical scripting (Harris *et al.*, 2003) of what Carlzon (1987) called the critical moments of truth.

More Than Just a Passing Fashion?

Pine and Gilmore's reliance on examples from Disney and Starbucks contributed to the widely held impression that experience management was showy and superficial. Ritzer (2004) criticises as inauthentic the experience management emphasis on staging performances. Holbrook (2001) refers dismissively to experiential marketing theories such as Pine and Gilmore's and Schmitt's, as 'a gloriously upbeat, positive and opportunistic picture of consumer culture full of millennial optimism'. Prahalad and Ramaswamy (2004) call for strategies to go beyond experiential marketing 'a la Disney...which they considered was still production centric' and saw the customer as 'a human prop in a carefully staged performance'.

This is arguably unfair to the authors of *The Experience Economy* who in fact stress that experiences are events that engage individuals in a personal way and that the most valued forms of experience do not just entertain but offer the prospect of some kind of personal transformation, for example, health, fitness or the development of sporting or cultural skills. Perhaps the cause of experience management has not been well served by its adoption by a range of management writers and consultants each offering their own recipes for business transformation (Schmitt, 1999, 2003; Shaw, 2005; Smith & Wheeler, 2002). In contrast, few academic authors have taken up research into the managerial as opposed to the behavioural, sociological and psychological aspects of the consumer experience paradigm.

This was initially true in tourism, where destination management appeared slow to accept the implications of this perspective. King (2002: 107) criticised destination marketing organisations for being too focused on promoting the physical attributes of the destination, despite travel being 'increasingly more about experiences, fulfilment and rejuvenation than about places and things'. Williams (2006) called for a change of emphasis which focused less on destinations and more on the consumers themselves. Tourism and hospitality marketing, he felt, had failed to take up the fundamental challenge to the orientation of marketing that the experience concept offers.

Experience Management 10 Years After

How, then, does the progress of experience management now seem, 10 years after? Has Pine and Gilmore's analysis proved correct? Has the experience sector grown in the way they predicted? How far have the concepts been accepted by leisure and tourism managers, or by the sectors' academic community? Does experience management and marketing indeed deliver the sustainable competitive advantage they promised? Or were the critics quoted earlier right that it was just a passing fashion in an era of unprecedented economic growth? Each of these questions would need its own research programme in order to produce definitive answers, and it is perhaps disappointing that few of them has been addressed either by contributors to this book or to recent academic journals. This chapter can only provide an impressionist account of some of the issues in the hope of stimulating debate.

Increased competition in the age of the internet

One aspect of Pine and Gilmore's analysis has certainly proved increasingly correct since the book was published. Adoption of the internet is now stabilising at around 70% of the adult population in developed countries (European Travel Commission, 2009) and has indeed proved to be 'the biggest force towards commoditisation known to man' (Pine & Gilmore, 1999: 10). As home shopping has become accepted as safe and reliable, the impact has been felt over many retail sectors including books and music. In the travel sector, flights and accommodation are indeed treated as commodities by people searching the websites of low-cost airlines and their affiliated networks of hotel bed-banks, car-hire and other services for the cheapest offers, regardless of which brand they carry. This is likely to intensify in the current recession as business travellers too trade down to economy class or low-cost carriers. The internet has also increased competition for destinations and made it even harder than it already was (Morgan, 1995) for DMOs to differentiate themselves from a homogeneous mass of generic beach, city, ski or rural destinations.

The growth of experience products

It is, therefore, not surprising that many of them are using experiences as the vehicle for this differentiation. In this book, Haven-Tang and Jones describe the attempt, by the Wales Tourist Board and others, to develop and market 'a sense of place' as a way of delivering unique experiences in rural areas. Experience-themed marketing campaigns have recently been undertaken by among others Greece and Canada (Hudson & Ritchie, 2009). Research among DMOs found the concepts and practices of experience management accepted to some degree at least in destinations in UK, Sweden and Spain (Morgan *et al.*, 2009). On a recent visit to Denmark, I learnt that the city of Aalborg, once proud to market itself as an industrial centre (the 'City of the Smoking Chimneys'), now promotes itself with the strap-line 'Full of Experiences'.

There have also been no shortage of 'experience products' which aim to provide something extraordinary, something which will stand out from everyday life and from all the competition for people's spare time and disposable income (Morgan & Watson, 2007). In our book, McClinchey and Carmichael examine the way the neighbourhood festivals create visitor experiences through the interaction of meanings created by the place, the local community and the visitors themselves.

The need for rigorous evaluation

A recent edition of the Journal of Hospitality Marketing and Management on leisure experiences included literary trails (Macleod *et al.*, 2009), urban precincts (Griffin & Hayllar, 2009), museums (Chan, 2009), cross-cultural shopping (Hartman *et al.*, 2009) and wine tourism (Pikkemaat *et al.*, 2009) among its examples of experience products. The editors of that edition say that this suggests that 'tourism marketing may be embarking on a more sophisticated phase in which the concern is to understand, appeal to and satisfy customers' tourist experiences, rather than base business success on the perceived features or endowments of tourist destinations' (Scott *et al.*, 2009: 108). However, we feel it would be rash to claim that research to date has come up with sustained evidence of the success of such experience-led strategies beyond individual case studies. Experience management still needs to move beyond the Pine and Gilmore level of anecdotal citing of high-profile brands like Disney and Starbucks.

Staged performance or authenticity?

Such research could usefully explore the relative success of so-called authentic and stimulated environments. The experience management emphasis on staging performances has been criticised, for example, by Ritzer (2004), as inauthentic (see also Ritzer & Liska, 1997). This kind of value judgement has its roots in the anthropological based work of writers who equated travel with pilgrimage, a journey in search of spiritual goals or self-discovery (Graburn, 1989) and saw tourism and leisure sites as sacred spaces (Schechner, 1988, Turner, 1974) set apart for the sharing of socially significant experiences. From this perspective, authentic experiences and places are those which retain the essence of what is held to be sacred, in contrast to staged authenticity which has lost its 'real meaning' and became 'commercialised' (Cohen 1988; Lewis & Bridger, 2000, MacCannell, 1976; Ritzer & Stillman, 2001). Some later writers argue that authenticity is a subjective term and part of the negotiation of the meanings of the experience (Uriely, 2005). Wang (1999) came up with the term 'existential authenticity' to distinguish between the feeling that the tourist has that he is experiencing something real and authentic, and the reality that much of his experience is in fact staged managed by the tourism industries.

On the other hand, the success of many completely simulated environments such as theme parks, shopping malls, waterfront developments, sports and music arenas and even whole resorts such as Las Vegas or South Africa's Sun City leads one to question how important the search for authenticity is to many segments of the tourism market. Do tourists take a post-modern ironic or ludic approach to these environments, enjoying the overt artificiality of the designs and entering into the mood they create? Do they seek them out precisely because they are artificial and offering fun and fantasy as a break from the realities of normal life? Or is their appeal simply that they offer a safe place in which to relax and enjoy themselves with their friends (Morgan & Watson, 2009)? This is an area of research that might guide developers and managers of leisure and tourism facilities to get the balance of authenticity and fantasy right for their particular target markets.

Sustainable competitive advantage or another form of commodification?

An evaluation of experience-based products and marketing strategies might also include the extent to which they create repeat visits and loyal customers. There is evidence to the contrary, certainly among the young. Morgan and Xu (2009) found that student travellers do not intend to return to the places where they have had their most memorable experiences so far but instead dream of travelling further and more adventurously in the future. As Richards and Wilson (2003) put it, their experiences serve to give them 'a thirst for more travel' as they build a 'travel career' choosing increasingly challenging destinations as they get older. In another article, Richards and Wilson (2006) suggest that, in cultural tourism at least, competition to offer tourist experiences through cultural events, quarters and exhibitions is leading to a commodification or McGuggenheimisation effect. In this kind of market, experience products become taken for granted, just as service quality was in Pine and Gilmore's thesis, leading to a search for yet more active, creative and engaging forms of tourism product.

Barriers to the implementation of experience management strategies

There is also a need for further research into the barriers that prevent the full implementation of experience management. Two of these are highlighted in the current volume. First, there is the problem that the leisure and tourism sectors contain large numbers of small- and medium-sized enterprises. As Haven-Tang and Jones describe, training modules by the Wales Tourist Board to encourage distinctive tourist experiences through fostering a unique sense of place for Monmouthshire have had a low take up from SMEs in the county. There is a paradox here in that good small businesses can give a place a very distinctive character and leave tourists feeling that they have met the real authentic locals, but equally, poor, unprofessional service can ruin the quality of the experience. As one of Morgan *et al.*'s (2009: 211) interviewees explained: 'Persuading individuals to look beyond their own businesses [is difficult] all they think of is bed-nights and occupancy, and getting them to think outside that box is a problem'.

The other problem is that of the staff. The people who serve the tourists in hotels, bars and restaurants, and are, therefore, the on-stage cast in the performance, are generally temporary seasonal staff on low wages, frequently migrant workers from outside the region, and so have little stake in the business or motivation to stage a unique and memorable experience for the visitors.

In this book, Gibbs and Ritchie point out that to create a sense of theatre in restaurants would require the employment of technically skilled, professional, empowered front of house staff but that this would increase labour costs, as well as time costs. They suggest that this would also add value and generate word-of-mouth recommendations for the establishment, but any manager would have to balance the extra costs and the extra revenue from such a strategy.

In some sectors, such as call-centres, experience management has come to mean not empowerment but monitoring and control. Type 'Customer Experience Management' into a search engine and what comes up are the websites of companies offering software that monitors and records every on-line or telephone contact a particular customer has with the organisation. While this may be a way of ensuring the continuity of experience, in the cinematic sense, that Pine and Gilmore called for, it does not seem to offer much sense of theatre or personal engagement between the customer and the company.

However, some would argue that theatre and personal engagement are not actually what customers want from their everyday transactions: 'many customers are migrating away from face-to-face encounters with sales staff, not only to save money, but also to take greater control of the buying process' (Friedman & Goodrich, 1998: 38).

In leisure and tourism a number of authors have made the distinction between peak and supporting experiences (Quan & Wang, 2004) and called for more attention to be given to humble everyday pleasures (Carù & Cova, 2003) or mundane experiences (Hemmington, 2007).

As Gibbs and Ritchie say, customers may require differing experiences and differing levels of staff support and interaction across a range of situations. Experience management needs to move from a focus on staging performances to one on creating the space in which customers can stage, or co-create, their own experiences (Lugosi, 2008; Morgan *et al.*, 2008; Prahalad & Ramaswamy, 2004; Wearing & Wearing, 1996).

This is of increased importance in times of recession such as we are going through as this book is being written. Experience products are not necessarily luxury products, as some cynics suggest (Wheeller, 2007). If experiences are personal events involving benefits (Beard & Ragheb, 1983; Ryan, 2002) such as socialising, intellectual discovery, physical challenge or hedonic escapism, then in a recession people will not stop seeking them entirely. Instead they will look for ways of economising on the supporting elements, such as travel, accommodation and food, in order to continue to enjoy the core benefits. Identifying which elements of a leisure experience are still regarded as unique, essential and worth paying extras for, and which are the price-sensitive supporting elements, would seem a useful area of managerial research.

Fields for Future Research

In summary, from a managerial perspective, there are a number of areas of the leisure and tourism experience that would provide rich and fruitful fields for research:

- *The effect of the setting on the visitor experience.* This could draw on disciplines such as environmental psychology to explore, for specific settings, the extent to which visitors seek historic or contemporary authenticity, the extent to which they positively enjoy the escapist fantasies suggested by the design and the extent to which the setting merely provides a background for the creation of their own personal and social experiences.
- *The role of experience management in creating repeat visits.* If experience seeking is often linked to a thirst for novelty, how can managers persuade visitors to return to the same attraction or resort? The obvious answer is through product innovation but more cost effective strategies might be through creating a sense of community or social network, or enabling visitors to deepen their skills and knowledge each time they visit.
- *The role of SMEs in creating the visitor experience.* How do you engage busy small business owners in creating distinctive and memorable visitor experiences?
- *The staff customer interface.* Given that most leisure and tourism services rely on low-paid, temporary staff to serve the customers, how can you motivate and empower them to create extraordinary experiences? Linked with this would be research into what level of service and contact with staff, customers actually expect and appreciate in specific situations.
- *The trade-off between unique and memorable experiences and the supporting services that facilitate them.* Techniques like conjoint analysis (see e.g. Suh & Gartner, 2004) could be used to determine

in which elements of the overall experience are customers looking for the cheapest solution and what elements are valued as unique and therefore worth paying extra for.

From this incomplete agenda it would seem that the field of leisure and tourism experience management research is likely to interest academics and managers alike over the next 10 years. We hope this book will be useful to them as a starting point and a stimulus.

References

Beard, J. and Ragheb, M.G. (1983) Measuring leisure motivation. *Journal of Leisure Research* 15, 219–228.

Berry, L (1981) The employee as customer. *Journal of Retail Banking* 3, 33–40.

Berry, L., Zeithaml, V. and Parasuraman A. (1985) Quality counts in services too. *Business Horizons* 28, 44–52.

Bitner, M. (1992) Servicescapes: The impact of physical surroundings on customers and employees. *Journal of Marketing* 56, 57–71.

Booms, B. and Bitner, M. (1981) Marketing strategies and organisational structures. In J. Donnelly and W. George (eds) *Marketing of Services* (pp. 47–51). Chicago, IL: American Marketing Association.

Carlzon, J. (1987) *Moments of Truth*. New York: Harper Collins.

Carù, A. and Cova, B. (2003) Revisiting consumption experience: A more humble but complete view of the concept. *Marketing Theory* 3 (2), 267–286.

Chan, J.K.L. (2009) The consumption of museum service experiences: Benefits and value of museum experiences. *Journal of Hospitality Marketing and Management* 18 (2–3), 173–196.

Cohen, E. (1988) Authenticity and commoditization in tourism. *Annals of Tourism Research* 15, 371–386.

Csikszentmihalyi, M. (1975) *Beyond Boredom and Anxiety*. San Francisco, CA: Jossey-Bass.

European Travel Commission (2009) *New Media Trend Watch*. Online document: On WWW at http://www.newmediatrendwatch.com/world-overview/34-world-usage-patterns-and-demographics. Accessed 03.06.10.

Friedman, L. and Goodrich, G. (1998) Sales strategy in a multi-channel environment. *The Journal of Sales and Major Account Management* 1 (1), 38–48.

Graburn, N.H. (1989) Tourism: The sacred journey. In V.L. Smith (ed.) *Hosts and Guests: The Anthropology of Tourism* (2nd edn) (pp. 21–36). Philadelphia, PA: University of Pennysylvania Press.

Griffin, T. and Hayllar, B. (2009) Urban tourism precincts and the experience of place. *Journal of Hospitality Marketing and Management* 18 (2–3), 127–153.

Gronroos, C. (1985) Internal marketing - theory and practice. In T. Bloch, G. Upah and V. Zeithaml (eds) *Services Marketing in a Changing Environment* (pp. 41–47). Chicago, IL: American Marketing Association.

Grove, S.J. and Fisk, R.P. (1989) Impression management in services marketing: A dramaturgical perspective. In R. Giacalone and P. Rosenfeld (eds) *Impression Management in the Organisation* (pp. 427–438). Hillsdale, NJ: Lawrence Erlbaum.

Grove, S.J., Fisk, R.P. and Bitner, M.J. (1992) Dramatising the service experience: A managerial approach. In T.A. Swartz, S. Brown and D. Bowen (eds) *Advances in Services Marketing and Management* (pp. 91–121). Greenwich, CT: JAI Press .

Gyimóthy, S. (2000) Odysseys: Analysing service journeys from the customer's perspective. *Managing Service Quality* 10, 389–396.

Harris, R., Harris, K. and Baron, S. (2003) Theatrical service experiences: Dramatic script development with employees. *International Journal of Service Industry Management* 14, 184–199.

Hartman, K.B., Meyer, T. and Scribner, L.L. (2009) Retail and service encounters: The inter-cultural tourist experience. *Journal of Hospitality Marketing and Management* 18 (2–3), 197–215.

Hemmington, N. (2007) From service to experience: Understanding and defining the hospitality business. *Service Industries Journal* 27 (6), 747–755.

Holbrook, M.B. (2001) Times Square, Disneyphobia, HegeMickey, the Ricky principle, and the downside of the entertainment economy. *Marketing Theory* 1 (2), 139–163.

Holbrook, M.B. and Hirschman, E.C. (1982) The experiential aspects of consumption: Fantasies, feelings and fun. *Journal of Consumer Research* 9, 132–139.

Hudson, S. and Ritchie, J.B. (2009) Branding a memorable destination experience. The case of "Brand Canada" *International Journal of Tourism Research* 11, 217–228.

King, J. (2002) Destination marketing organizations - connecting the experience rather than promoting the place. *Journal of Vacation Marketing* 8 (2), 105–108.

Lewis, D. and Bridger, D. (2000) *The Soul of the New Consumer: Authenticity-What We Buy and Why in the New Economy.* London: Nicholas Brealey.

Lovelock, C. (1981) Why marketing management needs to be different for services. In J. Donnelly and W. George (eds) *Marketing of Services* (pp. 5–9). Chicago, IL: American Marketing Association.

Lugosi, P. (2008) Hospitality spaces, hospitable moments: Consumer encounters and affective experiences in commercial settings. *Journal of Foodservice* 19, 139–149.

MacCannell, D. (1976) *The Tourist: A New Theory of the Leisure Class.* New York: Schocken.

Macleod, N., Hayes, D. and Slater, A. (2009) Reading the landscape: The development of a typology of literary trails that incorporate an experiential design perspective. *Journal of Hospitality Marketing and Management* 18 (2–3), 154–172.

Morgan, M. (1995) Homogenous products: The future of established resorts. In W. Theobald (ed.) *Global Tourism: The Next Decade* (pp. 363–377). Oxford: Butterworth Heinemann.

Morgan, M. (2004) From production line to drama school: Higher education for the future of tourism. *International Journal of Contemporary Hospitality Management* 16, 91–99.

Morgan, M., Elbe, J. and de Esteban Curiel, J. (2009) Has the experience economy arrived yet? The views of destination managers *International Journal of Tourism Research* 11, 201–216.

Morgan, M. and Watson, P. (2007) Resource guide: Extraordinary experience. UK Higher Education Academy Hospitality, Leisure, Sport and Tourism Network. Online document: On WWW at http://www.heacademy.ac.uk/assets/hlst/documents/resource_guides/extraordinary_experiences.pdf. Accessed 03.06.10.

Morgan, M. and Watson, P. (2009) Understanding the Bournemouth experience: A free-elicitation approach. *Presentation to the Tourist Experiences: Meanings, Motivations, Behaviours Conference*, Preston: University of Central Lancashire, April 1–4.

Morgan, M., Watson, P. and Hemmington, N. (2008) Drama in the dining rooms: Theatrical perspectives on the foodservice encounter. *Journal of Foodservice* 19, 111–118.

Morgan, M. and Xu, F. (2009) Student travel experiences, memories and dreams. *Journal of Hospitality and Marketing Management* 18 (2–3), 216–236.

Pikkemaat, B., Peters, M., Boksberger, P. and Secco, M. (2009) The staging of experiences in wine tourism. *Journal of Hospitality Marketing and Management* 18 (2–3), 237–253.

Pine, B.J. and Gilmore, J.H. (1999) *The Experience Economy: Work is Theatre and Every Business is a Stage*. Boston, MA: HBS Press.

Plog, S. (2001) Why destination areas rise and fall in popularity. *Cornell Hotel and Restaurant Administration Quarterly* 42 (3), 13–24.

Poon, A. (1993) *Tourism, Technology and Competitive Strategies*. Wallingford: CABI.

Porter, M. (1980) *Competitive Strategy: Techniques for Analysing Industries and Competitors*. New York: Free Press.

Prahalad, C.K. and Ramaswamy, V. (2004) *The Future of Competition: Co-creating Unique Value with Customers*. Boston, MA: Harvard Business School Press.

Quan, S. and Wang, N. (2004) Towards a structural model of the tourist experience: An illustration from food experiences in tourism. *Tourism Management* 25, 297–305.

Richards, G. and Wilson, J. (2003) *New Horizons in Independent Youth and Student Travel*. A Report for the International Student Travel Confederation (ISTC) and the Association of Tourism and Leisure Education (ATLAS) International Student Travel Confederation. Amsterdam: ATLAS.

Richards, G. and Wilson, J. (2006) Developing creativity in tourist experiences: A solution to the serial reproduction of culture? *Tourism Management* 27, 1209–1223.

Ritzer, G. (2004) *The McDonaldization of Society* (Revised New Century Edition). London: Pine Forge Press.

Ritzer, G. and Liska, A. (1997) 'McDisneyization' and 'post-tourism': Complementary perspectives on contemporary tourism. In C. Rojek and J. Urry (eds) *Touring Cultures: Transformations of Travel and Theory* (pp. 96–112). London: Routledge.

Ritzer, G. and Stillman, T. (2001) The post-modern ballpark as a leisure setting: Enchantment and de-McDonaldization. *Leisure Sciences* 23, 99–113.

Ryan, C. (ed.) (2002) *The Tourist Experience* (2nd edn). London: Continuum.

Schechner, R. (1988) *Performance Theory*. London: Routledge.

Schmitt, B.H. (1999) *Experiential Marketing: How to Get Companies to Sense, Feel, Think, Act, and Relate to Your Company and Brands*. New York: Free Press.

Schmitt, B.H. (2003) *Customer Experience Management: A Revolutionary Approach to Connecting with your Customers*. Hoboken, NJ: John Wiley.

Scott, N., Laws, E. and Bokkesberger, P. (2009) The marketing of hospitality and leisure experiences. *Journal of Hospitality Marketing and Management* 18 (2–3), 99–110.

Shaw, C. (2005) *Revolutionize Your Customer Experience*. Basingstoke: Palgrave Macmillan.

Smith, S. and Wheeler, J. (2002) *Managing the Customer Experience: Turning Customers into Advocates*. Harlow: FT Prentice Hall.

Suh, Y.K. and Gartner, W.C. (2004) Preferences and trip expenditures – a conjoint analysis of visitors to Seoul, Korea. *Tourism Management* 25 (1), 127–137.

Turner, V.W. (1974) *Dramas, Fields and Metaphors*. Ithaca, NY: Cornell University Press.

Uriely, N. (2005) The tourist experience: Conceptual developments. *Annals of Tourism Research* 32, 199–216.
Wang, N. (1999) Rethinking authenticity in tourism experience. *Annals of Tourism Research* 26, 349–370.
Wearing, B. and Wearing, S. (1996) Refocusing the tourist experience: The flaneur and the choraster. *Leisure Studies* 15 (4), 229–243.
Wheeller, B. (2007) Vague, vogue and vacuous. *Keynote Presentation to the Extraordinary Experiences Conference*, Bournemouth: Bournemouth University, September 3–4, 2007.
Williams, A. (2006) Tourism and hospitality marketing: Fantasy, feeling and fun. *International Journal of Contemporary Hospitality Management* 18 (6), 482–495.

Index

active vs. passive viewer 100, 103, 107, 109-110, 111-112, 211

adventure tourism *xv*, *xix*, 11-13, 89-90, 92, 102, 103, 106, 112, 169-170, 211

aesthetics 108, 109, 137, 168, 184, 190, 211

anticipation *xviii*, 3, 6, 9, 12-13, 21, 63-64, 69-74, 117, 183, 206 (*see also* expectation; *and* recollection)

Arnould, R. 6, 13-14, 17-18, 20, 47, 84, 139

art/artisans/artists 46, 66, 111, 126, 174-175, 183-184, 191, 205, 211, 215
– galleries 47, 174
– of the theatre 188 (*see also* restaurants, as theatre; *and* theatre)

arts and crafts 174-175, 176-177, 204, 207

attitudes *xix*, *xx*, 7, 11, 13, 48, 54, 92, 137, 139, 166, 189 (*see also* behaviour; beliefs; motivation; perception; *and* values)

attractions 46, 55, 60, 68, 69, 113, 174, 176, 204, 207, 219
– management 6, 21

authenticity *xvii*, *xviii*, *xx*, *xxi*, 4-5, 7, 14-15, 22, 27-42, 50, 60, 63, 68-69, 73, 86, 90, 92, 101-102, 113-114, 126, 128, 130, 131, 137, 164-165, 170, 174, 177, 188-189, 193-196, 202, 204, 207, 211-215, 220, 223-226

authentic self (*see* identity, authentic self)

autoethnography *xix-xx*, 100-103, 118-119, 125-131

backpackers/hikers 36, 45, 154 (*see also* lifestyle travellers)

bars (*see* food and drink, pubs)

behaviour *xvi*, *xvii*, *xx*, 10, 11, 14, 20, 28, 33, 36, 44, 46, 47, 48, 53-54, 55, 60, 61, 84, 100, 118, 120, 122, 129, 130, 137, 138, 139, 141, 210, 221 (*see also* attitudes; beliefs; perception; motivation; *and* values)
– service 193-195

beliefs *xx*, 12, 20, 36, 62, 127, 139, 167, 176 (*see also* attitudes; behaviour; motivation; perception; *and* values)

bistro (*see* restaurants; *see also* food and drink)

Bitner, M.J. 185, 218, 220

blogs (*see* communities, virtual; *see also* Internet)

branding 49, 52, 74, 143, 145, 165, 203, 215 (*see also* destination image; *and* marketing)

cameras (*see* photography; *see also* memorabilia; *and* visual culture)

Canada *xviii*, 60, 64-66, 69, 70, 74, 222

capital
– cultural 111, 112, 163, 176, 188
– natural 163, 167, 169, 170-171, 175-177
– physical 9-10, 163, 170, 171, 175, 176, 177, 221
– social 165-167, 168-169, 176
– socio-cultural 163, 176

Caribbean 66, 70, 202, 213-215

Clawson, M. 4, 6, 8, 83, 117, 118, 123, 206

co-creation 86-87, 187

Cohen, E. *xvii*, 3-5, 6, 12, 14, 27-42, 137, 211, 222

commercialisation 16, 45, 49, 87, 99, 100, 102, 103, 104, 105, 108, 113, 166, 175, 189, 191, 196

commodification/commoditisation *xv*, 10-11, 29, 31, 37, 59-60, 68, 73, 202-205, 211-215, 219-220, 222, 224

communities *xiii*, *xviii*, 47, 54, 59, 61, 63, 64, 65, 67, 69, 82, 88, 93, 109, 164-165, 169, 177, 215
– Amish *xx*, 143-158
– ethnic *xviii*, *xix*, *xx*, 60, 63, 65-66, 69-74 (*see also* ethnicity)
– host/local 165-167, 169, 173-174, 175, 176-177, 207, 215
– Native North American Indian 102-103, 212-213
– rural *xx*, 143, 147, 155, 163-167, 169, 170, 171, 172-177, 222
– sense of community 65, 67, 68-72, 166, 176, 226 (*see also* sense of place)
– virtual 21, 50, 53-54, 81, 107, 225 (*see also* Internet)

community festivals (*see* festivals)

community involvement 10, 13, 88, 166, 176, 177, 187

competitive
– advantage *xv*, *xvii*, *xxi*, 163, 166, 167, 175-178, 205, 220, 221, 224
  sustainable *xv*, *xxi*, 221, 224-226
– strategies 59, 81, 139, 164, 166, 167, 219, 221, 223, 224

connectivity (*see* communities, virtual; *see also* Internet)

consumer experiences *xvii*, 3-77, 210
– dimensions of 3-26

231